DAUGHTERS OF GOD

SCRIPTURAL
PORTRAITS

S. MICHAEL WILCOX

Deseret Book Company
Salt Lake City, Utah

Library of Congress Cataloging-in-Publication Data

Wilcox, S. Michael.
    Daughters of God : scriptural portraits / S. Michael Wilcox.
        p.   cm.
    Includes bibliographical references and index.
    ISBN 1-57345-352-8
    1. Women in the Mormon sacred books.   I. Title.
BX8622.W55   1998
289.3'2'0922—DC21   98-10268
                                                                               CIP

Printed in the United States of America

10   9   8   7   6   5   4   3   2   1   72082 - 6315

To my wife and my mother,
from whom every good thing of my life has flowed

CONTENTS

Acknowledgments ix

Foreword xi

The Portrait Gallery of the Scriptures 1

THE HALLS OF THE OLD TESTAMENT

1　Eve, the Help Meet and Life-Giver 7

2　The Price of Virtue 22

3　Sarah and Hagar, Mothers of Two Nations 24

4　Fleeing Spiritual Babylon 32

5　Preservers of a Lineage 35

6　The Worth of a Covenant Wife 39

7　Mothers of Israel 51

8　The Women Who Saved Moses 60

9　An Inheritance in the Promised Land 69

10　Women of the Reign of the Judges 75

11　Charity Seeketh Not Her Own 86

12　Women of Devotion and Understanding 91

Contents

13 Women of Tragedy 102

14 Trusting in the Prophets 116

15 Contrasting Queens 129

16 Three Queens of the East 138

17 More Precious Than Rubies 147

18 Surviving the Crucible of Suffering 154

19 The Daughters of Zion 157

20 Fair As the Moon, Clear As the Sun 160

THE HALLS OF THE NEW TESTAMENT

21 Mary, the Chosen and Precious Vessel 169

22 Elisabeth and Anna, Aged Women of God 180

23 Three Women Who Loved Jesus 188

24 Seeking the Blessings of the Savior 201

25 Hope for the Penitent 214

26 Names Written in the Book of Life 224

THE HALLS OF LATTER-DAY SCRIPTURE

27 Courage in the Wilderness 239

28 Reviving Old Secrets 243

29 Women of Faith and Sacrifice 247

30 Many Hearts Died, Pierced with Deep Wounds 259

31 Vienna Jaques, a Woman of Consecration 266

32 Lucy Mack Smith, the Mother of the Prophet 269

33 Emma Hale Smith, an Elect Lady 273

The Corridors of Time 290

Sources 293

Index 297

ACKNOWLEDGMENTS

I wish to express my deepest and warmest gratitude to the many women whose encouragement and valuable help have been so graciously given. Special thanks go to Sheri Dew for her constant support and to Suzanne Brady for her friendship and untiring editorial insight and labor.

FOREWORD

Each year as I have interacted with hundreds of young adult and adult women from different parts of the country, I have repeatedly heard cries for help from sisters who have not understood clearly what the Lord expects of them. Some of them have been angry because they have been hurt or mistreated in some fashion. Many have had questions about the role of the Latter-day Saint woman in today's world. These sisters have been a constant reminder that women today face challenges and opportunities unheard of in their grandmothers' day, and their changing circumstances bring a flurry of new and confusing problems. How they need help from a gospel context to meet their problems in a complex world!

Daughters of God: Scriptural Portraits is invaluable in helping to bring a deepened spiritual understanding to the heart of every daughter of God. Within these pages are messages that illustrate the concerned love of a kind Heavenly Father for his daughters. We are constantly reminded, as the lives of our sisters in the scriptures are unfolded, that God desires each of his daughters to be happy and feel worthwhile.

Regrettably, ours is a time when the divine role of motherhood is often regarded as a second-class occupation. Women frequently expect too much of themselves, and they come up wanting when their expectations (usually imposed by others) are not met. In a world that would homogenize men and women—their roles, their occupations, their perspectives—I am especially grateful that a book such as this has been written to clarify our vision and illustrate the divine perspective God intended women to have. The women of the scriptures teach us lessons that are timely, applicable, and valuable. From Eve to Emma, the effects of a woman's influence and the power she has to inspire those around her make the world a better place in which to live.

These women of old call to the women in modern times, beckoning us to see the sameness in our struggles. We live in a time when women have more opportunity, more time, more conveniences, and more possibilities to extend their influence and use their talents than ever before. It is often difficult to choose the place where we will put our energies. I am grateful that through a sensitive, caring, thought-provoking author, we are brought to recognize the values common to women through the ages—and to be shown, in a most stunning way, that the women of the scriptures have relevant answers for many of our most perplexing problems.

Teachers and leaders alike will benefit from the insights of this writing, not only to better understand the needs of women but to see the value of women in God's eyes.

MAURINE J. TURLEY
Young Women General Presidency, 1984–87

THE PORTRAIT GALLERY
OF THE SCRIPTURES

Women in the Church today find themselves in many different situations. Some are married and rearing families. Some are single parents who struggle to rear children on their own. Some find fulfillment in marriage but for one reason or another have no children. Some are married to men who are not members of the Church or who are less active. Some women are divorced, some have not married, and some are widows. Some are older women nearing the end of their lives, and some are young women just learning what it means to be a daughter of God. Some have all the material comforts. Some live in poverty. But each situation a Latter-day Saint woman faces is reflected in the scriptures.

Elder Boyd K. Packer said, "The right things, those with true spiritual nourishment, are centered in the scriptures" (Regional Representatives' Seminar, 2 April 1982, 1–2). Great lessons can be learned from the wonderful sisters of the past who faced their challenges with dignity and faith. We can also learn from those who distorted their potential or in other ways failed to reach it. We all can learn much from the women the Lord chose for his gallery. I am confident that if we will study these women of the scriptures, there will be kindled in our hearts a deep respect for all the daughters of our Heavenly Father.

As each woman passes from one stage of life to another, she will find women in the scriptures to give her additional understanding. And in the midst of all the discussions regarding the roles of women, let us avail ourselves of the most trustworthy of guides—the holy scriptures and the Holy Spirit.

On occasion, while teaching classes of young women, I hold up a mirror and ask them who they see. They often smile hesitatingly before they say their own names. I ask them to look more closely, and we begin talking about the women described in the scriptures. "Can you see Rebekah in your own countenances? Do you see Ruth, or Hannah, or Mary?"

I want them to see in themselves the courage, compassion, and faith of their ancient sisters both well-known and obscure. The images of these past daughters of God are reflected in the lives and faces of Latter-day Saint women.

At the end of my mission, I stopped in Paris to visit the Louvre. I was overwhelmed by the size of the museum. The gallery was divided into rooms, and I dashed through, seeking out the most famous pieces. As I moved from room to room, I was aware there were many other works of art hanging on the walls. Some were very small, some were finely detailed, and others were only sketches. I recall wondering, as I hurried by, why some of these very small and seemingly unfinished portraits were hanging in the museum at all.

Years later, I visited the National Gallery of Art in Washington, D. C., with my wife. Laura knew art much better than I. We spent the better part of a day in the gallery. We visited each room and studied almost every painting. As in the Louvre, there were well-known works of art as well as others of which I had never heard. There were sketches with little detail, but as we examined them closely, I realized why they were included. The painting that most inspired me was a relatively obscure one hanging in an unobtrusive place in a minor room of the gallery.

Similarly, the pages of holy writ contain portraits preserved for us to study. There are finely detailed portraits that dominate whole walls of their respective rooms, and there are small, relatively unfinished portraits or faintly lined sketches that attract little attention.

We often hurry through the scriptural gallery, stopping only at the well-known, more complete portraits of Ruth, or Esther, or Mary. But as we hurry from room to room, we glimpse other portraits. They lack details and are often faint. Among them are the faces of Shiphrah and Puah, Rhoda, Priscilla, Vashti, Lamoni's queen, and the daughters of Zelophehad.

I have tried to visit the scriptural gallery as I did the National Gallery of Art. I wanted to discover why the Lord chose to add each portrait to his collection. I have learned that some of the most inspiring portraits are the small, faintly lined sketches, hanging in minor rooms.

I have known many wonderful women in my life. Because my parents divorced when I was a baby, I was reared solely by my mother. I grew up with my sisters, who also taught me a great deal. These women, with whom I shared my first nineteen years, graced my life with the power of their examples.

When I married, my education of refinement, compassion, and faithfulness continued, this time guided by the wonderful example of my wife. Our first children were girls. I love Sarah, Martha, Eve, and Abish because I saw their qualities first in the women closest to me.

This book is an attempt to share some of the lessons I have learned from the women of the scriptures. It is a personal odyssey, a thematic journey of discovery, rather than a scholarly commentary or a comprehensive explanation. Other truths are to be found in the lives of these women, for we will never exhaust the riches of the scriptures. I have diligently tried to apply the stories in an edifying manner, but they are personal applications. Please accept this book for what it is intended to be—lessons one man has learned from the women whose lives are recorded in the scriptures. I sincerely pray that my examination of their lives will create respect and gratitude for the wonderful daughters of God.

THE HALLS
OF THE OLD
TESTAMENT

CHAPTER 1

EVE, THE HELP MEET
AND LIFE-GIVER

No other woman in the scriptures has been more misunderstood than Eve. But when we closely examine the scriptural record and the words of latter-day apostles and prophets, we discover Eve's true likeness and noble character, which teach us many edifying lessons.

In my institute classes, I write on the board the words *helpmate*, *helpmeet*, and *help meet* and ask which the Lord used when he first spoke of Eve. Students are usually surprised to learn that the correct scriptural description of Eve is *"help meet"* (Moses 3:18). Eve was introduced as a help for Adam because "it was not good that the man should be alone" (Moses 3:18).

The word *help* is translated from a Hebrew root meaning "to surround, to protect, and to aid" (*New Strong's Exhaustive Concordance of the Bible*, 87). We have a stereotype of the man as the protector, but the wife also surrounds, protects, and aids her husband. The spirit and influence of wives and mothers make our homes places where we are surrounded by peace and love and protected from the contention, temptations, and opposition of the world.

There have been times in my own life, when through the buffetings of mortality, I have been sustained by the single thought that as long as I was Laura's husband, all was well. The world could take every other thing, but it could not take that relationship from me as long as I remained faithful. My desire to be worthy of her companionship in the eternities has been a strong motivation in my life to live to be worthy of celestial glory. This thought has surrounded me with protection against trial and temptation.

A "help" that surrounds and protects is also a powerful expression of a woman's role as mother. The very name *Eve* means "mother," and the first commandment given to Adam and Eve was to "multiply, and replenish the earth" (Moses 2:28). A fundamental power in rearing children is the surrounding and protecting aid a mother provides.

The word *help* thus increases our understanding of the incalculable contribution women make to their families, their communities, and their nations.

In describing Eve as a help for Adam, the Lord adds the adjective *meet*. In this context *meet* means "equal to, suitable for, becoming, right, fit, worthy, sufficient, competent, well-placed, necessary, proper, fulfilling, and satisfying." Eve was all of this to Adam. She was equal to him. She was suitable, becoming, and of value. Her help and companionship were right. She was fit, worthy, sufficient, and competent. She was well-placed beside Adam, a necessary and proper companion. Her help was fulfilling and brought satisfaction.

Meet also suggests that Eve would complement Adam, would make him complete. The Lord desires husbands to view their wives as the best, most wonderful thing in their lives. They are not whole without them.

What we learn from the story of Adam and Eve about the proper relationship of men and women is amplified by the Lord's description of the marriage of Adam and Eve through the metaphor of the rib.

BONE OF MY BONES

President Spencer W. Kimball indicated that "the story of the rib, of course, is figurative" ("Blessings and Responsibilities of Womanhood," 71). President George Albert Smith said: "In showing this relationship, by a symbolic representation, God didn't say that woman was to be taken from a bone in the man's head that she should rule over him, nor from a bone in his foot that she should be trampled under his feet, but from a bone in his side to symbolize that she was to stand by his side, to be his companion, his equal, and his helpmeet in all their lives together" (cited in Lee, *Ye Are the Light of the World*, 284).

Adam understood the Lord's metaphor. He viewed his wife as so closely knit to him that he considered her his own flesh and bone (see Moses 3:23). Paul added insight to this story when he counseled husbands to nourish and cherish their wives as they would their "own flesh" (Ephesians 5:29).

Adam stated further that a man should leave his parents and cleave unto his wife (see Moses 3:24). President Harold B. Lee indicated that Adam's words "were undoubtedly just what they sound like. They were very likely the words spoken by Adam reciting the vows of the first marriage upon this earth" (*Decisions for Successful Living*, 125). We can imagine how Eve felt to hear her husband pronounce these words of commitment.

The phrase "bone of my bones and flesh of my flesh" may also suggest the wife is now part of her husband's family. When a man and woman marry, they become part of each other's families, as though they had been born into those families.

THEY WERE BOTH NAKED AND WERE NOT ASHAMED

The image of being naked or clothed is a common symbol used in the scriptures. Eve and Adam "were both naked . . . and were not ashamed" (Moses 3:25). In a figurative sense, Eve might have been saying, "Adam, I am not hiding anything. There is nothing in my past or in my thoughts that I am ashamed for you to discover." Adam, in turn, could say the same to Eve. The example of Eve and Adam teaches us that we should come to the altar of the temple unashamed. Because we all make mistakes, the Lord has given us the blessings of the Atonement to make us clean again. In Hebrew, the word *atonement* means "to cover." If we sincerely repent, the Atonement makes it possible to begin and maintain the type of marriage in which we are not hiding things from each other—in which we can live together "naked and not ashamed."

The portrait of Eve teaches us many truths about the relationship between wives and husbands. Yet many daughters of Eve do not have the opportunity of a marriage relationship in this life. President Spencer W. Kimball gives us modern revelation on this point: "Just as those who do not hear the gospel in this life, but who would have received it with all their hearts had they heard it, will be given the fulness of the gospel blessings in the next world—so, too, the women of the Church who do not in this life have the privileges and blessings of a temple marriage, through no fault of their own, who would have responded if they had an appropriate opportunity—will receive all those blessings in the world to come" (*Teachings of Spencer W. Kimball*, 295).

THE SERPENT BEGUILED ME, AND I DID EAT

Eve often has been overly condemned or overly excused for her role in the Fall. But rather than judge Eve, we can learn valuable lessons from this daughter of God.

Elder James E. Talmage wrote: "Eve was fulfilling the foreseen purposes of God by the part she took in the great drama of the fall; yet she did not partake of the forbidden fruit with that object in view, but with intent to act contrary to the divine command, being deceived by the sophistries of Satan" (*Articles of Faith*, 69; see also 1 Timothy 2:14). Because Eve was deceived by Satan and transgressed the law, many people have condemned her. Yet how many of us have been "beguiled" by the adversary? How many of us have partaken of "forbidden fruit"? How many of us have been "deceived by the sophistries of Satan"? Eve did not do anything all human beings have not done.

Yet when Eve partook of the fruit of the tree of the knowledge of good and evil, the consequences furthered the Father's plan. Of all people who ever were deceived by the adversary, Eve is, perhaps, the one least worthy of condemnation. She took responsibility for her transgression. She did not make excuses. She simply confessed: "The serpent beguiled me, and I did eat" (Moses 4:19). She did not rationalize or hide what she had done. We can learn much from Eve's response to the Lord.

As Latter-day Saints we have modern revelation that gives us additional knowledge about Eve's role in the Fall. In the Book of Mormon, Lehi teaches us the importance of the Fall and its relationship to agency and the Atonement of Jesus Christ. We learn that the fall of Adam and Eve is a central part of the plan of salvation. The Prophet Joseph Smith taught that Eve's act was not a sin because God had decreed it (see Ehat and Cook, *Words of Joseph Smith*, 63). Likewise President Joseph Fielding Smith taught: "I never speak of the part Eve took in this fall as a sin, nor do I accuse Adam of a sin. . . . This was a transgression of the law, but not a sin . . . , for it was something that Adam and Eve had to do!" (*Doctrines of Salvation*, 1:114–15).

President Brigham Young also said we ought not to condemn Eve for her transgression and should be thankful for the consequences of it: "We [as Latter-day Saints] also understand . . . why God permitted Mother Eve to partake of the forbidden fruit. We should not have been here today if she had not; we could never have possessed wisdom and intelligence if she had not done it. It was all in the economy of heaven, and we . . . should never blame Mother Eve, not the least" (*Journal of Discourses*, 13:145).

Modern revelation also teaches us that Eve understood the importance of the Fall. Elder Dallin H. Oaks said that "our first parents understood the necessity of the Fall" (Conference Report, October 1993, 98). After she had been put outside the Garden, had borne children, and learned that the sacrifices they had been offering pointed to the great sacrifice of the Savior, Eve beautifully expressed her deep understanding and joy over the Fall: "Were it not for our transgression we never should have had seed, and never should have known good and evil, and the joy of our redemption, and the eternal life which God giveth unto all the obedient" (Moses 5:11). Elder Oaks observed that we as Latter-day Saints "celebrate Eve's act and honor her wisdom and courage in the great episode called the Fall" (Conference Report, October 1993, 98).

Often we speak of two great commandments given in the Garden of Eden: Multiply and replenish the earth and refrain from partaking of the forbidden fruit (see Moses 2:28; 3:16–17). Yet there was a third commandment: God had commanded Adam and Eve to remain with each other (see Moses 4:18). Adam partook of the fruit in order to remain with Eve, as well as to multiply and replenish the earth. Given the choice of Eden or Eve, Adam chose Eve. I have known people who have chosen a perceived Eden over an Eve. How grateful we ought to be for the courage of both Eve and Adam and the power of their examples.

THY SORROW AND THY CONCEPTION

The false belief still circulates that women endure the pains of childbearing as a punishment for Eve's partaking of the forbidden fruit. But, to paraphrase the second Article of Faith, Latter-day Saints believe that women will be punished for their own sins and not for Eve's transgression.

After the Fall, the Lord told Eve there would be two major consequences for her: He would "multiply [her] sorrow and [her] conception," and her "desire" would be to her husband and he would "rule" over her (Moses 4:22). Yet each consequence is a blessing, not a curse. The serpent was "cursed" and the ground was "cursed," but not Adam or Eve (see Moses 4:20, 23).

The words *sorrow* and *conception* obviously refer to childbearing. In the mortal world Eve would bear children. She later said that "were it not for our transgression we never should have had seed" (Moses 5:11). The ability and opportunity to bear children is a great blessing, but the Lord told Eve that her sorrow would be multiplied.

We tend to interpret *sorrow* in this context as meaning almost exclusively the pain of pregnancy and the labor of childbirth. Yet the same Hebrew word is used in the Lord's decree to Adam: "Cursed is the ground for thy sake; in *sorrow* shalt thou eat of it all the days of thy life" (Genesis 3:17; emphasis added; see also Moses 4:23).

The Hebrew word translated "sorrow" has many meanings. It can be translated "labor, toil, worrisomeness, or pain." The root word means "to carve, fabricate, or fashion." The bearing of children would involve a depth of toil, worry, and pain Eve had not experienced in the Garden of Eden. When a child is born, the labor and worry, and sometimes even the pain, continue far beyond pregnancy and birth, but few women have viewed this as a curse. The Lord was simply telling Eve she would be a mother.

Childbearing encompasses both bringing children into the world through birth and then bearing the children throughout life by caring for them and teaching them the principles of righteousness. I have watched my wife bear our five children. Tremendous pain has been involved, but each time there were tears of joy and wonder at the birth. Each new life is a great blessing, in spite of the sorrow. My wife told me, "When the pain and effort is over, and they lay that newborn child in your arms, there is no feeling in all the world like it. It is the purest joy I have ever experienced." Eve realized that it was better for her and for Adam to pass through the sorrow of mortality that they might know good from evil, understand the joy of their redemption, and receive the blessings of posterity.

SAVED IN CHILDBEARING

The apostle Paul added wonderful insight to the Lord's words concerning Eve when he stated: "Notwithstanding she shall be saved in childbearing, if they continue in faith and charity and holiness with sobriety" (1 Timothy 2:15). In the Joseph Smith

Translation the verse reads, "Notwithstanding *they* shall be saved in childbearing" (JST 1 Timothy 2:15; emphasis added).

The words "saved in childbearing" may imply the physical preservation of many women in giving birth, but I believe there is also something more profound being taught here. The word *saved* refers also to spiritual salvation. When childbearing is combined with faithfulness, charity, holiness, and sobriety, the combination is, with the atonement of Christ, saving. That interpretation was suggested by President Joseph F. Smith (see *Gospel Doctrine*, 288–89).

I came to understand this point more fully in the months before our last son was born. This was a time of great sacrifice and toil for my wife. Our four other children (ages four, eight, nine, and eleven) made great demands on her time and energy, as did the responsibilities of running a home and serving in Church callings. Not only was she bearing a child but she was still bearing four others.

As I watched the love and labor of my wife, Paul's words came into my mind. It seemed that the Spirit whispered, "That which your wife does is an act of righteousness so great that it is saving in and of itself. No other single act is greater, except the atonement of the Savior."

The act of bearing children is indeed a significant act of devotion and faithfulness. Women sacrifice much physically, emotionally, and spiritually to bear children. The sacrifice, love, devotion, and labor of righteously rearing children to the Lord helps to mold and refine a woman's character. It amplifies all that is godlike and noble within her.

Many women, through no fault of their own and for various reasons, will not enjoy the blessing of children in this life. The Lord is mindful of their pain and struggles. The prophets have taught that no eternal blessing will be denied to those who live worthily. Elder Melvin J. Ballard said: "God bless those mothers who are not yet permitted, through no fault of their own, to be mothers in very deed, but who are mothers at heart. The Lord looks upon the hearts of men and women, and their intent, and they shall be judged according to their will and their desires. Such mothers shall not go through eternity childless" (Hinckley, *Sermons and Missionary Services of Melvin Joseph Ballard*, 206–7).

President Brigham Young taught the same truth: "Many of the sisters grieve because they are not blessed with offspring. You will see the time when you will have millions of children around you. If you are faithful to your covenants, you will be mothers of nations" (*Discourses of Brigham Young*, 200).

Although without the blessing of children in this life, women can develop the saving qualities of motherhood which are inherent to their natures. Sister Patricia Holland noted that "some women give birth and raise children but never 'mother' them. Others, whom I love with all my heart, 'mother' all their lives but have never given birth. All of us are Eve's daughters, whether we are married or single, maternal or barren; and we can provide something of that divine pattern, that maternal prototype for each other and for those who come after us" (*On Earth As It Is in Heaven*, 94).

THE LIFE-GIVER

"And Adam called his wife's name Eve, because she was the mother of all living; for thus have I, the Lord God, called the first of all women, which are many" (Moses 4:26).

Eve's name in Hebrew means "life-giver." Both Adam and the Lord considered this the most appropriate and worthy name to give the first woman of many women, the "mother of all living." There is dignity in the thought that the first woman's name was essentially the title of mother.

Joseph Smith taught that "the 7th verse of 2nd chapter of Genesis ought to read—God breathed into Adam his spirit [i.e. Adam's spirit] or breath of life; but when the word 'rauch' applies to Eve, it should be translated lives" (*Teachings of the Prophet Joseph Smith*, 301).

Life-giver is an appropriate name because women not only give birth to children but continue to give life to their families and others. My mother gave me the gift of life when she gave me birth, but she continued to give me life as I grew, through her example, teachings, sacrifices, and love. Even today she continues to give me life through her counsel and wisdom.

Sister Patricia Holland gives added insight to what it means to be a life-giver. "Eve was given the identity of 'the mother of all living'—years, decades, perhaps centuries before she ever bore a child. It would appear that her motherhood preceded her maternity, just as surely as the perfection in the Garden preceded the struggles of mortality. I believe *mother* is one of those very carefully chosen words, one of those rich words, with meaning after meaning after meaning after meaning. . . . I believe with all my heart that it is first and foremost a statement about our nature" (*On Earth As It Is in Heaven*, 94).

There is a difference between the labor of Eve and the labor of Adam. The Lord told Adam, "By the sweat of thy face shalt thou eat bread" (Moses 4:25). Whatever our occupations in this life may be, there will come a time when they will not be necessary. None of the means by which men eat bread by the sweat of their face will continue in the eternities. Our occupations allow us to live and learn. They edify and instruct, but they are essentially aspects of the telestial world in which we live.

On the other hand, Eve's role as life-giver is eternal and celestial. It was revealed to Joseph Smith that the life-giving power of women fulfills "the promise which was given by my Father before the foundation of the world, and for their exaltation in the eternal worlds, that they may bear the souls of men; for herein is the work of my Father continued, that he may be glorified" (D&C 132:63). Adam shared in this great work, but Eve was the primary life-giver. Her labor would not change after the resurrection. Is it any wonder the adversary has tried so diligently to demean the labor that Eve and her daughters perform? Is it any wonder that he has tried to convince both women and men that the temporal labor of the lone and dreary world is more important than the eternal labor of a celestial one?

THY DESIRE SHALL BE TO THY HUSBAND

The Lord told Eve the second consequence of the Fall was, "Thy desire shall be to thy husband, and he shall rule over thee" (Moses 4:22). This verse has also been much misunderstood and has sometimes even been used to justify unrighteous dominion in marriage.

Part of the reason this verse has troubled people is that they emphasize "rule" instead of "desire." *Desire* is a beautiful word suggesting the nature of Eve's righteous feelings for her husband. The origins of the Hebrew word translated *desire* add to our understanding. The word means "to long for, to stretch out towards, to yearn for, to flow towards." This was not a curse but a blessing.

Before their marriage, daughters often ask for a father's blessing. Imagine if a father laid his hands on his daughter's head and said, "I bless you that you will always feel a desire toward your husband. You will long to be with him in time and in eternity. Your heart will stretch out to him in love. Your love will fill your lives until you become one. I also bless you that he will preside in righteousness and honor, protecting and sustaining you and your children." If a daughter received such a blessing, would she feel her father had cursed her?

Too much emphasis has been placed on the word *rule*. President Spencer W. Kimball said: "I have a question about the word *rule*. It gives the wrong impression. I would prefer to use the word *preside* because that's what he does. A righteous husband presides over his wife and family" ("Blessings and Responsibilities of Womanhood," 72). The Lord revealed the principles of righteousness by which a man presides in his home by virtue of the priesthood. Among these principles are persuasion, long-suffering, gentleness, meekness, love unfeigned, kindness, and pure knowledge (see D&C 121:34–46). That is the type of rule a righteous man exercises and a righteous wife desires.

We must remember that when the Lord spoke of desire and rule to Eve, he was speaking of Adam, the great Michael who had helped Jehovah create the earth. This was a righteous son of God.

The Lord was telling Eve that as she entered the fallen world to bear and rear children and to grow through her experiences in mortality, she would be watched over, cared for, and protected by the righteous love of a noble husband. How ironic that men would use this verse as license to exercise unrighteous dominion over their wives. A wife's desire, like a husband's authority, will die if it is based on anything other than the principles of righteousness.

Our Father in Heaven must have been pleased as he watched Eve's desire for Adam grow throughout the long years of their mortal existence. Eve's desire toward her husband is one of the most beautiful aspects of her portrait.

IN THE LONE AND DREARY WORLD

Eve left the Garden of Eden with her husband, Adam, to begin her journey through mortality. The Lord did not drive or thrust them out but used a gentler term, saying, "I, the Lord God, will *send* [them] forth from the Garden of Eden" (Moses 4:29; emphasis added). We also are sent forth by our Father in Heaven to learn the great lessons of mortality. Eve's life after the Fall gives us wonderful insights that can help us set proper priorities.

The final outcome of Eve's life was a deep unity with Adam. In Moses 5 we read of Eve and Adam's activities in the lone and dreary world. Each of their activities suggests their unity. The Lord commanded them to remain together, and they lived in such a way that they desired to remain with each other.

LABOR

"Adam began to till the earth, and to have dominion over all the beasts of the field, and to eat his bread by the sweat of his brow, as I the Lord had commanded him. And Eve, also, his wife, did labor with him" (Moses 5:1). In the daily responsibilities of the home and family, Eve and Adam worked together. The verse suggests this work included care of the crops and the flocks. It also would have included the maintenance of the home and many other tasks.

Some of the most enjoyable times my wife and I share come when we work together. We have put up wallpaper, planted trees and flowers and gardens, painted fences, reupholstered furniture, hung curtains, washed windows and dishes, and so on. These times of shared labor foster the unity and enjoyment that comes from shared responsibility.

MULTIPLY AND REPLENISH

"And Adam knew his wife, and she bare unto him sons and daughters, and they began to multiply and to replenish the earth" (Moses 5:2). Eve became a mother and a grandmother. That was the second important focus of Eve's life. Bringing children into the world involves a physical oneness between husband and wife, but it also involves much more. Bearing and rearing children can create unity between a husband and wife. The Lord did not give the commandment to multiply and replenish the earth solely to provide bodies for his spirit children. He also knew that of all the labors a couple share, parenting is the most conducive to unity. Parents simply must work together to be effective.

THEY CALLED UPON THE NAME OF THE LORD

"Adam and Eve, his wife, called upon the name of the Lord" (Moses 5:4). Adam and Eve worshiped together. When problems with their children developed, they "ceased not to call upon God" (Moses 5:16). Jointly they appealed to the Lord for guidance. Though they did not at first have full comprehension of the Father's plan, they offered the required sacrifices.

Eve also "heard the voice of the Lord" (Moses 5:4). She was obedient to his commandments and offered the firstlings of the flock with her husband. It is apparent from the account in Moses that Eve participated with Adam in offering sacrifices (see Moses 5:5). Eve also felt a sense of gratitude to the Lord, for we read, "Adam and Eve blessed the name of God" (Moses 5:12).

What a sweet thing it is to kneel in prayer with our spouses and children, to sit in the celestial room of the temple with each other, or to read the scriptures together. The example of Eve and

Adam teaches us another essential element of unity: their mutual devotion to God made them one.

THEY MADE ALL THINGS KNOWN

Eve and Adam also taught their children together. In Moses 5:12 we read, "And Adam and Eve blessed the name of God, and they made all things known unto their sons and their daughters." The Lord commanded them to teach their children the gospel (see Moses 6:57–59). This counsel is not only given for the sake of rearing righteous children, but also because of the unity it fosters between husband and wife. Children need the approach, input, and unique abilities of both parents as they grow in the gospel.

THEY MOURNED AND REJOICED TOGETHER

Perhaps Eve experienced no sorrow greater than the sorrow some of her children and grandchildren created through their rebellion. There is a certain poignancy in Eve's words as she "conceived and bare Cain." With the rebellion of some of her children already apparent, Eve said, "I have gotten a man from the Lord; wherefore he may not reject his words. But behold, Cain hearkened not, saying: Who is the Lord that I should know him?" (Moses 5:16). "Adam and his wife mourned before the Lord, because of Cain and his brethren" (Moses 5:27). Adam and Eve are together before the Lord in their sorrow.

Many daughters of God today know the sorrow of having a child who has gone astray or rejected the teachings of the gospel. We learn from Eve that when we have problems with our children we should "[cease] not to call upon the Lord" (Moses 5:16). Eve also teaches us that shared sorrow can bring unity. A husband and wife can pull together and draw strength from each other as they pray for their struggling child. Even mourning and sorrow can bind two souls together.

What a contrast to the situation with Cain is shown in these words: "Adam knew his wife again, and she bare a son, and he called his name Seth. . . . And God revealed himself unto Seth, and he rebelled not, but offered an acceptable sacrifice" (Moses 6:2–3). We can imagine Eve's joy in the righteousness of her son.

Eve and Adam both mourned and rejoiced together before the Lord as they taught their children. Their sorrows and joys contributed to the binding of their hearts and the oneness of their souls. They were viewed by the Lord as being one as they labored to form an eternal unit.

Eve was the first woman, the first help meet, the first life-giver. As we pause to take a final look at her portrait, we see one who was a true "help" to her husband, one who was "meet" for the varied tasks of her life. We see one who began marriage with nothing to conceal. We see one who confessed without guile or excuse. Before us is a woman who continued to strive for salvation through bearing and rearing children in righteousness, a woman who was filled with desire toward her husband, who longed for, stretched toward, and overflowed with love for him as they labored to form an eternal unit. We see a woman who became one flesh with her companion by laboring, multiplying and replenishing, worshiping, teaching, and at times even mourning with him.

Truly, the portrait of Eve depicted in scripture both ancient and modern inspires wonder and awe and deep respect for the woman who was called "the mother of all living" (Genesis 3:20; Moses 4:26). Her image is repeated in the countenances of her life-giving daughters in the Church today.

CHAPTER 2

THE PRICE OF VIRTUE

No journey through the gallery of scriptural portraits would be complete without stopping at the sketch of the daughters of Onitah. Before telling of his own rescue from the priest of Elkenah, Abraham recounted the courage and conviction of the daughters of Onitah. Abraham was spared to become the father of the faithful, the founder of the chosen lineage of Israel, but no angel freed the daughters of Onitah from the altar: they gave the ultimate sacrifice. In their faces we see the value of virtue.

Abraham related: "It was the custom of the priest of Pharaoh . . . to offer up upon the altar which was built in the land of Chaldea, for the offering unto these strange gods, men, women, and children" (Abraham 1:8). Often the victims of human sacrifice were those who, like Abraham, opposed the priest of Elkenah or refused to worship his false gods. "Now, this priest had offered up upon this altar three virgins at one time, who were the daughters of Onitah, one of the royal descent directly from the loins of Ham. These virgins were offered up because of their virtue; they would not bow down to worship gods of wood or of stone, therefore they were killed upon this altar" (Abraham 1:11).

The daughters of Onitah gave their lives for virtue. The word *virtue* as used in the scriptures means much more than chastity;

in Hebrew it suggests valiancy, valor, and strength. Like their counterparts Shadrach, Meshach, and Abednego, these magnificent women show us that virtue is the refusal to worship anything but the true God of heaven.

It is easy to see why virtue is associated with chastity, for chastity creates confidence and strength. The Lord counseled, "Let virtue garnish thy thoughts unceasingly; then shall thy confidence wax strong in the presence of God" (D&C 121:45). Many ancient rites of idol worship included immoral practices. That these three daughters were virgins suggests they would not sacrifice their chastity to the false gods of the day. The daughters of Onitah are a wonderful example of chastity as well as of virtue. It is worth giving one's life for.

As we pass to the other portraits in the hall of Genesis we carry with us the images of three valiant young women, martyrs who gave their lives because of their virtue and devotion to God.

CHAPTER 3

SARAH AND HAGAR,
MOTHERS OF TWO NATIONS

Two of the great portraits of Genesis are those of Sarah and Hagar. Through trials and hardships, both women learned to trust in the Lord. Ultimately, both became mothers of great nations.

SHE HAD NO CHILD

We are introduced to Sarah with these words: "But Sarai was barren; she had no child" (Genesis 11:30). Many sisters know the anguish those words convey. We see the desire for children powerfully illustrated in the portraits of Sarah, Rebekah, Rachel, Hannah, and Elisabeth. Understanding the depth of this desire helps us appreciate one aspect of Sarah's greatness: her faithful, patient waiting for the Lord to fulfill his promise.

SHE JUDGED HIM FAITHFUL WHO HAD PROMISED

Paul praised Sarah by using her as an example of faith. "Through faith also Sara herself received strength to conceive seed, and was delivered of a child when she was past age, because she judged him faithful who had promised" (Hebrews 11:11). Sarah had faith that the Lord would fulfill his promise of children as numberless as the sands of the sea or the stars of the heavens. She waited years for the Lord to grant her desire. Her example gives hope to those who have been promised blessings from the Lord and have not yet received them.

The scriptures suggest Sarah desired children before she and Abraham left Ur for Haran. The Pearl of Great Price tells us Abraham was "sixty and two years old when [he] departed out of Haran" for the land of Canaan (Abraham 2:14). Sarah was ten years younger, making her fifty-two. Surely many years of waiting for children are contained in the words "but Sarai was barren; she had no child" (Genesis 11:30).

In Haran, Abraham had been promised he would be blessed with posterity. "I will make of thee a great nation, . . . and in thee shall all families of the earth be blessed" (Genesis 12:2–3; see also Abraham 2:9–11). Sarah knew the promise. The Lord assured Abraham that "he that shall come forth out of thine own bowels shall be thine heir." He then showed Abraham the stars and said, "Look now toward heaven, and tell the stars, if thou be able to number them: and he said unto him, So shall thy seed be" (Genesis 15:4–5).

In her desire for children, Sarah instructed Abraham: "Behold now, the Lord hath restrained me from bearing: I pray thee, go in unto my maid; it may be that I may obtain children by her" (Genesis 16:2). In the Doctrine and Covenants we learn that "God commanded Abraham, and Sarah gave Hagar to Abraham to wife. And why did she do it? Because this was the law; and from Hagar sprang many people" (D&C 132:34). At this point Sarah must have thought the promise would be fulfilled through another woman's child.

Hagar conceived Ishmael, "and when she saw that she had conceived, [her mistress] was despised in her eyes" (Genesis 16:5). Knowing the Lord commanded Abraham to marry Hagar helps us understand why Sarah told her husband, "My wrong be upon thee: I have given my maid into thy bosom; and when she saw that she had conceived, I was despised in her eyes: the Lord judge between me and thee" (Genesis 16:5). Sarah had obeyed the

Lord, and now she was despised. When Abraham told Sarah, "Thy maid is in thy hand; do to her as it pleaseth thee," Sarah "dealt hardly with her" (Genesis 16:6).

When Abraham was ninety-nine and Sarah eighty-nine, the Lord again promised Abraham would become the "father of many nations" (Genesis 17:4) and changed his name from Abram to Abraham. The Lord also announced that Sarai, whose name would be changed to Sarah, would bear a son and would be a "mother of nations" (Genesis 17:15–16). At this wonderful news, "Abraham fell upon his face, and laughed, and said in his heart, Shall a child be born unto him that is an hundred years old? and shall Sarah, that is ninety years old, bear?" (Genesis 17:17). In his translation of the Bible, Joseph Smith changed the word *laughed* to *rejoiced*.

Later, when three messengers appeared and told Abraham that Sarah would have a son, Sarah laughed within herself, saying, "After I am waxed old shall I have pleasure, my lord being old also?" Her question was answered with a question. "Is any thing too hard for the Lord?" (Genesis 18:12–14).

The name Isaac means literally "he laughs." Did Sarah laugh in unbelief, or, like Abraham, did she rejoice at news so wonderful it was almost beyond belief? Perhaps she felt like the apostles when the resurrected Christ first appeared. "They yet believed not for joy, and wondered" (Luke 24:41).

After years of prayer and waiting, the promise of the Lord was to be fulfilled. The object of Sarah's patience and faith was to come to pass.

DECISIONS OF CHARACTER ASIDE FROM SYMPATHY

Josephus tells us that Sarah "loved Ishmael, who was born of her own handmaid Hagar, with an affection not inferior to that of her own son" (*Antiquities of the Jews*, 36). When Isaac was born, Sarah "saw the son of Hagar the Egyptian, which she had born unto Abraham, mocking" (Genesis 21:9). Paul explained that "He that was born after the flesh [Ishmael] persecuted him that was born after the Spirit [Isaac]" (Galatians 4:29).

What a dilemma for Sarah. She loved the boy Ishmael, and she knew that Abraham loved both Hagar and Ishmael, his son. But she feared for the well-being of Isaac. If Ishmael continued to persecute Isaac, all Sarah had lived for could have been lost. Isaac's life and Ishmael's eternal salvation would have been in danger. The promises of the birthright could have been lost.

Sarah pondered the dilemma and made a difficult decision. She asked Abraham to send Ishmael and Hagar away, "for the son of this bondwoman shall not be heir with my son, even with Isaac" (Genesis 21:10). Joseph Smith spoke of such difficult decisions when he addressed the first Relief Society. He said, "There must be decision of character, aside from sympathy" (*Teachings of the Prophet Joseph Smith*, 202).

This was such a moment. Natural sympathy would not send away a lone woman and a beloved child into the wilderness. Indeed, "the thing was very grievous in Abraham's sight" (Genesis 21:11). But the words of the Lord to Abraham indicate His hand in Sarah's decision: "And God said unto Abraham, Let it not be grievous in thy sight because of the lad, and because of thy bondwoman; in all that Sarah hath said unto thee, hearken unto her voice" (Genesis 21:12). The Lord then assured Abraham He would care for Hagar and Ishmael.

Sarah's "decision of character" proved wise in time. Both boys grew to become fathers of great nations. Sarah's decision ultimately saved them both.

ETERNITY WAS OUR COVERING AND OUR ROCK

Sarah lived in a dangerous world, especially for a woman. If there was no safety in Ur, Egypt and Canaan offered no greater assurances. Famine drove Sarah and Abraham into Egypt. Here, the lust of the Egyptian men, especially the Pharaoh, placed both Sarah and Abraham in a difficult position. The Lord counseled Abraham to tell the Egyptians that Sarah was his sister or else they would kill him and take his wife. (Because Sarah was Abraham's niece, she could in that time and culture legitimately be called his sister.) Sarah trusted her husband's revelation and the Lord's solution to their dilemma.

What were her thoughts when she "was taken into Pharaoh's house" because of her beauty? (Genesis 12:15). This also was a test of faith in the Lord's protecting power. Sarah submitted to the test, and the Lord preserved her.

Sarah and Abraham put their trust in the Lord and found joy. As they journeyed from Ur to Haran, from Haran to Canaan, and then down into Egypt and back to Canaan, they tell us, "Eternity was our covering and our rock and our salvation" (Abraham 2:16). The words *covering*, *rock*, and *salvation* are strongly associated with the Lord Jesus Christ. Sarah and Abraham relied on his loving care. They worshiped him and offered sacrifices. Abraham says they "called on the Lord devoutly, because we had already come into the land of this idolatrous nation" (Abraham 2:18).

We, too, live among a violent, carnal, "idolatrous people" (Kimball, "False Gods We Worship," 6). The example of Sarah provides comfort and counsel for us today. We can listen for the Lord's voice, obey his counsel, and rely on his care.

STRANGERS AND PILGRIMS

Paul taught that Abraham and Sarah "looked for a city [the city of Zion] which hath foundations, whose builder and maker is God . . . and confessed that they were strangers and pilgrims on the earth" (Hebrews 11:10, 13).

Sarah and Abraham knew of the peace, righteousness, and safety of the city of Enoch. They were not blessed to live in such a society, but they never stopped trying to build it within their own lives. They received the promise from the Lord that they would one day find that better country. Until that day they remained strangers to the corruption around them, pilgrims seeking a better country, and not ashamed of the God they worshiped. They had come out of the wickedness of Ur and would not return. We can learn much from this example of Sarah and Abraham.

AN EXAMPLE OF HOLY WOMEN
WHO TRUSTED IN GOD

As did Paul, Peter used Sarah as an example for the sisters of his day. Peter counseled the women that their adorning "not be that outward adorning of plaiting the hair, and of wearing of gold, or of putting on of apparel; but let it be the hidden man of the heart, in that which is not corruptible, even the ornament of a meek and quiet spirit, which is in the sight of God of great price. For after this manner in the old time the holy women also, who trusted in God, adorned themselves, being in subjection unto their own husbands: even as Sara obeyed Abraham, calling him lord: whose daughters ye are, as long as ye do well" (1 Peter 3:3–6).

We know Sarah was beautiful, but the focus of her life was the beauty of righteousness, which only God and those who look more deeply see.

Sarah's portrait gives us strength and inspiration. It reminds us that faith in the Lord and in his counsel is the only sure way of surviving an evil world. It teaches us to make eternity our covering and our rock and our salvation, of the need to be strangers and pilgrims, always seeking that better world and trusting the promise that one day we will find it. "Patience and faith in the Lord's promises will always bring their fulfillment even though one must wait many, many years," she seems to whisper. We learn from her that difficult decisions, even painful ones, must be made. Her portrait teaches us that through life's trials and hardships we will be blessed, if we learn to trust in the Lord and patiently wait for his promised blessings.

HAGAR, SEEN AND HEARD OF GOD

The lines of character etched in the portrait of Hagar's face reveal dignity and courage won through trial. The scriptures often speak of the "reproach" of women—that of not being able to bear a child. Since Hagar could bear the child Sarah could not, Hagar wrongly assumed a superior attitude to her mistress.

The scriptures report that "Sarai dealt hardly with her" and "she fled from her face" (Genesis 16:6). There are many ways we flee when corrected. All of us are undoubtedly aware of people who have fled from the fellowship of the Church because of real or perceived offenses.

A friend of mine serving as a bishop related the following experience: "A sister came into the office, desiring a temple recommend. She wanted to see her daughter married in a few weeks. I would have loved to grant her the recommend, but she had not paid tithing or attended meetings.

For one month she came to sacrament meeting and then handed me a check for fifty dollars, explaining it was her tithing. I tried to explain I would love to issue her a recommend, but could not until there was a pattern of activity in her life.

"I didn't have much of a chance. As soon as she heard I would not issue her a recommend at that time, she rose from her seat, chastised me for being a bad bishop, and walked out of the office. I followed her down the hall trying to get her to return so I could explain, but she would not let me. I drove to her house, but neither she nor her husband would speak with me. I tried calling on the phone; they would not listen. Months and years went by, but the family would not speak to me. I had 'dealt hardly' with them, and to this day they place the burden of their own inactivity on my shoulders."

Hagar was counseled by an angel, "Return to thy mistress and submit thyself under her hands" (Genesis 16:9). She returned to submit to Sarah.

If more members of the Church followed Hagar's example, activity in the Church would increase. How wonderful if husbands and wives could also apologize and admit their faults. If parents and children followed Hagar's example, families would be strengthened and alienation overcome. Even Hagar's name suggests the association of this act with her life, for the name *Hagar* means "flight." Perhaps she would have been more properly named *return*.

The Joseph Smith Translation of the Bible sheds an interesting light on the story of Hagar's flight. The angel asked Hagar,

"Knowest thou that God seest thee? And she said, I know that God seest me, for I have also here looked after him" (JST Genesis 16:15–16). Hagar learned the Lord was watching over her. He knew why she had fled; he knew her thoughts and desires. Before he sent her back, the Lord assured her: "I will multiply thy seed exceedingly, that it shall not be numbered for multitude" (Genesis 16:10).

When Hagar and Ishmael were sent away after the birth of Isaac, the Lord once again saw the plight of Hagar and took care of her, and he reaffirmed that Ishmael would be made a great nation. As she was struggling to survive, it was important for Hagar to know that the Lord was aware of her and her son. Alone, and "the water . . . spent in the bottle," Hagar placed Ishmael under a bush and removed herself from him to pray. "Let me not see the death of the child. And she sat over against him, and lift up her voice, and wept. And God heard the voice of the lad; and the angel of God called to Hagar out of heaven, and said unto her, What aileth thee, Hagar? Fear not; for God hath heard the voice of the lad where he is. Arise, lift up the lad, and hold him in thine hand; for I will make him a great nation. And God opened her eyes, and she saw a well of water; and she went, and filled the bottle with water, and gave the lad a drink" (Genesis 21:15–19).

The Lord heard the prayers of Hagar and of Ishmael. Alone, struggling to survive, and sometimes desperate, many women lift up their voices as did Hagar and cry out to the Lord in behalf of their children. Sometimes the answers do not come until "the water is spent in the bottle." I can testify that the Lord hears the prayers of these women and their children. He knows of their problems and pain. He knows their fears. Many women in the Church today rear their children alone for reasons that are far different from those that sent Hagar into the wilderness. But it is my fervent hope that they will find comfort and encouragement in the portrait of Hagar and know that there is a God in heaven who sees, hears, and provides for the Hagars and Ishmaels of the world as well as for the Sarahs and Isaacs.

CHAPTER 4

FLEEING SPIRITUAL BABYLON

There is no question that the sketch of Lot's wife is one the Lord would have us study. The Savior himself referred to her. One of the great tragedies of Genesis is that of Lot's family.

The world of Genesis was wicked and dangerous. Lot and Abraham dwelt together, but as their flocks grew, Abraham, wishing to avoid contention, suggested they separate and gave Lot the choice of where he wanted to dwell. "Lot lifted up his eyes, and beheld all the plain of Jordan, that it was well watered every where. . . . Then Lot chose him all the plain of Jordan. . . . And Lot dwelled in the cities of the plain, and pitched his tent toward Sodom" (Genesis 13:10–12).

If we are not careful, we too may unwisely pitch our tents toward Sodom. Then we too may find that the things of the world pull apart the fabric of our family.

When the Lord decided to destroy Sodom, he made his intentions known to Abraham and sent messengers to remove Lot's family. The men of the city surrounded Lot's house and demanded he surrender the messengers. When he refused, the men of Sodom also demanded Lot's two virgin daughters. At this moment perhaps Lot would have liked to rethink his decision to "[pitch] his tent toward Sodom." The messengers saved the family from the mob and told Lot to warn his extended family. "Lot went out, and spake unto his sons in law, which married his daughters, and said, Up, get you out of this place; for the Lord will destroy this city. But he seemed as one that mocked unto his sons in law" (Genesis 19:14). It seems that Lot had family in Sodom who refused to believe his message and died in the destruction.

LOOK NOT BEHIND THEE

When the angels brought Lot and his family out of Sodom, they counseled the family, "Escape for thy life; look not behind thee" (Genesis 19:17). Lot escaped to Zoar, and Sodom was destroyed, "but his wife looked back from behind him, and she became a pillar of salt" (Genesis 19:26).

When Jesus warned his disciples about the destruction of Jerusalem he told them to flee the city without delay. They were not to return for their possessions. He added, "And he that is in the field, let him likewise not return back. Remember Lot's wife" (Luke 17:31–32). Apparently, Lot's wife returned to the city.

The Savior counsels us to not look back to the things of the world we are leaving. If we seek the temporal things of Sodom we shall lose the eternal things of the Lord.

FLEE SPIRITUAL BABYLON

In the Doctrine and Covenants the Lord warns: "Go ye out from among the nations, even from Babylon, from the midst of wickedness, which is spiritual Babylon." He then adds a reference to Lot's wife: "And he that goeth, let him not look back lest sudden destruction shall come upon him" (D&C 133:14–15). When you leave the world, leave it for good. Don't look back! Don't hesitate! Don't return to wickedness!

When my mother was younger, she left the principles of the gospel for a time. As I was growing up, she warned me against the things of the world, assuring me that there was nothing desirable in the "large and spacious building." "Learn from me," she would say. "Don't be foolish as I was. Stay in the Church. Only in the gospel is there true happiness." These were powerful words. But what impressed me the most, and still does, is that I could never see my mother as a rebellious person. The only Norma Wilcox I knew was a faithful and righteous woman.

During her less active years, my mother reached a time when she began to explore the truths of the Book of Mormon. Its power softened her heart and created a hunger for knowledge. One evening she prayed to know the nature of God. The Lord answered her prayer, and her whole life began to change from that night on. She never looked back. She left all the trappings, attitudes, desires, habits, and thoughts of "spiritual Babylon" and "fled to Zion." This is why I found it so hard to believe she had ever been anything but totally committed to the gospel of Jesus Christ.

We have all met individuals who surprise us by indicating there were times in their lives when they were less than dedicated. It is hard to picture them as anything but the committed, righteous people we know. Their present lives testify to the principle of never looking back.

The Lord wants his children to live virtuous lives. Most of the women of the scriptures follow this pattern. Some may pitch their tents too close to Sodom or spend time in spiritual Babylon. But when the messengers come to bring them out, they neither linger nor look back. With their eyes focused on the celestial kingdom, they "press forward with a steadfastness in Christ, having a perfect brightness of hope, and a love of God and of all men" (2 Nephi 31:20).

Lot's wife made the mistake of looking back. Her life teaches us a great lesson by showing us the consequences of her mistake. We can learn from her to flee spiritual Babylon and never look back.

CHAPTER 5

PRESERVERS OF A LINEAGE

Not all of the portraits in the Bible are easy to understand. Among those more difficult ones are the portraits of women in the Old Testament who preserve a lineage. These portraits are complicated and can be hard to understand in our day. Yet there are still lessons we can learn from them.

LOT'S DAUGHTERS:
THE NEED TO MAINTAIN BALANCE

On either side of Lot's wife we see the faces of his daughters. Lot fled with his two daughters to a little city called Zoar. After the destruction, he left Zoar and "dwelt in the mountain, and his two daughters with him; for he feared to dwell in Zoar: and he dwelt in a cave, he and his two daughters" (Genesis 19:30).

At this point in the narrative, the Prophet Joseph Smith added important explanation. "And the first-born dealt wickedly, and said unto the younger, Our father has become old, and we have not a man on the earth to come in unto us, to live with us after the manner of all that live on the earth; therefore come, let us make our father drink wine, and we will lie with him, that we may preserve seed of our father. And they did wickedly, and made their father drink wine that night: and the first-born went in and lay with her father; and he perceived not when she lay down, nor when she arose" (JST Genesis 19:37–39). The next night the younger daughter did the same thing, and both became pregnant by their father. The two children born of these unions were Moab and Ammon, the fathers of the Moabites and Ammonites.

In the Old Testament culture it was extremely important to preserve the lineage, name, and seed of the father (see Genesis 38; Numbers 27:1–7; Ruth 4:14). That one should be cut off without seed to declare his generation was a great tragedy (see Isaiah 53:8).

YE SHALL NOT ADD, NEITHER SHALL YE DIMINISH

We can learn a great lesson from Lot's daughters. They surely knew that there were still people living on the earth, because they had just left Zoar. In addition, they had heard the messengers say that the Lord would destroy Sodom, not all places. The desire to perpetuate a lineage is righteous. But any law, counsel, commandment, or desire will produce wickedness if taken to extreme. All the requirements of the Lord must be kept in balance.

Moses told the children of Israel, "Ye shall not add unto the word which I command you, neither shall ye diminish ought from it, that ye may keep the commandments of the Lord your God" (Deuteronomy 4:2; see also Revelation 22:18–19).

The principles of the gospel are like a tightrope. Satan does not care which side of the rope we fall off. Fanatical zeal is as useful to him as rebellion or apathy. To help us walk the principles correctly, the Lord gives us the gift of the Holy Ghost. This gift is like the balancing pole the tightrope walker uses to remain balanced. All of our lives we are making adjustments, with the help of the Spirit, to stay in balance.

Occasionally we meet someone in the Church today who is off balance. I remember a sister who strongly believed in the Word of Wisdom. Many fast and testimony meetings she preached the Word of Wisdom. She believed that observing the Word of Wisdom included eating whole wheat ground on a home mill and avoiding all processed foods. She felt meat should not be eaten at all and natural herbs should be used for medicine rather than drugs prescribed by competent physicians. She was zealous in her beliefs and went to great lengths to convince others. She had "added" to the Word of Wisdom.

The daughters of Lot got way off balance. They were too zealous in the need to perpetuate their father's name and therefore "dealt wickedly." When we add to a principle, we often diminish from another. In this case Lot's daughters diminished the law of chastity in their desire to perpetuate a lineage.

TAMAR

The image of Tamar is an enigma, especially when seen through the ages that separate us. It is difficult to condone Tamar's actions; however, it is her father-in-law, Judah, who carries the burden of condemnation. All of Judah's lineage, including the Savior's, are traced to Tamar. If the manner in which she saved this line is not laudatory, her desire to "raise up seed" is understood in ancient and modern culture.

Judah had arranged for the marriage of Tamar to his eldest son, Er. Er was slain, and Onan, the next son, was instructed by Judah to "go in unto thy brother's wife, and marry her, and raise up seed to thy brother" (Genesis 38:8). Onan refused and died also because "the thing which he did displeased the Lord" (Genesis 38:10). Tamar was promised she would be given to the next son, Shelah, when he was old enough. Shelah grew up, but Tamar remained in her father's house, unmarried, childless, and forgotten.

Tamar laid aside her widow's garments, "covered her with a vail, and wrapped herself, and sat in an open place, which is by the way to Timnath" (Genesis 38:14). Judah saw her and thought she was a harlot. "And he turned unto her by the way, and said, Go to, I pray thee, let me come in unto thee; (for he knew not that she was his daughter in law)" (Genesis 38:16).

Tamar must have been aware of a moral laxity in her father-in-law or her plan would have been ridiculous. Her actions seem

strange to us, yet her desire for posterity and the need to perpetuate a family name were compelling.

Tamar demanded Judah pledge his signet, bracelets, and staff.
"And he gave it her, and came in unto her, and she conceived by
him" (Genesis 38:18). Tamar knew if she was found pregnant she
could expect harsh treatment. Her only hope for mercy would be
proof that Judah was the father of her child, and that she had
sought the preservation of a lineage and acted according to the
law of her time.

When word of Tamar's pregnancy was sent to Judah, he said,
"Bring her forth, and let her be burnt" (Genesis 38:24).

This incident illustrates the double standard for the chastity
of women and of men. Both Judah and Tamar had lost their
spouses, but whereas it seemed acceptable for Judah to go in to a
harlot, his daughter-in-law was to be burnt for the same sin.

When Tamar "was brought forth, she sent to her father in
law, saying, By the man, whose these are, am I with child: and she
said, Discern, I pray thee, whose are these, the signet, and
bracelets, and staff" (Genesis 38:25).

Judah's own words when he was presented with his property
are, perhaps, the best assessment of Tamar. He said: "She hath
been more righteous than I; because that I gave her not to Shelah
my son" (Genesis 38:26).

Twins were born to her. She named them Pharez and Zarah.
All genealogies of the tribe of Judah, including the lineage of
David, the kings of Judah, and the Savior, trace back to Pharez or
Zarah. Tamar is mentioned by name in the Savior's genealogy as
recorded in Matthew (see Matthew 1:3) and is mentioned by the
people and elders who surround Ruth and Boaz at their marriage.
"Let thy house be like the house of Pharez, whom Tamar bare
unto Judah, of the seed which the Lord shall give thee of this
young woman" (Ruth 4:12).

It is not insignificant that the Savior chose for his lineage to
come through Tamar. Perhaps he is teaching us that we should
not judge the actions of others too harshly, for we do not know
their circumstances or motivations.

CHAPTER 6

THE WORTH OF A
COVENANT WIFE

As the story of Rebekah begins, Abraham charges his servant with finding a righteous woman to be Isaac's wife, and therefore one of the great matriarchs of Israel. Anxious to see his son married within the covenant, Abraham had his servant swear that he would "not take a wife unto my son of the daughters of the Canaanites" but would "go unto my country, and to my kindred, and take a wife unto my son Isaac" (Genesis 24:3–4).

It was a long and dangerous trip to Haran. Josephus describes the journey as follows: "It requires much time to pass through Mesopotamia, in which it is tedious travelling, both in winter for the depth of the clay, and in summer for want of water; and, besides this, for the robberies there committed, which are not to be avoided by travellers but by caution beforehand" (*Antiquities of the Jews*, 38).

But holy men need holy women to stand by their sides. Brigham Young taught, "There is not a young man in our community who would not be willing to travel from here to England to be married right, if he understood things as they are; there is not a young woman in our community, who loves the Gospel and

wishes its blessings, that would be married in any other way"
(*Journal of Discourses*, 11:118).

Abraham and Isaac believed this truth. Rebekah was worth a
long and dangerous journey, just as Rachel and Leah were worth
that same journey in the next generation. The story of Esau also
illustrates this great principle. Esau lost his birthright because he
was content to marry from among the Canaanites.

THE MAN WONDERING AT HER HELD HIS PEACE

As the servant approached the well at Haran, he presented
the Lord with his plan for finding the right woman for Isaac. "O
Lord God of my master Abraham, I pray thee, send me good
speed this day, and shew kindness unto my master Abraham.
Behold, I stand here by the well of water; and the daughters of
the men of the city come out to draw water: And let it come to
pass, that the damsel to whom I shall say, Let down thy pitcher, I
pray thee, that I may drink; and she shall say, Drink, and I will
give thy camels drink also: let the same be she that thou hast
appointed for thy servant Isaac" (Genesis 24:12–14).

As a father of three boys, I have prayed earnestly that the
Lord would lead them to righteous young women. Our Father in
Heaven can show no greater kindness to a young man than to
help guide him to marry a worthy woman.

The servant prayed for a reassuring sign. The young woman
not only would give him a drink, which was a common courtesy
of the time, but she would volunteer to water his ten camels.
Camels drink a considerable amount. The young woman who
volunteered to do this would be kind, hospitable, and courteous.
The right wife for Isaac would pass this test.

According to Josephus, the servant went to the well and
asked water of several young women, "but while the others
refused, on pretence that they wanted it all at home, and could
spare none for him, one only of the company rebuked them for
their peevish behaviour towards the stranger, and said, What is
there that you will ever communicate to any body, who have not

so much as given the man some water? She then offered him water in an obliging manner" (*Antiquities of the Jews*, 38).

We read that Rebekah "went down to the well, and filled her pitcher, and came up"; furthermore, "she hasted, and let down her pitcher upon her hand, and gave him drink" (Genesis 24:16, 18). To reach wells in the Middle East, one must often descend numerous steps to reach the water. The fact that she hasted further testifies to her character.

Rebekah displayed a natural generosity, kindness, and eagerness to serve a stranger. Then, "when she had done giving him drink, she said, I will draw water for thy camels also, until they have done drinking. And she *hasted,* and emptied her pitcher into the trough, and *ran* again unto the well to draw water, and drew for all his camels" (Genesis 24:19–20; emphasis added).

If we visualize this scene, we begin to understand the next words of the story: "And the man wondering at her held his peace, to wit whether the Lord had made his journey prosperous or not" (Genesis 24:21). We admire Rebekah and love her immediately not only for her kindness but for the eagerness with which it was given. She was truly a woman worthy of being the progenitor of a lineage responsible to draw precious living water and offer it to the strangers of the world. Her descendant, Jesus, would one day offer living water to a woman of Samaria and, in time, to all of us.

Isaiah said, "Therefore with joy shall ye draw water out of the wells of salvation" (Isaiah 12:3). We have all seen modern Rebekahs run to draw living water for a Primary or Young Women class. I have watched many of my students leave their studies and graciously draw living water for people of many different countries. Every time we see these modern Rebekahs coming up from the well with their pitchers dripping, we, like Abraham's servant, wonder at seeing such unrehearsed demonstrations of character.

I often recall the time in my life when I was trying to find my own Rebekah. I had dated Laura for a short time and felt she was the woman with whom I desired to spend eternity. I traveled to

Canada to visit her at her parent's home. When we walked into church Sunday morning, I was pushed aside by the rush of people who wanted to see her. For at least five minutes I stood off to the side and wondered at her. Everyone loved her. She spoke softly to all the older members of the ward and hugged them in greeting. Little children came up to her. She knew all their names and stooped to hug and kiss them. There was such spontaneity in this scene. I saw her ability to love and to show genuine concern for others. I saw their love for her, which could only have been built by years of kindness and courtesy. I asked her the next morning to marry me.

This image of my wife holds a tender spot in my memory. I have seen similar scenes in many different places with different people, but I love this memory the best. Of all the memories I have of my wife throughout our marriage, this is one of the sweetest.

I WILL GO

Abraham's servant placed earrings and bracelets on Rebekah and asked her if there was space in her father's house. Rebekah replied, "We have both straw and provender enough, and room to lodge in" (Genesis 24:25). Remember, the servant had not yet introduced himself. The servant "bowed down his head" and thanked the Lord for "his mercy and his truth" for leading him correctly (Genesis 24:26–27). Then we read, "And the damsel ran, and told them of her mother's house these things" (Genesis 24:28).

At the house, the servant related his story to Rebekah's family, who agreed to let Rebekah be Isaac's wife, for "the thing proceedeth from the Lord" (Genesis 24:50). The next morning the servant desired to begin the long and dangerous return journey, but Rebekah's brother and mother wanted her to "abide with [them] a few days, at the least ten." After that she could go. But Abraham's servant said, "Hinder me not, seeing the Lord hath prospered my way; send me away that I may go to my master. And they said, We will call the damsel, and enquire at her mouth" (Genesis 24:55–57).

What were Rebekah's thoughts during this time? Would she not also have desired ten days with family members she would never see again? Yet, "they called Rebekah, and said unto her, Wilt thou go with this man? And she said, I will go" (Genesis 24:58).

In Rebekah's willingness to obey the Lord's will, we are reminded of Mary's sweet words, "Behold the handmaid of the Lord" (Luke 1:38). Her words also echo the Savior's own words in the premortal existence when he said, "Here am I, send me" (Abraham 3:27).

President Howard W. Hunter spoke with admiration of Rebekah's choice: "We have, then, examples from the scriptures of how we should consider and evaluate the commandments of the Lord. If we choose to react like . . . Rebekah, . . . our response will be, simply, to go and do the thing that the Lord has commanded" (Conference Report, October 1982, 83–84; see also 1 Nephi 3:7).

Prior to her departure, Rebekah was given a blessing. The words of that blessing echo one given to Abraham (see Genesis 22:17) and indicate Rebekah and her family knew of the Abrahamic covenant and understood the significance of her marriage to Isaac: "Thou art our sister, be thou the mother of thousands of millions" (Genesis 24:60).

When Isaac went out to meet the returning caravan, Rebekah "lighted off the camel . . . took a vail, and covered herself." This was proper modesty. "And Isaac brought her into his mother Sarah's tent [implying that Rebekah became the matriarch of the family], . . . and he loved her" (Genesis 24:64–65, 67).

SHE WENT TO ENQUIRE OF THE LORD

Rebekah shared with other noble women of the scriptures a deep desire for children, but for twenty years, Rebekah, like Sarah, had no child. "Isaac intreated the Lord for his wife, because she was barren: and the Lord was intreated of him, and Rebekah his wife conceived. And the children struggled together within her; and she said, If it be so, why am I thus? And she went to enquire of the Lord" (Genesis 25:21–22). Perhaps Rebekah sensed the significance of the struggle within her. Perhaps, like most mothers, she was anxious about her children. She enquired of the Lord and received an answer.

When questions arose in their lives, the women of the scriptures sought counsel. Latter-day Saint women do the same. When my daughter was young, she fell on a glass and severed a nerve in her arm. She was worried about the doctor's warning that she might never use her hand again. He was afraid the muscles would die before the nerve could regenerate. She asked for a blessing and then went to her room. The next morning, she announced: "I know that my hand will be all right. I asked Heavenly Father, and he told me the nerve would grow in time." Her faith was rewarded, and the nerve regenerated in a miraculously short amount of time.

Women across the Church, like Rebekah, enquire of the Lord. In his own way and his own time, he answers them. The knowledge the Lord gave to Rebekah about Jacob and Esau guided her in maintaining the birthright line. The answers women receive today also guide the futures and destinies of those they love.

ISAAC WAS SPORTING WITH REBEKAH HIS WIFE

Rebekah was "very fair to look upon" (JST Genesis 24:16). As with Abraham and Sarah, Isaac and Rebekah feared that Isaac would be killed for his wife's beauty. Following the example of Abraham and Sarah, Isaac and Rebekah told Abimelech, "king of the Philistines unto Gerar," that Rebekah was Isaac's sister (Genesis 26:1). This stratagem worked well until "Abimelech . . . looked out at a window, and saw, and, behold, Isaac was sporting with Rebekah his wife" (Genesis 26:8). Although the word *sporting* can have a sexual meaning, it does not always carry that connotation. In Hebrew it is the same word that is translated "laugh" in the story of Sarah and Abraham. The *New Strong's Exhaustive Concordance of the Bible* gives the meaning of *sporting* as "to laugh outright (in merriment or scorn)" and the meaning of *to sport* as "to laugh, mock, play, make sport" (99).

The scriptures so often show the serious nature of women and men. It is refreshing to know Rebekah and Isaac enjoyed each other's company. There are times of laughter in marriage. We can be assured that many scriptural women also enjoyed such moments of merriment and play.

WHAT GOOD SHALL MY LIFE DO ME?

Scriptural evidence testifies that Rebekah loved both her sons intensely, but she knew by revelation that Jacob had been chosen of the Lord. As they grew, this knowledge was confirmed by the different qualities each developed. When Esau "took to wife Judith the daughter of Beeri the Hittite, and Bashemath the daughter of Elon the Hittite," his decision was a "grief of mind unto Isaac and to Rebekah" (Genesis 26:34–35). Josephus indicates that Esau contracted these marriages on his own, without consulting his parents (*Antiquities of the Jews*, 39).

Esau's marriages help explain why Rebekah would dress Jacob in Esau's clothes to make him seem to Isaac to be Esau. Perhaps Rebekah chose this deception because she felt Isaac's preference for the hunting abilities of Esau would cause him to bestow on Esau that which she knew by revelation belonged to Jacob. Perhaps elements are missing from the story. Elder Erastus Snow explained Rebekah's actions in this way:

"From the story that is told of Rebekah helping her son Jacob to get the first blessing from his father Isaac, on purpose to secure the birthright from his brother Esau, many would be inclined to think that deceit, dishonesty and unrighteous means were employed to secure it, and they perhaps wonder why it should be so. This was really not the case; it is only made to appear so in the eyes of those who do not understand the dealings of God with man, and the workings of the Holy Spirit to being about His purposes. There was neither unrighteousness in Rebekah nor in Jacob in this matter; but on the contrary, there was the wisdom of the Almighty, showing forth his providences in guiding them in such a manner as to bring about his purposes, in influencing Esau to transfer his birthright to Jacob, that He might ratify and confirm it upon the head of Jacob; knowing as He did that Jacob and his seed were, and would be, more deserving of the birthright, and would magnify it in its true spirit. While Esau did not sense nor appreciate his condition and birthright; he did not respect it as he should have done, neither did he hearken to the counsels of his father and mother, on the contrary, he went his own way with a stubborn will, and followed his own passions and inclinations and took to wife one of the daughters of the Canaanites whom the Lord had not blessed; and he therefore rendered himself unacceptable to God and to is father and mother. . . . The Lord therefore saw fit to take it from him, and the mother was moved upon to help the younger son to bring about the purpose of the Lord" (*Journal of Discourses*, 21:370–71).

This story centers on the marriage covenant. It is introduced with Rebekah's "grief of mind" over Esau's marriages, and it ends with Rebekah asking Isaac to send Jacob to Haran to marry one of her brother Laban's daughters. "And Rebekah said to Isaac, I am weary of my life because of the daughters of Heth: if Jacob take a wife of the daughters of Heth, such as these which are of the daughters of the land, what good shall my life do me?" (Genesis 27:46). Rebekah shows us the strong desire that her children marry within the covenant and fulfill its responsibilities.

One of the greatest sorrows women bear is the incorrect decisions of their children. Just as the death of a loved one reveals to us how much we love them, Rebekah's grief of mind revealed the intensity of her love.

Rebekah's grief is one many of us bear at one time or another, in differing degrees of intensity. The power of the scriptures is in their ability to show us the sorrows and the strengths of wonderful people so that we may understand we are not alone in our challenges. Rebekah's last recorded words are a poignant cry that her child marry within the covenant. Isaac heeded her cry and sent Jacob to Haran to find a wife from the daughters of Laban.

Rebekah is one of my favorite women in the scriptures. We learn much from her. We see in her the worth of a covenant wife, as well as her desire for her children to marry in the covenant.

Here is a woman who without hesitation responded to the will of the Lord with the simple words, "I will go." Her example encourages us to enquire of the Lord to receive direction for our lives and answers to our questions. May her features remain long in our minds and in our hearts.

NOAH'S GRANDDAUGHTERS: THE DAUGHTERS OF GOD AND THE SONS OF MEN

The grief Rebekah felt when her son Esau chose to marry one of the daughters of Heth may have mirrored the grief felt by Noah and his wife over the marriages of their granddaughters outside the covenant. Although this decision often brings heartache, it is very common. Priesthood leaders and friends frequently find themselves comforting women who have made similar choices. My heart goes out to these women. The lesson this portrait teaches is one of the plain and precious truths of the Old Testament restored in the Pearl of Great Price.

In the book of Moses we read that "Noah and his sons hearkened unto the Lord, and gave heed, and they were called the sons of God" (Moses 8:13). A son of God was one who accepted the plan of salvation, acted upon its truths, received priesthood ordination, and hearkened to the counsels and words of the Lord.

By contrast those who would not listen to or obey the gospel were called the "sons of men." The granddaughters of Noah married men who were not obeying the gospel.

"And when these men [the sons of God] began to multiply on the face of the earth, and daughters were born unto them, the sons of men saw that those daughters were fair, and they took them wives, even as they chose. And the Lord said unto Noah: The daughters of thy sons have sold themselves; for behold mine anger is kindled against the sons of men, for they will not hearken to my voice" (Moses 8:14–15).

The expression "sold themselves" is very strong. We might add the word *short* to the expression to clarify its meaning. They had denied themselves numerous blessings, including the wonderful blessings associated with the eternities. Their decision also affected their children and grandchildren until the Flood.

Brigham Young spoke of this type of decision when he said: "How is it with you, sisters? Do you distinguish between a man of God and a man of the world? . . . The love this Gospel produces is far above the love of women; it is the love of God—the love of eternity—of eternal lives" (*Journal of Discourses*, 8:199–200). Marriages must be entered into in which a woman can love her husband and love God without conflict. For a daughter of God to accept anything less is to sell herself short.

That does not apply only to marriages to men who are not Church members. Some members of the Church are not worthy of temple blessings. To become a son of God requires more than just baptism; it requires "hearkening unto the Lord, and [giving] heed." Often such a marriage is entered into with great hope that the "son of men" will in time see the beauty of the gospel and change. Surely he will become a "son of God." That result is the exception, however, not the general rule.

Daughters of God face the dilemmas caused by such a marriage for various reasons. Some, when they decided to marry, perhaps did not appreciate the great blessings of the temple but now desire those blessings in their lives. Others may have joined the Church after marriage, and their husbands have not yet followed them into the waters of baptism. Whatever the reasons, it is important for us not to judge each other based upon a husband's or a wife's membership or activity in the Church. We should love and fellowship each other regardless of circumstances.

PETER'S COUNSEL

When faced with the concerns of marriages not in the covenant, due largely to the conversion of the wife but not of the husband, Peter counseled, "Likewise, ye wives, be in subjection to your own husbands; that, if any obey not the word, they also may without the word be won by the conversation of the wives; while they behold your chaste conversation coupled with fear" (1 Peter 3:1–2). Peter counseled the sisters to live so righteously that their example of the fruits of the gospel would win the husbands to conversion. The term *conversation* means "conduct" (1 Peter 3:2 note b). Although a wife cannot take away agency or bear the responsibility of her husband's choices, she can be an example. There is nothing more powerful in changing a husband than the righteous example of his wife.

PAUL'S COUNSEL

When Paul faced similar concerns among the Corinthian Saints he counseled them: "If any brother hath a wife that believeth not, and she be pleased to dwell with him, let him not put her away. And the woman which hath an husband that believeth not, and if he be pleased to dwell with her, let her not leave him. For the unbelieving husband is sanctified by the wife, and the unbelieving wife is sanctified by the husband. . . . For what knowest thou, O wife, whether thou shalt save thy husband? or how knowest thou, O man, whether thou shalt save thy wife?" (1 Corinthians 7:12–14, 16).

Paul gave the same hope Peter did. From time to time this hope is rewarded. One of the finest couples I know began marriage as did the granddaughters of Noah, but the wife desired the full blessings of the gospel, and eventually her husband chose to enter the waters of baptism.

COUNSEL OF MODERN PROPHETS

Brigham Young offered the following counsel: "Were I a woman possessed of great powers of mind, filled with wisdom, and, upon the whole, a magnanimous woman, and had been privileged with my choice, and had married a man, and found myself deceived, he not answering my expectations, and I being sorry that I had made such a choice, let me show my wisdom by not complaining about it. . . . By seeking to cast off her husband—by withdrawing her confidence and goodwill from him, she casts a dark shade upon his path, when, by pursuing a proper course of love, obedience, and encouragement, he might attain to that perfection she had anticipated in him" (*Journal of Discourses*, 7:280).

President Spencer W. Kimball echoed the advice given by his predecessors. "I can understand quite fully the problems that have arisen in your family life because of your conversion to the gospel of Jesus Christ. . . . It has always been so and sadly the future will continue to see it so. . . . It would be our hope that, instead of bringing a chasm between your husband and you, the gospel could be the welding link that could bring you close together and finally into an unalterable, unterminating relationship with your precious children. . . . It seems to me that your position would be to become the perfect wife and the perfect mother and make your husband love you so intensively that he would never give thought to the possibility of losing you for eternity, and that you would so thoroughly and properly rear your children so that their father would never entertain the thought of a possible loss of them. . . . In my experience of many years, I have seen many unbelieving spouses finally brought into the Church in great happiness in the cases where there was long-suffering and deep understanding and much patience" (*Teachings of Spencer W. Kimball*, 309–10).

For those who have not yet married, the granddaughters of Noah provide a strong warning about the importance of marrying in the covenant. For those who are married to nonmembers or less active husbands, for whatever reason, the counsel of prophets both past and present offers encouragement and hope for someday enjoying the blessings of a covenant marriage. In all marriages, husbands and wives should share each other's support, love, and respect. They should enjoy being together. We see this illustrated beautifully in the portrait of Rebekah.

CHAPTER 7

MOTHERS OF ISRAEL

The next great women presented in the gallery are the sisters Rachel and Leah, whose portraits hang side by side. Their account contains one of the most beautiful love stories in all of literature, one that reemphasizes the worth of a covenant wife.

THE WORTH OF A VIRTUOUS WOMAN

"And Laban had two daughters: the name of the elder was Leah, and the name of the younger was Rachel. Leah was tender eyed; but Rachel was beautiful and well favoured. And Jacob loved Rachel; and said [to Laban], I will serve thee seven years for Rachel thy younger daughter" (Genesis 29:16–18). What is the worth of a virtuous woman? Proverbs answers, "Her price is far above rubies" (31:10). Jacob was willing to give seven years' work for Rachel. As it turned out, he also worked seven years for Leah. In this manner he provided the dowry demanded by custom. What would it mean to a wife to know her husband had labored seven years for her?

Wilford Woodruff understood the worth of a righteous woman. He taught, "Bless your souls, if you lived here in the flesh a thousand years, as long as Father Adam, and lived and labored all your life in poverty, and when you got through, if, by your acts, you could secure your wives and children in the morning of the first resurrection, to dwell with you in the presence of God, that one thing would amply pay you for the labors of a thousand years" (*Journal of Discourses*, 21:284). A man courts a woman for a short while to win her for time, but he must court her for a lifetime to win her for eternity.

I do not find it hard to understand Jacob's labors or his feeling that they "seemed unto him but a few days" (Genesis 29:20). I can imagine my Father in Heaven asking me, as Laban asked Jacob, "Because thou art my [son], shouldest thou therefore serve me for nought? tell me, what shall thy wages be?" (Genesis 29:15). I would answer, "I will serve thee all my life and into eternity for the companionship of thy daughter Laura." What greater reward could one ask?

SURELY THE LORD HATH LOOKED UPON MY AFFLICTION

All this was good for Rachel, but what about Leah? How must she have felt? Through the deception of Laban, Leah was married to Jacob. Leah must have been involved in the plan, for one word from her would have stopped everything. We do not know how much freedom she had in the matter or how she felt. She did know the character of Jacob and the birthright promises. It would be understandable if she wanted to have a noble husband and be "the mother of thousands of millions" (Genesis 24:60).

There is a certain justice in the marriage of Leah and Jacob. Jacob had deceived his own father and brother to secure the birthright. He could certainly understand the deception worked by Laban and Leah, even though he cried, "What is this thou hast done unto me?" (Genesis 29:25). Jacob, however, agreed to work another seven years, and Laban allowed him to marry Rachel a week later.

Jacob "loved . . . Rachel more than Leah" (Genesis 29:30). Josephus wrote, "Now Lea[h] was sorely troubled at her husband's love to her sister; and she expected she should be better esteemed if she bare him children: so she entreated God perpetually" (*Antiquities of the Jews*, 41).

In a sense, the Lord compensated Leah for her sorrow. "When the Lord saw that Leah was hated, he opened her womb: but Rachel was barren" (Genesis 29:31). *Hated* is a strong word. The word translated as *hated* means "not favored" in Hebrew.

Leah bore Jacob four sons. At this time and in this culture, having sons was very important. Leah's naming of her sons reveals her pain that Jacob does not favor her, as well as her recognition that God had blessed her. At Reuben's birth she said, "Surely the Lord hath looked upon my affliction; now therefore my husband will love me." The name *Reuben* means "Look, a son." When Simeon was born she said, "Because the Lord hath heard that I was hated, he hath therefore given me this son also." *Simeon* means "hearing." Leah named her next son *Levi*, meaning "joined or pledged," and said, "Now this time will my husband be joined unto me, because I have born him three sons." Then Leah bore Judah and said, "Now will I praise the Lord." The name *Judah* means "praise" (Genesis 29:32–35). Later, Leah bore two more sons, Issachar and Zebulun, and a daughter named Dinah. "Now will my husband dwell with me, because I have born him six sons" (Genesis 30:20).

The Lord understands the sorrow of women who feel their husbands do not favor them. In our modern world there are not two wives in the same family, but a wife may compete against her husband's hobby, his work, his friends, or even in some tragic cases, another woman. In his mercy and compassion, the Lord does what is possible to alleviate some of the pain these circumstances create.

GIVE ME CHILDREN, OR ELSE I DIE

Leah envied Rachel's favor in Jacob's eyes, and Rachel envied Leah her sons. "When Rachel saw that she bare Jacob no children, Rachel envied her sister; and said unto Jacob, Give me children, or else I die" (Genesis 30:1). Rachel's desire for children was as great as any other woman's in the scriptures, and no other woman in the scriptures expressed this desire more fervently. It is a righteous desire lodged deep in the souls of the daughters of God. Many latter-day Rachels hunger for children that they cannot bear. Not all women will have this hunger satisfied in this life, but the Lord will bless them eternally for their desires.

Life has a way of reaching a certain equality. The Lord will extend his compensating mercy. Rachel eventually bore two sons, Joseph and Benjamin. Though she did not bear six sons, as her sister did, she was the mother of the chosen son, Joseph, who became one of the foremost prophets in the Old Testament. She had other noble descendants, including Joshua, Samuel, Jonathan, and Esther. The apostle Paul was a descendant of Rachel through Benjamin. Lehi, Nephi, and other Book of Mormon prophets descended from Rachel. Through Rachel came Joseph Smith and other great leaders of the Restoration.

Leah also had a noble posterity. Although some of her sons brought her pain with their choices, through them came such noble people as Moses, Caleb, Naomi, Boaz, David, Jehoshaphat, Hezekiah, Josiah, and Ezra. Leah also, through Mulek, had descendants who became part of the great story of the Book of Mormon. For generations the priesthood rested with Leah's descendants, the Levites. Most important of all, through Leah came the Messiah and his apostles.

Both Rachel and Leah were blessed greatly by the Lord in having a great and noble posterity.

EQUALITY OF TESTING

And what of Leah's "tender eyes" when compared to the "beautiful and well favoured" Rachel? Brigham Young taught: "Those who attain to the blessing of the first or celestial resurrection will be pure and holy, and perfect in body. Every man and woman that reaches to this unspeakable attainment will be as beautiful as the angels that surround the throne of God. If you can, by faithfulness in this life, obtain the right to come up in the morning of the resurrection, you need entertain no fears that the wife will be dissatisfied with her husband, or the husband with the wife; for those of the first resurrection will be free from sin and from the consequences and power of sin" (*Journal of Discourses,* 10:24).

In the eternities the love of Jacob for Rachel and Leah, as well as for Bilhah and Zilpah, and their love for him, will be celestial and eternal.

Elder Boyd K. Packer spoke of the equality of the testing we all undergo while in mortality. "Some are tested by poor health, some by a body that is deformed or homely. Others are tested by handsome and healthy bodies; some by the passion of youth; others by the erosions of age. Some suffer disappointment in marriage, family problems; others live in poverty and obscurity. Some (perhaps this is the hardest test) find ease and luxury. All are part of the test, and there is more equality in this testing than sometimes we suspect" (Conference Report, October 1980, 29).

Leah lived to see her children and grandchildren. Rachel died in childbirth. A husband and wife share a sweet and beautiful love in the first years of marriage. In the later years, a different kind of deep love and closeness develops, which comes from years of struggle and sacrifice together. Rachel received the blessings of the first years. Leah apparently was granted the blessings of the later ones. Although these compensating blessings may not have eased the daily existence of Leah at first, from an eternal perspective Leah and Rachel both were "well favored."

WHATSOEVER GOD HATH SAID UNTO THEE, DO

Jacob was told in a dream to "Return unto the land of thy fathers, and to thy kindred; and I will be with thee" (Genesis 31:3). Jacob detailed to his wives his reasons for desiring to leave Haran, ending with the Lord's words counseling him to return to his homeland. He then waited for his wives' views. Speaking of this moment, President Howard W. Hunter said: "When Jacob was instructed to return to the land of Canaan, which meant leaving all for which he had worked for many years, he called Rachel and Leah into the field where his flock was and explained what the Lord had said. The reply of Rachel was simple and straightforward and indicative of her commitment: 'Whatsoever God hath said unto thee, do' (Genesis 31:16)" (Conference Report, October 1982, 83).

This account presents a wonderful example of a family council. Jacob, Rachel, and Leah all gave their thoughts and expressed their willingness to do whatsoever God had said.

Before the family departed, Rachel took her father's images. Since she probably did not believe in the power of these images as gods, some suggest she did this because they were good luck charms or some type of heirloom. A more plausible explanation is that they served as a deed to property she felt was hers. Rachel and Leah both felt that their father had cheated them, and it is quite likely that Rachel therefore felt justified in taking some token of her inheritance rights. She soon gave them up, however, in order to "go up to Beth-el" (Genesis 35:3).

ARISE AND GO UP TO BETHEL

After Jacob and his family were settled in Canaan, the Lord commanded him to take his family to Bethel. On his way to seek a wife, Jacob had stopped at a place called Luz. There he had had a dream in which he saw a ladder or stairway reaching into heaven with angels ascending and descending. He made a vow to the Lord there and anointed a pillar in honor of the Lord. Jacob called this place Bethel, which means "house of God" (see Genesis 28:17–19). Bethel is one of the first temples identified in the Old Testament.

There is tremendous application for us today in the Lord's command to go to Bethel and in Jacob's response. Each man is charged with the responsibility of taking his wife and children to the temple, the Bethel of today. "Then Jacob said unto his household, and to all that were with him, Put away the strange gods that are among you, and be clean, and change your garments: And let us arise, and go up to Beth-el; and I will make there an altar unto God, who answered me in the day of my distress, and was with me in the way which I went" (Genesis 35:2–3).

They put away the strange gods, purified or cleansed themselves, and changed their garments. "And they gave unto Jacob all the strange gods which were in their hand, and all their earrings which were in their ears; and Jacob hid them under the oak which was by Shechem" (Genesis 35:4).

Rachel and Leah showed proper respect to both the Lord and his house. They buried the gods of the world deep in the earth before worshiping God at Bethel. We should examine our lives and see if we have any strange gods that need to be buried before we worship.

Rachel and Leah also gave up "all their earrings which were in their ears." There is nothing unrighteous in earrings, but apparently these earrings were inappropriate for Bethel. Some fashions today are also not appropriate for one who would go to the temple.

Elder Boyd K. Packer gave the following counsel relative to such fashions: "On occasions, when I have performed a marriage in the temple, there has been one there to witness it who obviously has paid little attention to the counsel that the Brethren have given about dress and grooming, about taking care not to emulate the world in the extremes of style in clothing, in hair length and arrangement, etc. I have wondered why it is that if such a person was mature enough to be admitted to the temple he would not at once be sensible enough to know that the Lord could not be pleased with those who show obvious preference to follow after the ways of the world" (*Holy Temple*, 74).

The Rachels and Leahs of today show their reverence for the temple by the styles they choose. Their respect for the temple garment, for instance, is not compromised in an attempt to keep abreast of fashions. Once they have been to Bethel, they leave worldly fashion behind.

Being clean encompasses both spiritual and physical cleanliness. Jacob, Rachel, and Leah needed to be cleansed from the world before they went up to Bethel. They changed their garments to signify they had cleansed themselves, just as we put on clean clothes after bathing and change our clothes when we enter the temple. The change of garments suggests a newness of life and a reverence for the Lord's house.

This trip to Bethel is the last we see of Rachel and Leah. Rachel died at Bethlehem giving birth to Benjamin. We do not know when Leah died, but she was buried in the Cave of Machpelah with Abraham, Sarah, Isaac, and Rebekah.

BILHAH AND ZILPAH: MOTHERS OF ISRAEL

Near the portraits of Leah and Rachel hang the two sketches of Bilhah and Zilpah, the handmaidens Laban gave to his daughters. There are few details in these sketches. Like Rachel and Leah, they bore children who became progenitors of tribes of Israel; they also would have buried the strange gods and earrings of the world to go up to Bethel.

When Rachel failed to bear children, like Sarah she arranged for the marriage of her handmaiden, Bilhah, to Jacob, "that I may also have children by her" (Genesis 30:3). "When Leah saw that she had left bearing, she took Zilpah her maid, and gave her Jacob to wife" (Genesis 30:9). Each of these handmaidens bore two children who fathered tribes of Israel.

Some have been troubled over this giving of maidservants to Jacob. Did Bilhah and Zilpah have any say in the matter?

Handmaids were servants attached to the family. Marriages would have been arranged for them. In all of Haran, Rachel and Leah could not have chosen a more righteous man for their handmaidens. Jacob was a great patriarch. Were they not invited to share in the covenants that were to be passed on through Jacob's lineage? Bilhah and Zilpah are nearly always called Jacob's wives. When Jacob went to meet Esau, all Jacob's wives and their children were presented as members of his household (see Genesis 33:3–7). Although they remained the handmaids of Rachel and Leah, much as Hagar remained a handmaid to Sarah, in their world this would not have been a demeaning role. It would have been a good marriage for them.

The Doctrine and Covenants implies that Bilhah and Zilpah are exalted with Jacob: "Abraham received concubines, and they bore him children; and it was accounted unto him for

58

righteousness, because they were given unto him, and he abode in my law; as Isaac also and Jacob did none other things than that which they were commanded; and because they did none other things than that which they were commanded, they have entered into their exaltation, according to the promises, and sit upon thrones, and are not angels but are gods" (D&C 132:37). A concubine was a wife who came to her marriage without a marriage contract or dowry, not a mistress or other immoral woman.

Bilhah and Zilpah hold an honored place as mothers of tribes of Israel. Although we have only sketches of these good women, the Lord carefully watched the lineage of his chosen people and placed Bilhah and Zilpah in places of honor.

The portraits of the wives of Jacob help us understand the worth of a covenant wife and to realize the compensating mercies of a loving Father in Heaven. As did other great women in the scriptures, the wives of Jacob—Leah, Rachel, Bilhah, and Zilpah—expressed their willingness to obey the Lord's directions without hesitation. When invited to worship the Lord at Bethel, they abandoned the things of the world forever.

We now pass on to other portraits, grateful for the lessons about facing life with dignity and hope that the wives of Jacob have taught us.

CHAPTER 8

THE WOMEN WHO SAVED MOSES

Adjacent to the hall of Genesis is a small room containing six sketches of the women who saved Moses. The beauty of their faces is worthy of admiration and reflection. Just as the Lord made Eve a "help meet," a surrounding and protecting force for Adam, Shiphrah and Puah, Jochebed, Miriam, Pharaoh's daughter, and Zipporah surrounded and protected Moses. Many are not familiar with their contributions.

SHIPHRAH AND PUAH:
OBEYING HIGHER LAWS OF CONSCIENCE

Since the days of Joseph, Israel's fortunes in the land of Egypt had changed drastically. Fearing the Israelites might become too powerful and revolt, Pharaoh decided upon a strategy to reduce the male population. "And the king of Egypt spake to the Hebrew midwives, of which the name of one was Shiphrah, and the name of the other Puah: And he said, When ye do the office of a midwife to the Hebrew women, and see them upon the stools; if it be a son, then ye shall kill him: but if it be a daughter, then she shall live" (Exodus 1:15–16).

BUT THE MIDWIVES FEARED GOD

Shiphrah and Puah faced a dilemma discussed again and again throughout history: Should an individual defy government when its commands are repugnant to moral sensibilities?

In the continuing debate between following conscience and following orders, it is wonderful that the first example of this presented in the Bible is that of Shiphrah and Puah. If they obeyed, they gained the favor of the king; if they disobeyed, they gained the favor of God and the approval of their own consciences.

"But the midwives feared God, and did not as the king of Egypt commanded them, but saved the men children alive" (Exodus 1:17). Their courage saved the life of Moses. To all who have justified cruelty, oppression, and suffering in the name of duty, Shiphrah and Puah witness that there is a higher law which must be obeyed, even at the cost of one's life. Fearing God is more important than fearing man, and duty to conscience must always guide our actions.

The king confronted Shiphrah and Puah with their disobedience. "Why have ye done this thing, and have saved the men children alive? And the midwives said unto Pharaoh, Because the Hebrew women are not as the Egyptian women; for they are lively, and are delivered ere the midwives come in unto them. Therefore God dealt well with the midwives" (Exodus 1:18–20). The midwives' excuse does not sound very convincing. That "God dealt well with the midwives" may suggest that the Lord had something to do with the king's acceptance of their explanation.

"And it came to pass, because the midwives feared God, that he made them houses" (Exodus 1:21). A large and righteous posterity, or "house," was considered one of the greatest blessings God could bestow.

As we contemplate the few strokes that delineate the images of Shiphrah and Puah, we seem to hear them say, "Do not justify evil by passing responsibility for your actions to those who demand them. Seek the Lord's approval over the compulsion of men."

JOCHEBED:
NOT AFRAID OF THE KING'S COMMANDMENT

During this time Moses was born to Amram and Jochebed. Again the courage and compassion of a woman saved Moses from destruction. Because the midwives would not kill the male children, "Pharaoh charged all his people, saying, Every son that is born ye shall cast into the river, and every daughter ye shall save alive" (Exodus 1:22). Josephus indicates, "If any parents should disobey him, and venture to save their male children alive, they and their families should be destroyed" (*Antiquities of the Jews*, 56). Jochebed was "not afraid of the king's commandment" (Hebrews 11:23). In Moses' own account we read: "And the woman conceived, and bare a son: and when she saw him that he was a goodly child, she hid him three months. And when she could no longer hide him, she took for him an ark of bulrushes, and daubed it with slime and with pitch, and put the child therein; and she laid it in the flags by the river's brink" (Exodus 2:2–3).

By placing Moses in the river, Jochebed demonstrated her faith in the protection of the Lord, as well as in her husband's revelations. Josephus indicates that Amram had received, through a dream, knowledge that his son was the promised deliverer of his people. He related this dream to his wife. After their three-month attempt to hide the baby they "determined rather to intrust the safety and care of the child to God, than to depend on [their] own concealment of him, which [they] looked upon as a thing uncertain, . . . but [they] believed that God would some way for certain procure the safety of the child, in order to secure the truth of his own predictions" (*Antiquities of the Jews*, 56). Their faith was rewarded through the intervention of Pharaoh's daughter.

PHARAOH'S DAUGHTER:
SHE HAD COMPASSION ON HIM

Pharaoh's daughter is one of the few women in scripture whose calling was prophesied before she was born. Joseph had prophesied: "A seer will I raise up to deliver my people out of the land of Egypt; and he shall be called Moses. And by this name he shall know that he is of thy house; for he shall be nursed by the king's daughter, and shall be called her son" (JST Genesis 50:29). Moses is an Egyptian name that means "son." As the ark rested in the flags at the river's brink, "the daughter of Pharaoh came down to wash herself at the river; and her maidens walked along by the river's side; and when she saw the ark among the flags, she sent her maid to fetch it. And when she had opened it, she saw the child: and, behold, the babe wept. And she had compassion on him, and said, This is one of the Hebrews' children" (Exodus 2:5–6).

By the Lord's foreknowledge of the natural sympathies of this particular woman, Moses was placed in the safest place in Egypt, Pharaoh's own house. The Lord knew before she was born that she would have compassion upon a crying baby. He knew she would desire to keep the child and rear him as her own. Once again, a woman of compassion defied unrighteous authority to save Moses' life.

Not only did she save his life but she was instrumental in preparing him for his great mission. The New Testament explains that "Pharaoh's daughter took him up, and nourished him for her own son. And Moses was learned in all the wisdom of the Egyptians, and was mighty in words and in deeds" (Acts 7:21–22). Part of the nourishing Pharaoh's daughter provided was education. Because Moses would lead his people and write the first five books of the Bible, the education Egypt could provide would have benefited him. Pharaoh's daughter fulfilled her premortal calling and played a significant role in the preparation of a great prophet.

I am familiar with a modern Pharaoh's daughter, a Latter-day Saint woman who has adopted "and nourished for her own" three children, in addition to the eight children she has given birth to. Two of the adopted children are of another race, and the third has Down's Syndrome. The environment of love and education she has provided have nourished exceptional children. May the many women who have adopted children and reared them as their own see the compassionate face of Pharaoh's daughter in their own countenance.

MIRIAM: AND HIS SISTER STOOD AFAR OFF

The fifth woman to play a role in the salvation of Moses was his older sister, Miriam. Her role, which continued well into the Exodus, began while she watched the ark of bulrushes in the flags of the river. "And his sister stood afar off, to wit what would be done to him" (Exodus 2:4). Miriam watched Pharaoh's daughter. She saw her lift her little brother out of the ark and hold him in her arms. She saw the compassion in her face.

Sensing all would be well, Miriam approached Pharaoh's daughter and asked, "Shall I go and call to thee a nurse of the Hebrew women, that she may nurse the child for thee? And Pharaoh's daughter said to her, Go. And the maid went and called the child's mother" (Exodus 2:7–8).

Thus it was through Miriam that Jochebed was able to nurse her own son until he was weaned. Who would have believed that within so short a time Moses would be back in his own house, nursed by his own mother, free from the Pharaoh's decree, and without need of hiding?

I SENT BEFORE THEE MIRIAM

At the time of the Exodus, Miriam again played a significant role in Moses' life. The Lord, in the book of Micah, places Miriam with Moses and Aaron at the head of the Exodus: "O my people . . . I brought thee up out of the land of Egypt, and redeemed thee out of the house of servants; and I sent before thee Moses, Aaron, and Miriam" (Micah 6:3–4). Modern counterparts to their roles might be leader of the Melchizedek Priesthood (prophet), leader of the Aaronic Priesthood (presiding bishop), and general president of the Relief Society. All were essential in leading the children of Israel out of Egypt, through the wilderness, and into the promised land.

When the Egyptians were drowned in the Red Sea, "Miriam

the prophetess, the sister of Aaron, took a timbrel in her hand; and all the women went out after her with timbrels and with dances. And Miriam answered them, Sing ye to the Lord, for he hath triumphed gloriously" (Exodus 15:20–21). Miriam is called a "prophetess," meaning she was filled with "the testimony of Jesus" (Revelation 19:10). She led the women in praising the Lord, just as Deborah, Hannah, and Mary sang hymns of praise and gratitude.

WE HAVE DONE FOOLISHLY

Miriam and Aaron used Moses' marriage to an "Ethiopian woman" as an excuse to challenge his leadership. They confronted him, saying, "Hath the Lord indeed spoken only by Moses? Hath he not spoken also by us?" (Numbers 12:1–2).

Undoubtedly the Lord had spoken by them in their respective callings; however, their complaints against Moses were inappropriate, and the Lord quickly set them straight. "The Lord spake suddenly unto Moses, and unto Aaron, and unto Miriam, Come out ye three unto the tabernacle" (Numbers 12:4).

When they arrived at the tabernacle, the Lord told Aaron and Miriam that he may speak to others "in a vision . . . [or] in a dream," but when he spoke to Moses he spoke "mouth to mouth" (Numbers 12:5–8). As a sign that her challenge of Moses had made her unclean, Miriam became leprous. Moses pleaded for her, and the Lord healed her, but she was shut outside the camp for seven days. She submitted humbly to the Lord's chastisement, and then returned, much as Hagar returned to Sarah. The people's great respect for Miriam is shown in Numbers 12:15. "And Miriam was shut out from the camp seven days: and the people journeyed not till Miriam was brought in again." Since the Lord himself directed the journeys of the people, this verse indicates it was his will that the people wait for Miriam's return.

The Lord's daughters, even those who are prophetesses, make mistakes, but they receive correction and repent. The Lord said, "As many as I love, I rebuke and chasten: be zealous therefore, and repent" (Revelation 3:19). The Lord does not choose leaders only because they are righteous; he also chooses them because they accept correction. Miriam had this ability. Those who cannot abide the Lord's rebukes will never be his leaders. A righteous woman may make mistakes, but she knows the Lord loves her and is willing to submit to him. As we face our own human fallibility and the numerous mistakes we make, it will help us to remember the portrait of Miriam.

ZIPPORAH: STANDING BEFORE THE LORD

We turn now to reflect on the features of the last woman in the six portraits of those who influenced the life of Moses. Zipporah was the daughter of Jethro, "high priest of Midian" (JST Exodus 18:1). Moses received from Jethro the Melchizedek priesthood and sound advice on delegation—we know from this that Zipporah was reared in an environment of righteousness and faith.

Moses defended Zipporah and her six sisters from shepherds who drove them away from the water they had drawn for their flocks. After this, "Moses was content to dwell with the man: and he gave Moses Zipporah his daughter. And she bare him a son" (Exodus 2:21–22).

We do not hear of Zipporah again until after Moses was called to deliver Israel. "And Moses took his wife and his sons, and set them upon an ass, and he returned to the land of Egypt: and Moses took the rod of God in his hand" (Exodus 4:20). Against one of the mightiest civilizations of the ancient world, God sent a man, his wife and children, and the rod of God.

We have only one story with any detail that involves Zipporah. The Joseph Smith Translation is a great help in understanding Zipporah's actions.

"And it came to pass, that the Lord appeared unto [Moses] as he was in the way, by the inn. The Lord was angry with Moses, and his hand was about to fall upon him, to kill him; for he had not circumcised his son" (JST Exodus 4:24).

How is it that a prophet of the Lord failed to obey such an important commandment? Some suggest Moses was so occupied with the Lord's work he had neglected this ordinance in behalf of his own family. Perhaps Moses' situation was similar to the one described in section 93 of the Doctrine and Covenants, when the Lord chastened the First Presidency, including Joseph Smith, for their misplaced priorities. The Lord told Frederick G. Williams, "That wicked one hath power, as yet, over you. . . . if you will be delivered you shall set in order your own house." Sidney Rigdon was told he had "not kept the commandments concerning his children" and that he must "first set in order thy house" (D&C 93:42–44). If Moses was to be delivered he needed to first "set in order [his] own house." If this was not done, the "wicked one" would have "power over" him.

What is the role of a wife when her husband has failed to set in order his own house? This is a delicate question and must be answered by each woman with the help of the Spirit. What is a woman to do when that failure has put him in jeopardy, either physically or spiritually? "Zipporah took a sharp stone and circumcised her son, and cast the stone at his [Moses'] feet, and said, Surely thou art a bloody husband unto me" (JST Exodus 4:25). The expression "bloody husband" can also be translated a "bridegroom of blood" and refers to a covenant (Exodus 4:25 note b). Zipporah was not expressing anger or exasperation. She appears rather to have been affirming a covenant relationship, almost as if she were saying to the Lord, "I have circumcised my son on behalf of my husband." Whether or not we fully understand Zipporah's actions, "the Lord spared Moses and let him go, because Zipporah, his wife, circumcised the child" (JST Exodus 4:26).

Women, in their role as help meets, often spare their husbands. They encourage, inspire, urge, motivate, exhort, counsel, advise, prod, beseech, advocate, goad, entreat, stimulate, persuade, influence, implore, sway, recommend, prompt, and invite their husbands, their sons, and others to do right. For Zipporah persuasion was not enough; action was required.

Many women save their husbands, sons, and others from foolishness, neglect, or lack of insight. The scriptures are full of examples. Eve helped Adam understand the necessity of partaking of the fruit. Sarah demanded the separation of Isaac and

Ishmael. Rebekah urged Isaac to send Jacob to Haran for a righteous wife. Rachel and Leah counseled with Jacob regarding the family's return to Canaan. Rahab recognized the true God of Israel and thereby saved her family. Deborah called and inspired Barak to deliver Israel. Hannah gave her son to the service of the Lord. Michal saved David's life; Abigail saved him from committing an act of revenge; Bathsheba reminded him that Solomon was chosen to reign in his stead. The Shunammite woman asked her husband to make a guest room for Elisha. Pilate's wife counseled him to set Jesus free. The list will continue to grow as long as men listen to righteous women.

Before leaving the room of Exodus we express silent gratitude for the lessons we have been taught from these beautiful portraits. We have learned from Shiphrah, Puah, and Jochebed not to compromise our own moral convictions or violate our conscience but to act with courage, faith, and compassion. We have learned from Pharaoh's daughter that if our heart is filled with natural empathy and tenderness, the Lord will use those qualities to further his work and bless his children. If the Lord knows we can receive correction, as did Miriam, he can mold us into effective leaders and productive servants. If men listen to the Zipporahs of their lives, those wonderful women will encourage them to righteousness while protecting them from their own foolishness, forgetfulness, neglect, or lack of vision. Moses was blessed by women who helped him fulfill his foreordained responsibilities. May God bless us all to be so encircled.

CHAPTER 9

AN INHERITANCE
IN THE PROMISED LAND

The next portraits we see are of six women who were blessed to receive an inheritance in Israel.

MAHLAH, NOAH, HOGLAH, MILCAH, AND TIRZAH: BRINGING CAUSES TO GOD

The five sisters Mahlah, Noah, Hoglah, Milcah, and Tirzah, women of the tribe of Manasseh, were the daughters of Zelophehad. They and their father wandered with Israel in the wilderness, where their father died. "He was not in the company of them that gathered themselves together against the Lord in the company of Korah; but died in his own sin, and had no sons" (Numbers 27:3).

Under the laws of inheritance during the time of Moses, the sons carried on their father's name and received his lands. The daughters of Zelophehad felt an injustice was being done. Their father had not rebelled, and they believed he should have an inheritance in the promised land through them. With faith in the justice of their cause "they stood before Moses, and before Eleazar the priest, and before the princes and all the congregation, by the door of the tabernacle of the congregation" (Numbers 27:2).

The courage to challenge the laws of their culture and make such a request must have come from a number of sources. Surely they supported each other. There is much strength when women unite together. Their courage also came from a belief in the Lord's prophet: They trusted Moses would hear their cause and make a wise and correct decision. They must also have found courage in the justice of their cause and in the knowledge that it was not selfish: "Why should the name of our father be done away from among his family," they reasoned, "because he hath no son? Give unto us therefore a possession among the brethren of our father" (Numbers 27:4).

The daughters of Zelophehad can inspire women of the Church to feel confidence in our prophets. The living prophets and apostles of today bring the causes of the sisters before the Lord as did Moses. They, like Moses, desire that women receive justice, equality, and the Lord's wisdom in every aspect of their lives. In an age of protest and criticism, these five young sisters show us a better way. Trusting in the Lord's prophet, they explained their concerns, then waited while he "brought their cause before the Lord" (Numbers 27:5).

The Lord told Moses, "The daughters of Zelophehad speak right: thou shalt surely give them a possession of an inheritance among their father's brethren; and thou shalt cause the inheritance of their father to pass unto them. And thou shalt speak unto the children of Israel, saying, If a man die, and have no son, then ye shall cause his inheritance to pass unto his daughter" (Numbers 27:7–8).

EVEN AS THE LORD COMMANDED

Everyone accepted the Lord's counsel until the "chief fathers of the families . . . of the sons of Joseph" saw a potential problem (Numbers 36:1). If Mahlah, Noah, Hoglah, Milcah, and Tirzah chose husbands from one of the other tribes, the land would pass to that tribe through their sons. Before long there would be little pockets of land within the boundaries of one tribal inheritance that belonged, through the marriage of daughters, to other tribes.

Moses again went to the Lord and brought back an addition to the earlier counsel. "This is the thing which the Lord doth command concerning the daughters of Zelophehad, saying, Let them marry to whom they think best; only to the family of the tribe of their father shall they marry. So shall not the inheritance of the children of Israel remove from tribe to tribe: for every one of the children of Israel shall keep himself to the inheritance of the tribe of his fathers. And every daughter, that possesseth an inheritance in any tribe of the children of Israel, shall be wife unto one of the family of the tribe of her father, that the children of Israel may enjoy every man the inheritance of his fathers" (Numbers 36:6–8).

Mahlah, Noah, Hoglah, Milcah, and Tirzah accepted the counsel of Moses. "Even as the Lord commanded Moses, so did the daughters of Zelophehad: for [they] . . . were married unto their father's brothers' sons . . . and their inheritance remained in the tribe of the family of their father" (Numbers 36:10–12).

The obedience of the daughters of Zelophehad stands as counterpoint to the murmurings and rebellions described in Exodus and Numbers. They represented the new generation whose faithfulness, courage, and trust in the prophets would carry Israel into the promised land and establish them as the Lord's people. As we take a final look at their portrait, we are reminded of the way faithful sisters of today strengthen one another, voice their concerns and bring their causes to the priesthood, and follow counsel.

RAHAB: BELIEF AMONG THE UNBELIEVERS

Next to the daughters of Zelophehad hangs the portrait of the harlot Rahab, a Canaanite woman from Jericho who hid Joshua's spies. Whatever her past, Rahab was held up in the New Testament by both Paul and James as an example of great faith. Rahab was a convert to the covenant of Israel, and in all probability accepted Israel's God without anyone to teach her. She is an example for thousands of converts who willingly change their lives when faith is born in their hearts. Rahab demonstrated her faith with works.

She also showed how one member of a family, who is willing to repent, can bring salvation to the rest. Rahab's story shows us that a woman from a wicked environment may still become a woman of integrity through repentance and righteous living.

I KNOW THAT THE LORD YOUR GOD, HE IS GOD

Word came to the king of Jericho that spies had lodged at Rahab's house, and he sent men to arrest them. Rahab hid the spies on the roof of her house under some flax. She then informed the men sent by the king that the spies were on their way across the Jordan River to the main camp of the Israelites. Her deception was successful, and the king's men searched for the spies between Jericho and the ford of the Jordan River.

Rahab then spoke to the spies on her roof. Her words proclaimed her faith, just as her actions demonstrated it. "I know," Rahab testified, "that the Lord hath given you the land, . . . for we have heard how the Lord dried up the water of the Red sea for you, when ye came out of Egypt; . . . the Lord your God, he is God in heaven above, and in earth beneath. Now therefore, I pray you, swear unto me by the Lord, since I have shewed you kindness, that ye will also shew kindness unto my father's house, and give me a true token: And that ye will save alive my father, and my mother, and my brethren, and my sisters, and all that they have, and deliver our lives from death" (Joshua 2:9–13). Others in Jericho may have feared the Israelites when they heard of the Lord's wonders, but Rahab accepted that the God who performed them was indeed the God in heaven above.

When James stated, "Shew me thy faith without thy works, and I will shew thee my faith by my works" (James 2:18), he used Rahab's actions as an example of faith demonstrated by works. Her life testifies that when we discover truth we must exercise faith and change.

SHE PERISHED NOT WITH THEM THAT BELIEVED NOT

Rahab is presented in sharp contrast to the Canaanites who were destroyed in the land of Israel. Paul spoke of Jericho's fall and of Rahab's faith: "By faith the walls of Jericho fell down, after they were compassed about seven days. By faith the harlot Rahab perished not with them that believed not, when she had received the spies with peace" (Hebrews 11:30–31).

I had the privilege of teaching the gospel to a modern Rahab in France during my mission. Like Rahab of Jericho, she did not have a virtuous past. But when we taught her the gospel, she, too, bore testimony, saying, "I know that . . . the Lord your God, he is God." Though she met with great opposition from those who did not believe, she refused to listen to them or to perish "with them that believed not."

Like Rahab of Jericho, this modern Rahab saved her family. She introduced them to the gospel, and in a short time we baptized her family into the Church. The joy I experienced in seeing the faith of this modern Rahab has been felt by nearly every missionary in the field. Many families now in the Church owe their salvation to the faith of women who first received the messengers with peace.

My own ancestor Harriet Austin accepted the gospel when it was first preached to her in New York state. When the call came to travel to Nauvoo, she packed her belongings and started down the road. Her father rode for miles after her, pleading with her to return, but Harriet never looked back. She refused to perish spiritually "with them that believed not."

SHE DWELLETH IN ISRAEL EVEN UNTIL THIS DAY

When the battle for Jericho was over, "Joshua saved Rahab the harlot alive, and her father's household, and all that she had; and she dwelleth in Israel even unto this day" (Joshua 6:25). It is one thing to accept the gospel; it is another to remain faithful. Many converts, as well as many born in the Church, do not dwell "in Israel even unto this day." Rahab appears to have endured to the end.

Conversion to the Church often requires new members to make substantial changes in their lives which take much hard work and faith to sustain. Many, like Rahab, remain faithful to the end. But some fall away and lose the blessings of the gospel. Brigham Young spoke of the unfortunate path of far too many converts when he said: "When the Gospel is preached to the honest in heart they receive it by faith, but when they obey it labor is required. To practice the Gospel requires time, faith, the heart's affections and a great deal of labor. Here many stop. They hear and believe, but before they go on to practice they begin to think that they were mistaken, and unbelief enters into their hearts" (*Journal of Discourses*, 16:40).

Like my ancestor Harriet Austin, Rahab never looked back and endured faithfully to the end. Because of her faith and courage, her descendants enjoyed the blessings of the covenant. He son was Boaz, the kind and gentle man who so lovingly cared for Ruth and Naomi. Only four women are mentioned by name in the genealogy of Jesus: Ruth, Bathsheba, Tamar, and Rahab (see Matthew 1:1–16).

The portrait of Rahab shows a woman who had the faith to go against the tide of evil and refused to perish spiritually with those who believed not. We see one who had the courage to change and a faith she was willing to demonstrate by her works, a woman who endured in her commitment to the truth and to the people she had accepted. May the portrait of Rahab provide hope for those whose faith leads them to make new commitments. May generations yet unborn honor them as Rahab's descendants honored her.

CHAPTER 10

———

WOMEN OF THE REIGN
OF THE JUDGES

We now see before us the portraits of the women of the book of Judges. First is the large portrait of the prophetess Deborah (see Judges 4:4). The last verse of the book of Judges reveals much about Deborah's world, the world of Jael, Jephthah's daughter, Samson's mother, and Delilah. "In those days there was no king in Israel: every man did that which was right in his own eyes" (Judges 21:25). That sounds hauntingly like our own expression, "Do your own thing."

DEBORAH: INSTILLING FAITH AND COURAGE

Deborah stands out as a woman of wisdom and integrity in a time of wickedness and foolishness. "The children of Israel came up to her for judgment" (Judges 4:5). In the scriptures "to judge" often means to minister or to serve. Deborah judged her people by drawing upon the spiritual gifts the Lord had given her.

Latter-day Saint women also live in an atmosphere of wickedness and foolishness. Deborah is an example to them of the necessity of being filled with the spirit of prophecy, of the testimony of Jesus (see Revelation 19:10), that their wisdom may guide their families, friends, and communities. I was honored to serve with several modern Deborahs while I was a bishop. Their wisdom was generally offered in private conversations. Their compassion, linked with the spirit of discernment, blessed and edified, and many came to them for judgment.

One sister in particular had great compassion and was blessed with the spirit of discernment. She seemed to know who in the ward needed help. She also was blessed with keen insight on how to alleviate their problems. Not only could she discern the spirits of others but she could also judge, much as I believe Deborah judged ancient Israel. Many, sensing her compassion and wisdom, sought her out, feeling she could understand their concerns. She listened to them and offered good counsel.

SHARING SPIRITUAL GIFTS

All sisters are given spiritual gifts through the Holy Ghost which enable them to bless the lives of others and contribute to the edification of the Church (see D&C 46:11). Often we are unaware of the power of our gifts, because we do not understand the many ways in which these gifts manifest themselves.

I recall one sister asking me about her patriarchal blessing, which told her she had the gift of healing. "I do not have the priesthood and have no desire to enter the medical field. What good is this gift to me?" she asked. As we talked, it became apparent that her gift had to do with spiritual and emotional healing.

Another had been told she had the gift of tongues. She had not gone on a foreign mission and never learned a second language. "What is the purpose of this gift?" she asked. As we talked she realized she had eloquence in the use of English, her own tongue. With this gift she had blessed the lives of many through her teaching and speaking abilities. The gifts of the spirit given to sisters of the Church enable them to "judge" the modern children of Israel much as Deborah must have used her gifts to judge ancient Israel. Latter-day Deborahs minister, guide, serve, and bless others.

I WILL SURELY GO WITH THEE

The verse I love most in the story of Deborah contains Barak's response when Deborah delivered to him the Lord's command to take ten thousand men and face an army with nine hundred iron chariots. "And Barak said unto her, If thou wilt go with me, then I will go: but if thou wilt not go with me, then I will not go." Deborah answered, "I will surely go with thee" (Judges 4:8–9).

Some interpret Barak's answer as evidence of a lack of faith or courage. I see it as his recognition of Deborah's faith and the strength she inspired. Modern Deborahs also inspire confidence and faith in others. Their support enables others to believe they can obey the Lord and fulfill his commandments, face great challenges and emerge victorious. How many times have we seen a mother's presence inspire a small child with the courage to face a congregation in his or her first talk, a wife inspire her husband in his new calling, or a young woman encourage a young man to faithfully serve a mission. Every time we witness this we see Deborah reborn.

With Deborah by his side, Barak and his ten thousand men descended Mount Tabor. The Lord flooded the valley, disabling the chariots. Sisera was defeated. Though Sisera had "his chariots and his multitude" (Judges 4:7), Barak had ten thousand men, Deborah, and the Lord. How could he fail?

A MOTHER IN ISRAEL

After the battle, Deborah sang a psalm of praise and love to the Lord. In this song she called herself by a special title, a title that is sometimes belittled today when everyone does that which is "right in his own eyes." Deborah sang, "The inhabitants of the villages ceased, they ceased in Israel, until that I Deborah arose, that I arose a mother in Israel" (Judges 5:7). The title "mother in Israel" is the most sacred title a woman will be honored to bear either in time or eternity.

The portrait of Deborah seems to say to us: "Use your gifts to bless the children of Israel who come to you for judgment and whom you serve. Inspire others, by your very presence, to obey the Lord, to keep his commandments, and to face great challenges. Choose the title mother in Israel above all others, for it is one of the most sacred titles you will be honored to bear either in time or in eternity."

JAEL: INTO THE HAND OF A WOMAN

Next to the portrait of Deborah is that of Jael, the woman who killed an enemy of her people by subterfuge.

After the battle between Barak and Sisera, "Sisera fled away on his feet to the tent of Jael the wife of Heber the Kenite." She gave him some milk and agreed to stand guard while he slept. "Then Jael Heber's wife took a nail of the tent, and took an hammer in her hand, and went softly unto him, and smote the nail into his temples, and fastened it into the ground: for he was fast asleep and weary. So he died" (Judges 4:17, 21).

To us, Jael's actions may seem shocking. Yet Deborah praised Jael, saying: "Blessed above women shall Jael the wife of Heber the Kenite be, blessed shall she be above women in the tent. . . . She put her hand to the nail, and her right hand to the workmen's hammer" (Judges 5:24–26).

To find in Jael's portrait a characteristic we can emulate, we must remember that the Lord commanded the Israelites to destroy the Canaanites for their wickedness and that Sisera "mightily oppressed the children of Israel" (Judges 4:3). Deborah had prophesied that "the Lord shall sell Sisera into the hand of a woman" (Judges 4:9). The word translated "sell" can also be translated "surrender," or "deliver." The Lord surely delivered Sisera into the hand of Jael.

It was important for Israel to realize the Lord could defeat their enemies with any means if they were only faithful. A lone woman could defeat the mightiest warrior. The theme of the weak defeating the mighty through the help of the Lord is repeated throughout the Old Testament. Jael's story teaches us that one need not be mighty to accomplish the Lord's work or to save her people. Many fought in the battle that day, but the Lord reserved the defeat of the general to a woman at home in her tent. Any woman may win the greatest victories in the spiritual battles against Satan, just as Jael triumphed over Israel's greatest enemy.

An important parallel in the scriptures to Jael's killing of Sisera is Nephi's killing of Laban. When the Spirit bade Nephi to slay Laban, he hesitated: "Never at any time have I shed the blood of man. And I shrunk and would that I might not slay him. And the Spirit said unto me again: Behold the Lord hath delivered him into thy hands. . . . Behold the Lord slayeth the wicked to bring forth his righteous purposes" (1 Nephi 4:10–13). Notice how similar the Spirit's words to Nephi—"the Lord hath delivered him into thy hands"—are to Deborah's prophecy that the Lord would "sell Sisera into the hand of a woman." As the Lord delivered Laban into Nephi's hand, so he delivered Sisera into Jael's hand. Perhaps Jael had a similar conversation with the Spirit before she took up the nail of the tent.

For most women service to the Lord and others will be through compassion, gentleness, and love. Regardless of the tools, however, the portrait of Jael reminds us all that the blow we strike against tyranny, oppression, or evil may be the one that will ensure victory.

JEPHTHAH'S DAUGHTER: THE WEIGHT OF A COVENANT

During the reign of the judges the Ammonites threatened the tribes of Israel living east of the Jordan River. They chose Jephthah to lead them in battle. Prior to the battle, Jephthah "vowed a vow unto the Lord, and said, If thou shalt without fail deliver the children of Ammon into mine hands, then it shall be, that whatsoever cometh forth of the doors of my house to meet me, when I return in peace . . . shall surely be the Lord's, and I will offer it up for a burnt offering" (Judges 11:30–31). Jephthah returned home in triumph "unto his house, and, behold, his daughter came out to meet him with timbrels and with dances:

and she was his only child; beside her he had neither son nor daughter" (Judges 11:34).

Some commentators have concluded that Jephthah offered his daughter as a human sacrifice. Others have concluded that she was not offered as a burnt offering, but devoted her life to the service of Jehovah. The latter seems a more plausible explanation. In the Old Testament, Jephthah is portrayed as one of the heroes of Israel, which would not have been true if he had participated in human sacrifice. In the New Testament, Paul extolled Jephthah as an example of faith along with Gideon, Barak, Samuel, and others (see Hebrews 11:32). Would Paul have done that if Jephthah had burned his daughter?

Jephthah was deeply distressed when his daughter appeared first to meet him. He "rent his clothes, and said, Alas, my daughter! thou hast brought me very low . . . for I have opened my mouth unto the Lord, and I cannot go back" (Judges 11:35). Dedicating his daughter to the service of Jehovah would have meant a life of virginity for her. The importance placed on lineage in the ancient world and the fact that she was his only child would only have added to Jephthah's anguish in losing her. She would be the end of his posterity.

"She said unto him, My father, if thou hast opened thy mouth unto the Lord, do to me according to that which hath proceeded out of thy mouth; forasmuch as the Lord hath taken vengeance for thee of thine enemies" (Judges 11:36). It is sometimes difficult to comprehend how strongly the people of the Old Testament felt about the taking of an oath or the fulfilling of a vow. Jephthah's daughter believed in the binding power of an oath, and she fulfilled her father's vow even though it meant a great sacrifice. How wonderful it would be if we felt the same way about our vows and covenants, especially those of the sacrament, endowment, and marriage. Though she did not make the oath herself, she honored it for her father's sake, both father and daughter believing their sacrifice was acceptable to the Lord.

Jephthah's daughter did ask her father, "Let this thing be done for me: let me alone two months, that I may go up and down upon the mountains, and bewail my virginity, I and my fellows. And he said, Go. . . . And it came to pass at the end of two months, that she returned unto her father, who did with her according to his vow which he had vowed: and she knew no man" (Judges 11:37–39).

The phrase "bewailed my virginity" and the phrase "she knew no man" immediately after we read that Jephthah "did with her according to his vow" have led many commentators to conclude she devoted her life to the service of Jehovah. In the New Testament, the widow Anna "departed not from the temple, but served God with fastings and prayers night and day" (Luke 2:37). Perhaps Jephthah's daughter served Jehovah in a similar fashion.

The sacrifice of Jephthah's daughter stands as a monument to the strength of a vow made before the Lord. We will continue to reflect on her portrait, seeking to fulfill our own vows, whatever the required sacrifice.

THE MOTHER OF SAMSON

The last part of Judges is dominated by Samson and his wife Delilah, but for me the sketch of his mother provides great inspiration.

Samson's mother was the wife of Manoah of the tribe of Dan. An angel appeared to her and said: "Behold now, thou art barren, and bearest not: but thou shalt conceive, and bear a son. Now therefore beware, I pray thee, and drink not wine nor strong drink, and eat not any unclean thing: for, lo, thou shalt conceive, and bear a son; and no razor shall come on his head: for the child shall be a Nazarite unto God from the womb: and he shall begin to deliver Israel out of the hand of the Philistines" (Judges 13:3–5).

A Nazarite was a consecrated man whose vow involved separation from the world and any uncleanliness. A Nazarite was known by the length of his hair (see Numbers 6:5). Samson's mother ran and told her husband about the angel, including the special instructions regarding her own separation while she carried the child.

Desiring to understand the requirements of bearing and

rearing this special son, both Manoah and his wife "intreated the Lord, and said, O my Lord, let the man of God which thou didst send come again unto us, and teach us what we shall do unto the child that shall be born" (Judges 13:8). The angel returned to Manoah's wife as she sat alone in a field. She ran and brought her husband, and the angel instructed them. When the angel left, Manoah said, "We shall surely die, because we have seen God." But his wife, showing greater discernment, replied, "If the Lord were pleased to kill us, he would not have . . . shewed us all these things, nor would as at this time have told us such things as these" (Judges 13:22–23). It is interesting to note that in this case the revelation came first to Samson's mother.

I am impressed with the unity of Samson's mother and father in desiring guidance to rear their child. Samson's mother wanted Manoah to hear the words of the angel spoken to her. They asked together for instructions regarding their son. It is important that a mother and father be united in rearing their children. Though couples may have differing views about bringing up their families, when parents seek the Lord's counsel, the desired unity usually comes naturally.

TEACH US WHAT WE SHALL DO UNTO THE CHILD THAT SHALL BE BORN

In addition to her discerning spirit, Samson's mother exemplified one of the most treasured aspects of a mother—the desire to rear her children in a manner pleasing to the Lord. She and her husband asked the Lord to "teach us what we shall do unto the child that shall be born." When the angel returned, they asked him, "How shall we order the child, and how shall we do unto him?" (Judges 13:8, 12).

What wonderful questions! Many righteous women have petitioned the Lord in like manner. Samson's mother and father were asking this question even before their child was born. The Lord has instructed us, "Bring up your children in light and truth" (D&C 93:40). If light and truth have not been taught in the early years, it is often too late.

We can be fairly confident Samson was taught in the way the Lord counseled. His faithful parents sought the Lord's guidance and tried to direct their son in the right course. Yet Samson's later behavior was a source of grief to his parents, for he broke many covenants of Israel as well as the covenants of a Nazarite. When he announced his desire to marry a Philistine woman, they replied, "Is there never a woman among the daughters of thy brethren, or among all my people, that thou goest to take a wife of the uncircumcised Philistines?" (Judges 14:3).

Although he was brought up to serve God, Samson's selfish, rebellious, and often childish ways led to his destruction. Sometimes, in spite of all parents do, children brought up in light and truth reject the faith of their parents. Many mothers today know this heartache. Though there may be some comfort in the knowledge that they sought the Lord and followed his counsel to the best of their ability, it often does not alleviate the pain and heartache parents feel over a wayward child. Elder Gordon B. Hinckley has said: "I recognize that there are parents who, notwithstanding an outpouring of love and a diligent and faithful effort to teach them, see their children grow in a contrary manner and weep while their wayward sons and daughters willfully pursue courses of tragic consequence. For such I have great sympathy" (Conference Report, October 1978, 27). On another occasion he taught: "If any of you have a child or loved one in that condition, do not give up. Pray for them and love them and reach out to them and help them" (*Teachings of Gordon B. Hinckley*, 54).

In the sketch of Samson's mother we see one who sought the Lord's inspiration in the rearing of her child even before he was born. May we follow her example and receive the comfort of knowing we sought to the best of our ability to follow the directions given us by the Lord.

DELILAH: THE MOCKERY OF FEIGNED LOVE

Although he had righteous parents who did as the Lord directed, Samson chose to reject their teachings and to associate with women who would lead him to destruction. He married a Philistine and consorted with harlots before encountering Delilah. Next to Jezebel, there is probably no more infamous woman in scripture than Delilah. We now turn to her portrait. In the gallery Delilah represents the woman who uses her physical powers in a seductive and unrighteous manner.

Many of the virtuous women whose portraits are in the scriptural gallery are described as being "exceedingly fair and beautiful," but they never used this beauty to arouse lust or to exercise unrighteous influence.

Men are warned against unrighteous dominion. Male dominion is often exercised by virtue of physical strength. Women, also, must avoid unrighteous dominion through using the influence of their physical endowments to manipulate, injure, or control. Delilah is an example of womanhood to be avoided.

In his instructions to men regarding the righteous use of priesthood, the Lord tells them to influence others only "by love unfeigned" (D&C 121:41). Feigned love is that which is manipulative, self-seeking, pretended, or deceptive. Women, as well as men, must avoid this type of love. Yet it was exactly that, feigned love, which Delilah used to bring Samson to his doom.

"And the lords of the Philistines came up unto her, and said unto her, Entice him, and see wherein his great strength lieth, and by what means we may prevail against him, that we may bind him to afflict him: and we will give thee every one of us eleven hundred pieces of silver" (Judges 16:5).

Delilah immediately set out to find the secret of Samson's great strength. "Tell me, I pray thee, wherein thy great strength lieth, and wherewith thou mightest be bound to afflict thee" (Judges 16:6). She must have been fairly confident of her power over him to ask so boldly and, of course, Samson himself was overconfident.

Samson should have learned from a previous experience with his Philistine wife and a wager regarding his riddle, but he toyed with Delilah by telling her various things she could do to "afflict" him. Delilah finally used the same line his Philistine wife had used earlier. His wife had said: "Thou dost but hate me, and lovest me not: . . . and she wept before him the seven days . . . and it came to pass on the seventh day, that he told her, because she lay sore upon him" (Judges 14:16–17). Delilah used the same tactic, and Samson gave in again. "She said unto him, How canst thou say, I love thee, when thine heart is not with me? thou hast mocked me these three times, and hast not told me wherein thy great strength lieth. And it came to pass, when she pressed him daily with her words, and urged him, so that his soul was vexed unto death; that he told her all his heart" (Judges 16:15–17).

Who was mocking whom? Delilah's heart was with not Samson but with the Philistine lords and their money. "When Delilah saw that he had told her all his heart, she sent and called for the lords of the Philistines. . . . And she called for a man, and she caused him to shave off the seven locks of his head; and she began to afflict him, and his strength went from him. And she said, The Philistines be upon thee, Samson . . . [and they] took him, and put out his eyes, and brought him down to Gaza, and bound him with fetters of brass; and he did grind in the prison house" (Judges 16:18–21).

The scriptures pointedly insist that Delilah was the first to "afflict" Samson. We see no compassion, no pity, no remorse. Motivated by greed and power, she betrayed Samson and received payment for a job well done. The image of Samson "sleep[ing] upon her knees," childlike and trusting as she called for the Philistines, adds to the image of her heartlessness (Judges 16:19). The writer of the book of Judges presented Samson as a man of great potential who failed but who can be pitied. Delilah is presented as a woman to be condemned.

Unlike Delilah, a righteous woman seeks to know the heart of the man she loves in order to help and support him, not to manipulate and destroy him. Her love is unfeigned. Delilah's brand of love is all too common. Let us be careful if we hear Delilah's words whispered in our own ears, and let us never use her strategy of deceit in our relationships. What a contrast the portrait of Delilah presents to the portraits of loving women we view next.

CHAPTER 11

CHARITY SEEKETH
NOT HER OWN

In a prominent place in the scriptural gallery hang two detailed and finely painted portraits, one of an older and one of a younger woman. A softness in their faces draws us instinctively. The story of Ruth and Naomi is one of the best loved stories in the Old Testament. It provides a marvelous contrast to the wickedness recorded in Judges and seems to foreshadow the peace and light of the New Testament. One can see the gentle and compassionate character of Jesus in both Ruth and Naomi.

RUTH AND NAOMI:
DEVOTION TO THE HAPPINESS OF OTHERS

The portraits of Ruth and Naomi teach us that kindness, self-lessness, and charity are their own reward. In a world where women often seek self-fulfillment through concentrating on their own desires,they lovingly remind us that self-fulfillment comes through selflessness. Ruth's entire motivation was to care for and love Naomi. Naomi's entire motivation was to care for and love Ruth.

Elimelech, Naomi, and their two sons traveled to the land of Moab to escape a famine in the land of Israel. Both sons were married to Moabite women, one to Orpah and the other to Ruth. In time, Naomi's husband and sons died, leaving the three women alone.

Naomi prepared to return to Bethlehem. Notice her selfless lack of concern about being an old single woman. She was concerned about Orpah and Ruth, who were young single women. In their time, both situations were serious. Yet "Naomi said unto her two daughters in law, Go, return each to her mother's house: the Lord deal kindly with you, as ye have dealt with the dead, and with me. The Lord grant you that ye may find rest, each of you in the house of her husband. Then she kissed them; and they lifted up their voice, and wept." When the two younger women told Naomi they desired to go with her, she replied: "Turn again, my daughters: why will ye go with me? are there yet any more sons in my womb, that they may be your husbands? Turn again, my daughters, go your way; for I am too old to have an husband. . . . Nay, my daughters; for it grieveth me much for your sakes that the hand of the Lord is gone out against me" (Ruth 1:8–13).

All three women wept. Orpah "kissed her mother in law" and returned to her family, "but Ruth clave unto her." Once again Naomi urged Ruth to think of her own needs, to return to her own people, her own land, and her own gods. But Ruth answered with the well-known words: "Intreat me not to leave thee, or to return from following after thee: for whither thou goest, I will go; and where thou lodgest, I will lodge: thy people shall be my people, and thy God my God: Where thou diest, will I die, and there will I be buried: the Lord do so to me, and more also, if ought but death part thee and me" (Ruth 1:14, 16–17).

That was not something Naomi had asked for. The power of Ruth's words is amplified when we remember how important it was in that time to be buried with one's people. Ruth relinquished the traditions of her own Moabite people in favor of the truths of Israel's God. Her words of devotion to Naomi were also words of commitment to Jehovah.

WHITHER THOU GOEST, I WILL GO

Ruth's words have a deeply personal meaning for me, for I have been the recipient of this type of love. My wife, Laura, was born in Alberta, Canada, and grew up there in a family who are fiercely proud of their Canadian heritage. We met at Brigham Young University, fell in love, and were married. Four years later I was transferred to Alberta and taught seminary there for three years. Because of concerns over retirement, the Church Educational System told us we needed to make a decision between teaching in Canada or in the United States. After counseling with each other and with the Lord, we decided to spend our lives in the United States.

I remember the last day we were in Canada. We had already sent our belongings ahead to Colorado in the moving van. The morning was dark and drizzling as we left for the border. No one said a word. The silence in the car seemed appropriate to the weather and the mood we were in. My wife looked out the window at the passing countryside, the familiar places she had known as a child and young woman. I did not know what to say.

As we crossed the border, her tears began to fall, and they didn't stop falling until we reached Great Falls, one hundred miles away. We didn't speak, but as I drove, listening to the rain on the windshield, the words of Ruth returned again and again to my mind.

Many Latter-day Saint women are modern-day Ruths. Often when they are married they give up the home of their childhood, the only home they have known and loved. When husbands are transferred or find new work, they travel to distant places to rear their families and contribute to the Church. They often long for home, family, and familiar landscapes, but, like Ruth, they follow those they love. I hope these women see Ruth in their own countenances.

SHALL I NOT SEEK REST FOR THEE?

Ruth and Naomi settled in Bethlehem. Because they were poor, Ruth gleaned in accordance with the law of Moses, gathering the leftover scattered stalks of grain. In the fields she met Boaz, who had heard of Ruth's selfless care of Naomi. Boaz did more than praise Ruth; he provided her food in the heat of the day and instructed the reapers to "let fall also some of the handfuls of purpose for her, and leave them, that she may glean them, and rebuke her not" (Ruth 2:16).

When Naomi heard Ruth had been in the fields of Boaz, she said, "My daughter, shall I not seek rest for thee, that it may be well with thee?" (Ruth 3:1). Naomi's concern was for the happiness of her daughter-in-law. She told Ruth to go to the threshing floor and ask Boaz to marry her to raise up children to Naomi's husband and son. I suspect Naomi knew Boaz would be a good and kind husband.

Boaz was amazed at the kindness of Ruth. "Blessed be thou of the Lord, my daughter: for thou hast shewed more kindness in the latter end than at the beginning, inasmuch as thou followedst not young men, whether poor or rich. And now, my daughter, fear not; I will do to thee all that thou requirest: for all the city of my people doth know that thou art a virtuous woman" (Ruth 3:10–11). Boaz knew Ruth could have married someone else, perhaps younger than himself, but I believe Ruth recognized the kindness, gentleness, and righteousness of Boaz and loved him.

A FULL REWARD BE GIVEN THEE

When he spoke to her in the field, Boaz expressed a desire that the Lord reward Ruth for her kindness: "The Lord recompense thy work, and a full reward be given thee of the Lord God of Israel, under whose wings thou art come to trust" (Ruth 2:12). How did the Lord recompense Ruth and Naomi for their unselfish love? Both women found companionship in their relationship, and the union of Ruth and Boaz was fruitful. Their child was named Obed, who was the father of Jesse, who was the father of David and other kings and through whom came the Savior. "Blessed is he through whose seed Messiah shall come" (Moses 7:53).

Part of Naomi's reward for her kindness to Ruth was the joy implied in the last reference to Naomi in the story. "And Naomi took the child, and laid it in her bosom, and became nurse unto it" (Ruth 4:16). I have seen the joy in the eyes of grandmothers as they take their grandchildren in their arms. If we could speak with Naomi, she might assure us this joy alone was sufficient recompense.

Perhaps the women of Bethlehem best understood the beauty of Ruth's relationship with Naomi, for they said at the birth of Obed, "Thy daughter in law, which loveth thee, which is better to thee than seven sons, hath born him" (Ruth 4:15). This love, so wonderfully expressed in the four short chapters of the Book of Ruth, has a godly quality. It seeks the happiness and welfare of others and finds its greatest fulfillment in their joy. The demonstration of this love, especially in the life and sacrifice of the Savior, is the central message of the scriptures.

In the images of numerous women who unselfishly care for elderly parents, or in older sisters who eagerly sacrifice for the happiness of younger ones, we see the images of Ruth and Naomi repeated. When we see the love of these modern daughters of God, we too feel like saying, "All the city of my people doth know that thou art a virtuous woman."

CHAPTER 12

WOMEN OF DEVOTION AND UNDERSTANDING

Near the portraits of Ruth and Naomi hangs the portrait of Hannah, who eventually became the mother of Samuel the prophet. In her face we see a beauty refined by sorrow. Close by is the portrait of Abigail, a wise counselor to David in the days before he became king.

HANNAH: GIVING A SON TO THE LORD

Hannah had two sources of trial: She was barren, and her husband Elkanah's other wife, Peninnah, "provoked her sore, for to make her fret, because the Lord had shut up her womb" (1 Samuel 1:6). Elkanah tried to console her, asking, "Am not I better to thee than ten sons?" (1 Samuel 1:8). But even a gentle and kind husband cannot diminish a woman's desire for children. Remember Rachel's impassioned cry, "Give me children, or else I die" (Genesis 30:1).

Hannah "wept, and did not eat [she was fasting]. . . . And she was in bitterness of soul." She said, "I am a woman of a sorrowful spirit. . . . out of the abundance of my complaint and grief have I spoken" (1 Samuel 1:7, 10, 15, 16).

All of us from time to time have felt like Hannah. She provides a beautiful example of what we can do when we find ourselves troubled with sorrow.

I POURED OUT MY SOUL BEFORE THE LORD

In conjunction with her fasting, Hannah took her heart full of grief and poured it out at the feet of the Lord: I "have poured out my soul before the Lord" (1 Samuel 1:15). There is great relief in openly sharing our sorrows. Hannah chose one of the best possible places to do this, at the house of the Lord.

Occasionally we hold back some of our grief, bitterness, sorrow, or complaint, because we don't want to appear ungrateful or to accuse or bother the Lord. In the midst of these thoughts, if we listen carefully, we may hear the voice of the spirit whisper, "The Lord already knows what is in your heart. You do not need to try and conceal it. Lay it at his feet." The Spirit will help us make the distinction between pouring out our souls to the Lord and murmuring or complaining to him.

HER COUNTENANCE WAS NO MORE SAD

Hannah exemplifies a trait I wish I had. I have seen it in many women. After listening to Hannah, Eli, the priest of the temple, expressed his desire that "the God of Israel grant thee thy petition that thou hast asked of him." Hannah then said, "Let thine handmaid find grace in thy sight. So the woman went her way, and did eat, and her countenance was no more sad" (1 Samuel 1:17–18). I do not believe Hannah had a full assurance that the Lord would give her a son, but she knew he had heard her petition. With faith she ended her fast and was "no more sad."

In Doctrine and Covenants 98:1–2, the Lord says, "Fear not, let your hearts be comforted; yea, rejoice evermore, and in everything give thanks; waiting patiently on the Lord, for your prayers have entered into the ears of the Lord of Sabaoth." In other words, "I have heard your prayers. I know your desires. Now go your way, be happy, be grateful, be patient, and in time I will work my will in your behalf."

It is difficult to wait for the Lord. It is especially difficult to wait without fear, feeling comforted and giving thanks. Yet those are the results of the Lord's final answer. The Lord's way sometimes appears backwards to us. We say, "Show me, Lord, and I will believe." He says, "Believe, and I will show you." We say, "Answer me in my distress, Lord, and I will rejoice and give thanks." He says, "Rejoice and give thanks, and I will answer you in your distress." Hannah attained that great level of faith, as described by those simple words, "So the woman went her way, and did eat, and her countenance was no more sad."

Joseph Smith wrote of this trusting faith: "Let us cheerfully do all things that lie in our power; and then may we stand still, with the utmost assurance, to see the salvation of God, and for his arm to be revealed" (D&C 123:17). The words "utmost assurance" mean we are assured that the Lord has heard our cries, accepted our efforts, and will answer in the proper time and manner. We will then cheerfully accept his will, even if it is not in accordance with our desires.

We often struggle with the idea of faith. We think that if only we had enough faith, the Lord would answer our prayers in the way that we want. We center our faith in the request. But we can't have faith in a request. Even if our request is righteous, our faith must center in the Lord Jesus Christ and in our Heavenly Father. Then, like Hannah, we can go our way, confident of the Lord's goodness.

In describing this truth I do not wish to underemphasize its balancing principle. The Savior also frequently taught us to continue to knock at heaven's gates. "And shall not God avenge his own elect, which cry day and night unto him, though he bear long with them?" (Luke 18:7). Again and again he teaches us, "Ask, and it shall be given you; seek, and ye shall find; knock, and it shall be opened unto you. For every one that asketh receiveth; and he that seeketh findeth; and to him that knocketh it shall be opened" (Luke 11:9).

SHE VOWED A VOW

In the midst of pouring out her grief, Hannah did another important thing. "She vowed a vow, and said, O Lord of hosts, if thou wilt indeed look on the affliction of thine handmaid, and remember me, and not forget thine handmaid, but wilt give unto thine handmaid a man child, then I will give him unto the Lord all the days of his life, and there shall no razor come upon his head" (1 Samuel 1:11). Notice the spirit of consecration in Hannah's prayer. This is no desperate bargaining with the Lord. Three times in the prayer she refers to herself as "thine hand-maid." Not only does Hannah belong to the Lord, but if he will grant her a son, she will give that son to the Lord.

Under the law of Moses, all firstborn males of both mankind and animals were dedicated to the Lord as a constant reminder of the atonement of the Father's firstborn son. Firstborn children were redeemed by the parents through a sum of money and an offering at the altar.

In offering Samuel to the Lord, Hannah completely gave her son to the Lord and dedicated him as a Nazarite "all the days of his life." That was a total consecration. Under the law of Moses, if a man wanted to make a special vow of dedication to God, he made what was called a Nazarite vow (see Numbers 6). The Nazarite was separated from things that were unclean. He drank no strong drink, and he let his hair grow as a sign for all to see that he was under a vow. The length of his hair would help others see the length of the vow. Hannah understood that as soon as the child was old enough, he would be presented at the temple. She would bear him and nurse him, but her time with him would be greatly restricted.

When we desire great blessings from the Lord, it is also appropriate to renew our vows of consecration to him. It is pleasing to the Lord when we acknowledge that we belong to him, and that all we possess is his.

While serving as a bishop I was approached by a couple who wanted most earnestly to have a child. I listened to the wife express her grief and thought, "Here is a modern Hannah." This wonderful woman had for a long time poured out her soul to God. They were now asking for a priesthood blessing. We prayed and fasted together and sought the Spirit of the Lord. In addition, this couple vowed a vow.

They told the Lord that if he granted them children, they would rear them in the manner he had prescribed. They would not fail to have family home evening each week. They would faithfully bring their children to church. Each day would find them on their knees with their children in family prayer. Each day they would turn the pages of the scriptures and teach their children. They themselves would attend the temple frequently to set an example and establish the temple as the center of their worship. They would be careful about the environment of their home.

Their desire was deep; their vow, sincere. Both the husband and the wife desired a blessing. No promise was given in the blessings. Rather, each blessing was a prayer, a request that the Lord look upon this wonderful couple and receive the earnest sincerity of their vow, knowing that any child placed in their family would receive spiritual care and attention. This couple now has four beautiful children. There is power in consecration; there is power in vowing a vow.

THE LORD HATH GIVEN ME MY PETITION

"Elkanah knew Hannah his wife; and the Lord remembered her. Wherefore it came to pass, when the time was come about after Hannah had conceived, that she bare a son, and called his name Samuel, saying, Because I have asked him of the Lord" (1 Samuel 1:19–20). Elkanah and Hannah had over the years gone to the temple at Shiloh to offer the yearly sacrifices. After the birth of Samuel, "Hannah went not up; for she said unto her husband, I will not go up until the child be weaned, and then I will bring him, that he may appear before the Lord, and there abide forever" (1 Samuel 1:22).

Hannah did not want to return to the Lord until she was able to fulfill her vow. In time Samuel was weaned, and Hannah returned to Shiloh, where she said to Eli, "For this child I prayed; and the Lord hath given me my petition which I asked of him: therefore also I have lent him to the Lord; as long as he liveth he shall be lent to the Lord" (1 Samuel 1:27–28).

Hannah promised to give her son to the Lord, and she did so, but the word *lent* makes that giving less permanent. Even though Samuel would now serve the Lord and belong to him, he also still belonged to her. Elder Matthew Cowley said, "How well the mothers know that life is eternal. How well she knew that in lending this child to the Lord for this life, that beyond and down through the ages of eternity, he would be her child, and she would be his mother" (Conference Report, October 1953, 107–8). Eli blessed Elkanah and his wife, saying, "The Lord give thee seed of this woman for the loan which is lent to the Lord" (1 Samuel 2:20).

Hannah saw Samuel when she went up to Shiloh for the annual sacrifices. Her love and devotion are shown in these simple words: "Moreover his mother made him a little coat, and brought it to him from year to year, when she came up with her husband to offer the yearly sacrifice" (1 Samuel 2:19).

Not only did Hannah perform her vow but she did it with a heart full of gratitude and a song of rejoicing. In 1 Samuel 2:1–10 we read the hymn of thanksgiving offered by Hannah as she lent her son to the Lord: "My heart rejoiceth in the Lord . . . ," she sang. "There is none holy as the Lord: for there is none beside thee: neither is there any rock like our God."

This portrait of a righteous woman dealing with grief or "bitterness of soul" would be incomplete without that prayer of thanksgiving. Hannah began by pouring out her soul in sorrow, and her story ends with the pouring out of her soul in thanksgiving. Hannah returned to give glory to God.

I HAVE LENT HIM TO THE LORD

I have tried to picture the moment when Hannah turned homeward after a last look at her son. She was returning him to his Father in Heaven, before she could enjoy the hundreds of small moments that are so endearing to a mother. Samuel was her first child, and though the Lord blessed her with three additional sons and two daughters, at this time she may have wondered if he would be her only child. How long did she linger? What could she say to a tiny son to express her love and the importance of what he was to do and why she must leave him?

We see Hannah reflected in the faces of thousands of Latter-day Saint mothers who give their sons and daughters to serve missions for the Lord. Although their children's service is for a set number of months, not a lifetime, there is still much of sacrifice and emotion in lending a child to the Lord.

Laura and I enjoyed a few moments with our eldest son at the airport when he was on his way to serve a mission in Brazil. Before we were quite prepared, it was time for him to board the plane. As a father, who knew by experience what awaited him, I was excited to see this day finally arrive. His mother, too, rejoiced in the goodness of his life and the experiences he would have, but the thought that she would not see him for two years produced some deep emotions.

She held onto him for a long time, trying to get two years' worth of embraces into one last long one. Then she kissed him, and he walked down the ramp to the plane. I stood to the side and watched her eyes follow our son. She did not turn her head until he had been out of sight for more than a minute. "I will not be able to touch him, or hear his voice, or see him for a long time," she said.

"He will write to us," I offered.

"I know, but he will still be gone."

How Hannah must have hungered for her yearly visits to see Samuel. How proud she must have been to see him in the new coat she took to him, to watch him grow and develop into the great man and prophet he became. She would have found comfort knowing she had lent him to the Lord, but she too was not able to touch him, or hear his voice, or see him for long stretches of time.

Hannah's portrait displays the features of a woman who knew

how to call on the Lord and overcome bitterness of soul. We see in her face a determination to keep the commitments she made with the Lord. May her image remind us that in lending our children to the Lord in this life, we will receive them beyond and down through the ages of eternity.

PENINNAH:
INCREASING THE PAIN OF THOSE WHO MOURN

Though merely a sketch, the image of Peninnah offers a warning. Peninnah was the other of Elkanah's two wives. She is identified as Hannah's "adversary" (1 Samuel 1:6). We do not know whether Peninnah was the first or second wife. The scriptures contain ample evidence of the stress plural marriage placed upon relationships. Peninnah and Hannah were challenged by it, as were Sarah and Hagar, and Rachel and Leah.

"Peninnah had children, but Hannah had no children" (1 Samuel 1:2). Instead of showing compassion for Hannah's barrenness, Peninnah "provoked her sore, for to make her fret, because the Lord had shut up her womb" (1 Samuel 1:6). She continued to do so, especially at the time of the yearly trip to Shiloh when the family made the sacrifices required by the law of Moses. "Year by year, when she went up to the house of the Lord, so she provoked her; therefore she wept, and did not eat" (1 Samuel 1:7).

Hannah's hymn of praise may indicate the type of provoking she received from Peninnah. "Talk no more so exceeding proudly; let not arrogancy come out of your mouth: for the Lord is a God of knowledge, and by him actions are weighed" (1 Samuel 2:3).

Peninnah teaches the cruelty of provoking others to greater sorrow by reminding them of their unfulfilled desires or inadequacies. Flaunting our own successes and joys often comes from our own sense of insecurity. It is a type of pride that gives little satisfaction while increasing pain in others. Women today do not face the difficulties associated with plural marriage, but from time to time they may be tempted to act as Peninnah.

I lived once in a ward in which there was a sister who was

very highly educated. She had written a well-respected dissertation and received a Ph.D. She was a good woman, but she used to cause the other women in the ward to "fret." Many of the other sisters had not had the opportunity of a university education, let alone a doctorate. Several had started degrees and then stopped when their children were born, or they had worked while their husbands completed schooling. This sister often reminded the others that they did not know all she knew. Sometimes she sat in class reading while another sister was teaching. These and other actions hurt the sisters of the ward and made them feel unimportant. It is well occasionally to recall the sketch of Peninnah and make sure we are not creating heavier burdens for others.

ABIGAIL: COUNSELOR OF UNDERSTANDING

The last portrait in this group is of a little-known woman named Abigail. She was married to Nabal, a man who was "churlish and evil in his doings," but Abigail was "a woman of good understanding, and of a beautiful countenance" (1 Samuel 25:3). A husband's churlish ways do not have to affect the nobility of his wife's character. The example of Abigail in 1 Samuel helps us comprehend what it means to be a woman of good understanding.

A WOMAN OF GOOD UNDERSTANDING

While David hid from the jealous obsession of Saul, he came in contact with Nabal. Even though David and his men were on the run, they did not harm any of Nabal's flocks or servants. Instead, the servants reported "the men were very good unto us, and we were not hurt, neither missed we any thing . . . : they were a wall unto us both by night and day, all the while we were with them keeping the sheep" (1 Samuel 25:15–16). David sent a message to Nabal requesting provisions for his men. Nabal returned a curt refusal. In a rage, David girded on his sword and led his men toward Nabal, swearing he would kill everyone before the next morning.

When Abigail learned this, she gathered the provisions and

went out to meet David. Falling at his feet she pleaded with him, saying: "Let thine handmaid, I pray thee, speak in thine audience, and hear the words of thine handmaid. . . . The Lord will certainly make my lord a sure house. . . . And it shall come to pass, when the Lord shall have done to my lord according to all the good that he hath spoken concerning thee, and shall have appointed thee ruler over Israel; that this shall be no grief unto thee, nor offence of heart unto my lord, either that thou hast shed blood causeless, or that my lord hath avenged himself" (1 Samuel 25:24–31).

Her beautiful plea softened David's heart, and he answered by recognizing her wisdom and good understanding. "Blessed be thy advice, and blessed be thou, which hast kept me this day from coming to shed blood, and from avenging myself with mine own hand" (1 Samuel 25:33).

Abigail had the type of vision that sees the consequences of decisions made in the heat of emotion, checks that emotion, and thus prevents sorrow and suffering. Abigail knew if David slaughtered her family he would regret his actions. She successfully reminded him of this.

Often when we are offended, we respond with anger. Like David, we gird on our swords, swearing to strike back. Decisions made in anger are rarely righteous and often bring sorrow and regret. The daily newspaper and the evening news show tragic examples of the results of rage. How much sorrow could have been eliminated had those involved listened to the Abigails in their lives and realized the regrets that would come?

Many a husband and father has been grateful for his wife's good understanding. When the relationship with a child would have been strained, or discipline too severely applied, these modern Abigails stand in the way and plead. They save their families from hurt. They show us that when our minds and hearts are calm, the Spirit can speak wisdom and peace to our souls.

David accepted Abigail's gifts and sent her home in peace. Soon David learned that Nabal had died. His admiration for Abigail was so great that he sent messengers and asked her to become his wife. Her response shows the humility that accompanied her good understanding. "Behold, let thine handmaid be a servant to wash the feet of the servants of my lord" (1 Samuel 25:41). But David was too wise to allow a woman of Abigail's understanding to be a servant; she became his wife. Ironically, David's passion and lack of good understanding later immersed him in grief and ultimately deprived him of Abigail herself.

In this world where sorrow and regret are often experienced by those who will not control their passions, we see the Lord's wisdom in including the portrait of Abigail in his scriptural gallery.

CHAPTER 13

WOMEN OF TRAGEDY

We next enter the room containing portraits that reflect great sorrow—sorrow that did not find the comfort experienced by Ruth, Naomi, and Hannah. Here, too, we learn important lessons.

One of Job's three friends said, "Man is born unto trouble, as the sparks fly upward" (Job 5:7). Suffering is all around us. Many women carry great burdens of sorrow; many are the victims of evil or live in circumstances that create pain. Often their suffering seems meaningless, and we may ask ourselves, "Why does a God of love allow such heavy burdens of agony and grief?"

The eternal purpose of our existence is to become like our Father in Heaven and his Son. Life is designed to help us become like them—perfect. Which experiences best increase love, compassion, mercy, kindness, and patience? Which experiences best focus the need for justice? Suffering creates and enhances those and other needful characteristics. When others sin against us, we learn to forgive and show mercy. When we see others suffer, compassion, empathy, and love are born in our hearts. James told the ancient Saints who were being persecuted to "count it all joy" when they faced "many afflictions," for "the trying of your faith worketh patience." He then counseled them to "let patience have her perfect work, that ye may be perfect and entire, wanting nothing" (JST James 1:2–4).

As the father of five children whom I love very much, I want them to acquire the qualities of godhood. I believe most parents would be willing to suffer any pain, if they knew that it was creating in their children the attributes of the Father and the Son. It is therefore not difficult for me to understand why the Father allows suffering, even great suffering, knowing that patience, mercy, compassion, empathy, and love are being created in his children.

Some allow suffering to turn them bitter and angry, but they are free to choose otherwise. Others become ennobled and refined through their sufferings. The women in this gallery suffered largely through the foolishness or evils of men. Much of their suffering is meaningless unless the memory of their pain helps keep mercy and kindness alive in our own hearts. I hope that those who now endure seemingly unexplainable indignities and pain in this mortal life will find comfort in these women of tragedy.

THE WIFE OF PHINEHAS: WHEN THE GLORY DEPARTS

The first portrait is a sketch of the wife of Phinehas, one of the wicked sons of Eli, who was the high priest in the days of Hannah. Her face is in the shadow cast by her husband and his brother Hophni, who were priests of the Lord and had responsibility at the tabernacle. They "were sons of Belial; they knew not the Lord" (1 Samuel 2:12). "Sons of Belial" means worthless or wicked people. They mocked the sacrifices of Jehovah, but, worse, imitating the immorality of the Canaanites, they "lay with the women that assembled at the door of the tabernacle of the congregation." Not only did they themselves indulge in wicked practices but they also made "the Lord's people to transgress" (1 Samuel 2:22, 24). Eli's feeble efforts to restrain his sons were not acceptable to the Lord, who called Samuel to replace Eli as the spiritual leader of Israel.

During a war with the Philistines, Hophni and Phinehas took

the ark onto the battlefield. In the ensuing battle, "the ark of God was taken; and the two sons of Eli, Hophni and Phinehas, were slain." When Eli heard the ark had been captured, "he fell from off the seat backward by the side of the gate, and his neck brake, and he died" (1 Samuel 4:11, 18).

Eli's "daughter in law, Phinehas' wife, was with child, near to be delivered: and when she heard the tidings that the ark of God was taken, and that her father in law and her husband were dead, she bowed herself and travailed; for her pains came upon her. And about the time of her death the women that stood by her said unto her, Fear not; for thou hast borne a son. But she answered not, neither did she regard it. And she named the child Ichabod, saying, The glory is departed from Israel: because the ark of God was taken, and because of her father in law and her husband. And she said, The glory is departed from Israel: for the ark of God is taken" (1 Samuel 4:19–22).

All we know of Phinehas's wife is what is sketched in these two verses. We do not know how she felt about her husband's evil practices; we know only that she mourned intensely the loss of the ark. From that, we may assume she was a good woman who understood that the ark symbolized the Lord's covenant with his people. As long as they followed his commandments and worshiped him, he would bless and protect them. When that covenant was broken, "the glory was departed."

A most joyous event in ancient Israel was the birth of a son. But if the covenant had been broken and the glory of the Lord had departed from Israel, even the birth of a son carried no joy. *Ichabod*, the name she chose for her newborn son, means "where is the glory?" She sorrowed over the death of her husband and her father-in-law, but she recognized the greater tragedy, a tragedy greater than her own impending death. The sketch of Phinehas's wife calls to us from the wall of the gallery and testifies, "When the covenant with the Lord is broken, all other sorrows are secondary, and joy is eclipsed by mourning."

MICHAL: CAUGHT BETWEEN TWO KINGS

Michal, a daughter of Saul, was caught up in the unrighteousness of her father. Saul promised David he could marry Michal if he provided a dowry of one hundred slain Philistines. He hoped David would be killed in his attempt to provide the dowry, but David doubled it, and Saul was forced to give him Michal. "And Saul saw and knew that the Lord was with David, and that Michal Saul's daughter loved him" (1 Samuel 18:28).

Michal's love saved David's life. "Saul also sent messengers unto David's house, to watch him, and to slay him in the morning: and Michal David's wife told him, saying, If thou save not thy life to night, to morrow thou shalt be slain. So Michal let David down through a window: and he went, and fled, and escaped." She then "took an image, and laid it in the bed, and put a pillow of goats' hair for his bolster, and covered it with a cloth" (1 Samuel 19:11–13). When messengers from Saul arrived to take David, Michal bought him more time by saying he was sick. The messengers returned to Saul, who sent them back, demanding they bring David up in his bed, "that I may slay him" (1 Samuel 19:15). By the time the ruse was discovered, David had found refuge with Samuel in Ramah.

When Michal had to choose between her husband and her father, she rightly chose her husband. Josephus adds that "she could not bear to live in case she were deprived of him" (*Antiquities of the Jews*, 136–37).

Michal is not mentioned in the account of David's fugitive years, but we discover later that "Saul had given Michal his daughter, David's wife, to Phalti the son of Laish" (1 Samuel 25:44). We do not know how Michal felt about this second marriage. What choices did she have? Why had David not rescued her?

After the death of Saul, his captain, Abner, placed Ishbosheth, one of Saul's sons, on the throne of Israel. But the tribe of Judah remained loyal to David, crowning him king in Hebron. For seven years there was civil war, and then messages were sent to David suggesting the reuniting of the tribes. David replied: "I will make a league with thee: but one thing I require of thee, that is, Thou shalt not see my face, except thou first bring Michal Saul's daughter, when thou comest to see my face" (2 Samuel 3:13).

Michal was taken "from her husband, even from Phaltiel the son of Laish. And her husband went with her along weeping behind her to Bahurim. Then said Abner unto him, Go, return. And he returned" (2 Samuel 3:15–16).

Perhaps David thought a son with Michal would help unite the tribes. Perhaps he still loved her. There is great pathos in the scene of her second husband weeping as he followed her to the border.

The last we hear of Michal is her reaction on the day David brought the ark of the covenant to Jerusalem. In his joy, David "danced before the Lord with all his might" (2 Samuel 6:14). Michal thought David's dancing was beneath the dignity of a king and let him know it. She greeted him with sarcasm, saying, "How glorious was the king of Israel to day, who uncovered himself to day in the eyes of the handmaids of his servants, as one of the vain fellows shamelessly uncovereth himself!" (2 Samuel 6:20).

David's answer was tinged with venom as he justified his behavior: "It was before the Lord, which chose me before thy father, and before all his house, to appoint me ruler over the people of the Lord. . . . and of the maidservants which thou hast spoken of, of them shall I be had in honour" (2 Samuel 6:21–22).

The exchange between David and Michal shows a definite breach in their relationship, and the next verse states, "Therefore Michal the daughter of Saul had no child unto the day of her death" (2 Samuel 6:23). Most commentators believe David refused to have a child with Michal at least partially as a result of her criticism.

The relationship between David and Michal had deteriorated from love to alienation. Unfortunately, that is all too common a pattern. The pressures placed upon the marriage of David and

Michal were extreme, yet clearly they shared some responsibility for the breakdown of their marriage. Nevertheless, we feel deeply for the unfairness in Michal's life. There are few sorrows so painful as the loss of a sweet and fulfilling love. Many women face similar situations, moved by forces and circumstances they cannot control and pained by the frailties and sins of others.

THE WITCH OF ENDOR: FEAR OF PUNISHMENT

Near the end of his life, Saul faced a battle with the Philistines. The Lord had not responded to his pleas, so "Saul [said] unto his servants, Seek me a woman that hath a familiar spirit, that I may go to her, and enquire of her" (1 Samuel 28:7).

His servants found a woman in Endor who had a familiar spirit. This woman was a medium, or spiritualist, who claimed to communicate with the dead (the Hebrew word translated *familiar* means "to mumble or prattle"). Any communication through such a person was from an evil source; nevertheless, Saul disguised himself and went to her under the cover of night.

The portrait of the witch of Endor teaches us a valuable lesson in addition to reinforcing the truth that righteous people shun such practices. When asked to bring up the dead, the woman replied, "Behold, thou knowest what Saul hath done, how he hath cut off those that have familiar spirits, and the wizards, out of the land: wherefore then layest thou a snare for my life, to cause me to die?" (1 Samuel 28:9).

The woman was cautious because the penalty for breaking the law against witchcraft was death. Saul swore to her that "as the Lord liveth, there shall no punishment happen to thee for this thing" (1 Samuel 28:10).

Assured that she would not suffer punishment, the woman proceeded. Then, upon discovering that her visitor was really Saul, the woman feared again for her life and cried "with a loud voice . . . saying, Why hast thou deceived me? for thou art Saul." Again reassured, she claimed to see an old man. "And Saul perceived that it was Samuel" (1 Samuel 28:12). The message was given that Saul and his sons would die in the battle.

Saul was deeply troubled. The woman responded that she had risked her life to obey him and reminded him of his promise that no harm would come to her. Both before and after her seance, the woman was concerned only with whether she would suffer punishment.

The witch of Endor is like many people in the world today. They are less concerned with right and wrong than with being caught or receiving punishment. At best, they are concerned with the legality rather than the morality of their actions. The witch of Endor reminds us not to think in these patterns but to make our decisions based on what is right and wrong. Morality, not fear of punishment, should direct our lives. Our desire should be to please our Father in Heaven.

Because so many think like the witch of Endor, it is well that her portrait hangs in the scriptural gallery. May the memory of her fears motivate us to a higher standard of thought and action.

RIZPAH: ENDURING PAIN BEYOND WORDS

Rizpah was another woman who suffered for the unrighteousness of Saul. Her suffering of Rizpah represents much of the heartache women endure. The portrait of Rizpah shows a woman caught by powerful forces that swept away her happiness and destroyed her peace. Early in her life she became one of Saul's concubines, a wife of lesser standing. She bore him two sons, Armoni and Mephibosheth.

"Then there was a famine in the days of David three years, year after year; and David enquired of the Lord. And the Lord answered, It is for Saul, and for his bloody house, because he slew the Gibeonites" (2 Samuel 21:1). Saul's "bloody house," who had sought to slay the Gibeonites despite Israel's covenant with them, must have included Rizpah's two sons Armoni and Mephibosheth.

When David asked the Gibeonites how he could right this wrong, they answered, "Let seven men of [Saul's] sons be delivered unto us, and we will hang them up unto the Lord in Gibeah of Saul" (2 Samuel 21:6). David delivered the two sons of Rizpah and the five sons of Merab, Saul's daughter, to the Gibeonites, who "hanged them in the hill" in the hometown of Saul (2 Samuel 4:9). There they left them. To see her sons' bodies, unburied, unprotected from the elements and from the birds and animals, was more than Rizpah could bear. She "took sackcloth, and spread it for her upon the rock, from the beginning of harvest until water dropped upon them out of heaven, and suffered neither the birds of the air to rest on them by day, nor the beasts of the field by night" (2 Samuel 21:10).

The execution of the seven sons and grandsons of Saul took place "in the beginning of barley harvest" (2 Samuel 21:9), which is in April. Some Bible commentators suggest that the rain was rain sent to end the famine, rather than the yearly rains, which usually begin in October. The image of Rizpah watching her sons' bodies day after day, whether for a few weeks or a few months, is an image of suffering that has few parallels.

Eventually word of Rizpah's vigil reached David. Her devotion reminded him of his love for Jonathan, and he realized he had never given Jonathan a proper burial in his tribal inheritance. So David "took the bones of Saul and the bones of Jonathan. . . . and they gathered the bones of them that were hanged" and buried them "in the country of Benjamin . . . in the sepulchre of Kish his father" (2 Samuel 21:12–14).

A friend of mine attended the viewing of a young man who had committed suicide after years of rebellion and unrighteous living. Toward the close of the evening, the mother, who had stood for hours while her friends offered whatever words of comfort they could find, bent over the body of her son, stroked his face, and gently kissed his cheek. "It was a gentle, tender moment," he said, "and I shall never forget it as long as I live." The face of this modern mother echoes the face of Rizpah. Their pain helps develop in us compassion and empathy. No mortal love is as deep as that of a mother for her child, no pain as poignant as that of a mother grieving over a lost child, whether that loss be spiritual or physical.

BATHSHEBA: THE CONSEQUENCES OF SIN

We turn now to the portrait of Bathsheba. There is nothing to suggest a romantic attachment between David and Bathsheba, only a satisfaction of David's desires. We do not know how much responsibility Bathsheba bore in the adultery with David, but regardless of the extent of her guilt or her feelings for David, her portrait shows the tragic results of sin.

The writer of 2 Samuel places the weight of the adultery with Bathsheba upon the shoulders of David. The first verse of 2 Samuel 11 suggests that if David had been where he should have been, the sin with Bathsheba would not have taken place: "And it came to pass, . . . at the time when kings go forth to battle, that David sent Joab, and his servants with him, and all Israel. . . . But David tarried still at Jerusalem" (2 Samuel 11:1). One evening, as he walked upon the roof of his house, he "saw a woman washing herself; and the woman was very beautiful to look upon" (2 Samuel 11:2). The Hebrew word translated *washing* in this passage is most often used to mean washing of the hands, feet, or face. This was a very modest society. For a woman to bathe, naked, in a place where she could be seen was highly unlikely.

David asked who the woman was and learned that she was the daughter of one of his most loyal men and the wife of another. Nevertheless, he "sent messengers, and took her; and she came in unto him, and he lay with her . . . and she returned unto her house. And the woman conceived, and sent and told David, and said, I am with child" (2 Samuel 11:4–5).

The sorrow of sin was surely compounded with the first fearful knowledge that she was with child. David tried to conceal the sin by sending for Uriah, whose words further indict David: "The ark, and Israel, and Judah, abide in tents; and my lord Joab, and the servants of my lord, are encamped in the open fields; shall I then go into mine house . . . to lie with my wife? as thou livest, and as thy soul liveth, I will not do this thing" (2 Samuel 11:11). Again, everyone was where he should have been, except David.

Because Uriah refused to sleep in his own house, David sent

him to the hottest part of the battle, where he was sure to be killed. I do not believe Bathsheba knew of David's murderous solution to their dilemma, for "when the wife of Uriah heard that Uriah her husband was dead, she mourned for her husband" (2 Samuel 11:26). What did Bathsheba feel when her submission to David was compounded by the murder of her husband? What were her thoughts when the son she bore died as Nathan prophesied? Did she feel responsibility or guilt for these deaths?

The sorrows of David's family may also have weighed upon Bathsheba. Soon after David's and Bathsheba's adultery, David's son Amnon raped his half-sister Tamar. David, perhaps hampered by the memory and guilt of his own sins, did nothing. When Absalom, Tamar's brother, murdered his half-brother Amnon in revenge, David again failed to act. The sins of his sons were too close to his own.

David apparently tried to compensate Bathsheba for her sorrow and pain by promising that their son Solomon would be king. There must have been satisfaction for Bathsheba when her son Solomon ascended the throne of David in humility and with great wisdom.

In Luke's lineage of Christ, considered to be the "natural descent through actual parentage" (LDS Bible Dictionary, 678), we read that Jesus is descended through Bathsheba's son Nathan. We know nothing of Nathan, but we hope that his life was one of integrity and that a measure of happiness was afforded Bathsheba through him and his posterity.

Bathsheba's life testifies to the tragedy of sin and immorality, whether she was a willing participant or a woman overwhelmed by pressure. How many times did that night of adultery come back to haunt her? When did its consequences end?

I am reminded of a young woman I met while I was a student at Brigham Young University. She had given in to pressure from a boyfriend before she came to college. She confessed her sins to the bishop and began the process of repentance. My wife and I were asked to help her while she worked her way back to full fellowship. I have never seen a person strive so hard to repent fully.

She became one of the sweetest, most modest and humble young women I have known. She began to feel peace and forgiveness and to look forward with hope.

She became engaged soon after. One evening she came to the house much troubled. "You know of my past," she said. "My fiancé does not. Do you think I should tell him?" I replied that it was obvious to anyone who looked at her that the Atonement had cleansed her and restored what she had lost. If the Lord would mention her sin no more, perhaps she should follow his example. On the other hand, if she felt that her past would be a barrier in the marriage, perhaps wisdom would advise revealing it.

A few days later she told us that she had decided to tell her fiancé. Late that night she knocked at our door. The young man had broken the engagement. She was devastated. "I feel unclean all over again," she cried.

We talked long into the night but could not find the words to ease her renewed suffering. Just before morning, she rose to leave. When she reached the door, she paused, and the room was filled with her pondering. At last she turned and asked a question that has haunted me ever since. "How long will I have to pay for my sins?"

She had repented of her sins, and the Savior had paid for them, but the consequences were still affecting her life. Like her, how many times did Bathsheba ask, "How long will I have to pay for my sins?" Did she eventually accept the Lord's atoning mercy and feel his forgiving love? The deep feelings of sorrow we feel as we gaze at her portrait are proper and good. May the empathy and compassion that arise naturally from the portrait of Bathsheba mold us in the pattern of our Savior while they warn us against the misuse of the Lord's precious gift of procreation.

TAMAR:
MOST DEAR AND PRECIOUS ABOVE ALL THINGS

The portrait of Tamar further testifies to the sacred nature of our God-given procreative power. Her portrait helps us to define the essence of love and its proper expression.

"Absalom the son of David had a fair sister, whose name was Tamar; and Amnon the son of David loved her." Amnon was Tamar's half-brother. His passion was so great "that he fell sick for his sister Tamar" (2 Samuel 13:1–2). A plan was devised to get Tamar alone with Amnon. Once alone "he took hold of her, and said unto her, Come lie with me, my sister. And she answered him, Nay, my brother, do not force me; for no such thing ought to be done in Israel: do not thou this folly. And I, whither shall I cause my shame to go? and as for thee, thou shalt be as one of the fools in Israel" (2 Samuel 13:11–13).

What is the "folly"? It is the deceitful assumption that love, even a love so strong that it makes one sick, is expressed by giving in to unlawful demands. Only fools believe Amnon's type of love is love and not its counterfeits, selfishness and lust. Tamar, because she was a virtuous woman, understood the difference.

No man ever compromised a woman and loved her when he did it. No man ever tried to force a woman, whether physically or through persuasion, and had her best interests at heart while he did it. Every act of immorality is inherently selfish and therefore an act not of love but of folly. If a man does not love a woman's virtue, he does not love her. The folly of believing intimate relations outside of marriage constitute love and can strengthen the relationship between a man and woman is quickly seen in the tragedy of Tamar.

As soon as Amnon's passion was spent, "Amnon hated her exceedingly; so that the hatred wherewith he hated her was greater than the love wherewith he had loved her. And Amnon said unto her, Arise, be gone." Tamar pleaded with Amnon, "but he would not hearken unto her. Then he called his servant that ministered unto him, and said, Put now this woman out from me and bolt the door after her" (2 Samuel 13:15–17).

"Tamar, my sister" soon became "this woman." President Gordon B. Hinckley said: "I heard Elder John A. Widtsoe . . . say, 'It is my observation that a young man and a young woman who violate the principles of morality soon end up hating one another.' I have observed the same thing. There may be words of love to begin with, but there will be words of anger and bitterness later" ("True to the Faith," 5).

The prophet Alma taught that the controlling, or bridling, of passion fills one with love: "See that ye bridle all your passions, that ye may be filled with love" (Alma 38:12). Amnon and the world believe just the opposite.

Although Tamar spoke of her shame, in the eyes of the Lord she was still virtuous. Her sorrow and mourning are a lesson to all who hold virtue as cheaply as the world does. "And Tamar put ashes on her head, and rent her garment of divers colours that was on her, and laid her hand on her head, and went on crying. . . . So Tamar remained desolate in her brother Absalom's house" (2 Samuel 13:19–20).

The Hebrew word translated *desolate* means "ruined, stunned, numbed, devastated, destroyed, or wasted." Both Tamar and Dinah, Tamar's counterpart in Genesis 34 who was defiled by Shechem, understood the value of that which Mormon called "most dear and precious above all things" (Moroni 9:9). Neither Amnon nor Shechem loved as he professed to.

It is a great evil of our time that wickedness is justified in the name of love. Does love break up homes? Does love fill a soul with guilt? Does love take children from a parent? Does love close the doors of the temple to a couple? Does love shrink our spirits and hinder our prayers? Does love render us desolate?

Love does none of these things, for as Paul taught, "Love worketh no ill to his neighbor: therefore love is the fulfilling of the law" (Roman 13:10).

POTIPHAR'S WIFE: PASSION PURSUING VIRTUE

Potiphar's wife is a rare example in the scriptural gallery of a woman who let lust consume her. Nothing Joseph said or did dissuaded her.

She resorted to the tactic used by Delilah. She pressured him relentlessly: "It came to pass, as she spake to Joseph day by day, that he hearkened not unto her, to lie by her, or to be with her" (Genesis 39:10).

A person consumed by lust is not easily dissuaded. When her final attempt failed, and he fled, leaving his garment in her hands, her passion turned to anger and hatred. Crying to the men of the house, she accused Joseph of an assault on her virtue. She kindled her husband's anger, and Joseph was cast into prison.

We do not know how many years Joseph stayed in prison. We do know that two years passed between the time Joseph interpreted the baker's and butler's dreams and his release from prison. Undoubtedly, Potiphar's wife found satisfaction in the knowledge that Joseph was paying for his refusal.

As a father, I have always worried about my daughters, hoping that the young men they meet and date will treat them with respect and decency. I have begun to worry about my sons, because it seems that young women today are much more forward in their relationships with young men than they used to be. As a bishop, I listened to nearly as many young men confess to sexual sin due to the advances of young women as to young women confessing sexual sin due to the advances of young men. Perhaps there is more relevance in this woman of ancient Egypt than we would like to admit. An occasional look at the portrait of Potiphar's wife reminds us of the high value a true daughter of God places on modesty and virtue.

THE PORTRAITS OF TRAGEDY

With some relief we leave these portraits of tragedy and distorted love, yet we may keep with us the lessons we have learned. If we have felt compassion, if we have gained a greater awareness of the far-reaching and often desolating consequences of giving in to our passions, then the moments we have spent gazing at the faces of these women will have been useful to us in our quest to become more like our Savior and our Father in Heaven.

CHAPTER 14

TRUSTING IN THE PROPHETS

As we enter the next room, we see five portraits, only two of which contain much detail, but we know the Lord placed them in his gallery so that we may learn from their lives. The four unnamed women associated with the ministries of Elijah and Elisha serve as foils to the wicked people of their times—that is, the strengths of one person contrast with the weaknesses of another. If we look carefully at stories involving righteous women in the scriptures, we often find their individual goodness contrasts with the general wickedness of their society. We have already seen what wonderful foils Ruth, Naomi, and Hannah present against the corrupt backdrop of Judges. In similar ways the righteousness of five women—the widow of Zarephath, the indebted widow, the woman of Shunem, the little maid of Naaman, and the prophetess Huldah—contrasts with the general wickedness in Israel during this time. These five women of compassion and faith also serve as foils for the evil Jezebel, her daughter, and other wicked women.

THE WIDOW OF ZAREPHATH:
TRUSTING A WIDOW'S HEART

The beautiful portrait of the widow of Zarephath is an important portrait in this grouping. In a recent general conference

Elder Jeffrey R. Holland praised this woman's act of faith (see Conference Report, April 1996, 39).

Elijah had called for a famine to bring Israel to repentance. He had been camping at the brook Cherith, where "the ravens brought him bread and flesh in the morning, and . . . in the evening." When the brook dried up, the Lord commanded Elijah to "arise, get thee to Zarephath, which belongeth to Zidon, and dwell there: behold, I have commanded a widow woman there to sustain thee" (1 Kings 17:6, 9). When Jesus was rejected in Nazareth, he said that "no prophet is accepted in his own country. But I tell you of a truth, many widows were in Israel in the days of Elias, when the heaven was shut up three years and six months, when great famine was throughout all the land; but unto none of them was Elias sent, save unto Sarepta, a city of Sidon, unto a woman that was a widow" (Luke 4:24–26).

Her food stores reduced to just enough for a final meal and fully anticipating that death would soon take her and her son, this woman would nevertheless still feed a stranger. Much of the power of this story is implied. It tells us that the life of this widow must have been filled with compassion and acts of mercy. The Lord knew the heart of this widow, and it may well be that he sent Elijah to her to ensure that she did not make her last meal and then die with her son in the famine.

SHE DID ACCORDING TO THE SAYING OF ELIJAH

Elijah arrived at the city gate where the widow was gathering sticks. He "called to her, and said, Fetch me, I pray thee, a little water in a vessel, that I may drink." Without hesitation, this faithful woman "was going to fetch it" when Elijah "called to her, and said, Bring me, I pray thee, a morsel of bread in thine hand" (1 Kings 17:10–11). The request is almost an afterthought, for she had already left for the water when he called to her. She cried out in apology and distress, "As the Lord thy God liveth, I have not a cake, but an handful of meal in a barrel, and a little oil in a cruse: and, behold, I am gathering two sticks, that I may go in and dress it for me and my son, that we may eat it, and die" (1 Kings 17:12).

"Fear not," Elijah said, "go and do as thou hast said: but make me thereof a little cake first, and bring it unto me, and after make for thee and for thy son. For thus saith the Lord God of Israel, The barrel of meal shall not waste, neither shall the cruse of oil fail, until the day that the Lord sendeth rain upon the earth. And she went and did according to the saying of Elijah: and she, and he, and her house, did eat many days" (1 King 17:13–15). There is no record of the conversation that resulted in Elijah's staying with the widow during the famine. Perhaps, believing his promise, she freely invited him to remain with her and her son.

The portrait of this poor widow teaches us to put the Lord first in our lives and trust his promises. Fulfilling his commandments must be our priority, even when obedience demands sacrifice or tests faith. We must believe and practice the counsel the Lord gave on the day the Church was organized: "Thou shalt give heed unto all [the prophet's] words and commandments which he shall give unto you as he receiveth them, . . . for his word ye shall receive, as if from mine own mouth, in all patience and faith" (D&C 21:4–5). It often takes both patience and faith to follow the prophet. The widow of Zarephath reminds us to trust in the Lord's promises.

NOW I KNOW THOU ART A MAN OF GOD

Blessings come from faith and service. "And it came to pass after these things, that the son of the woman . . . fell sick; and his sickness was so sore, that there was no breath left in him. And she said unto Elijah, What have I to do with thee, O thou man of God? art thou come unto me to call my sin to remembrance?" (1 Kings 17:17–18). How prone we are to remember our sins, to feel unworthy of the Lord's blessings, and to lay the trials of our lives at our own feet. We think to ourselves, If only I had been more dedicated, more righteous, I would not be suffering under this present distress. We fear we are somehow responsible for every affliction that comes our way. As he did for her, the Lord will assure us we are loved, that our sins we have repented of are not remembered, and that our present distress is not necessarily linked to past transgressions.

Elijah pleaded with the Lord to restore the life of the widow's son. "O Lord my God," Elijah prayed, "let this child's soul come into him again" (1 Samuel 17:21). Mindful of the widow's faith and her willingness to put his commandments first, the Lord heeded the prayer, "and the soul of the child came into him again, and he revived" (1 Kings 17:22). Elijah brought the child "and delivered him unto his mother: and Elijah said, See, thy son liveth. And the woman said to Elijah, Now by this I know that thou art a man of God, and that the word of the Lord in thy mouth is truth" (1 Kings 17:23–24).

I do not think the widow's last recorded words indicate a lack of faith. She had seen the daily miracle of the meal and the oil. This second miracle on her behalf was a further confirmation of all she believed. All of us need our faith reconfirmed, and the widow of Zarephath was no different. She did not ask for the miracle, but it strengthened her beliefs.

Her reaffirmation of faith reminds me of a poem by Robert Frost. In the first stanzas he describes a path through a forest. He wishes the trees stretched out forever and that he could walk the path and never return. Then he thinks about his friends and wishes they would join him on his journey. He concludes:

They would not find me changed from him they knew—
Only more sure of all I thought was true.

("Into My Own," *Poetry of Robert Frost*, 5)

The further I travel along the path of the gospel, the more I know it is true. Our faith is strengthened as we live and progress on the journey. From time to time we need to peer into the almost empty flour barrel, shake the cruse of oil, and ponder the Lord's compassion and power. Then we may echo the words of the widow of Zarephath: "Now by this I know that . . . the word of the Lord in thy mouth is truth" (1 Kings 17:24).

The Lord in his goodness and mercy will from time to time renew our faith and silence our fears. When we shake the cruse, we will hear the splash of oil. When we cry out to the Lord in anguish, we will hear the words, "See, thy son liveth." We then are invited to testify as does the portrait of the widow of Zarephath: "Now by this I know."

THE INDEBTED WIDOW:
MULTIPLYING WHAT WE HAVE

Elisha became the prophet after Elijah, and he performed a miracle in behalf of a faithful woman that is similar to the multiplication of the meal and oil. We turn to the portrait of this unnamed woman of faith.

"Now there cried a certain woman of the wives of the sons of the prophets unto Elisha, saying, Thy servant my husband is dead; and thou knowest that thy servant did fear the Lord: and the creditor is come to take unto him my two sons to be bondmen" (2 Kings 4:1).

The expression "sons of the prophets" means a follower of the prophets. This woman and her husband believed in the teachings of the prophets of Jehovah. They remained dedicated to Jehovah in a country where few had maintained their faith. When Elijah had cried in lonely anguish to the Lord after confronting the priests of Baal, the Lord assured him, "I have left me seven thousand in Israel, all the knees which have not bowed unto Baal, and every mouth which hath not kissed him" (1 Kings 19:18).

This good woman represents the seven thousand. Her faithful life made her deserving of a prophet's compassion and help. Josephus and others identify her as the widow of Obadiah, who had hidden the Lord's prophets from Jezebel. The debt she owed had been contracted in order to feed them while they were in hiding (see Josephus, *Antiquities of the Jews*, 198–99; 1 Kings 18:3–4).

When we read of miracles, we may think that the immediate faith of the person brought them about. Often, we discover that a long life of faithfulness preceded divine assistance. Faith is critical, but faithfulness may often be more important. Faithfulness produces faith.

LIVE THOU AND THY CHILDREN OF THE REST

The husband of this widow had died, leaving debts. The creditor, fearing the widow would not otherwise be able to pay, demanded her two sons as bondmen. When she asked Elisha for help, her situation was as desperate as that of the widow of Zarephath.

Elisha asked the woman what she had in her house. She answered, "Thine handmaid hath not any thing in the house, save a pot of oil." Elisha then had her borrow vessels from all her neighbors, "even empty vessels; borrow not a few. And when thou art come in, thou shalt shut the door upon thee and upon thy sons, and shalt pour out into all those vessels, and thou shalt set aside that which is full" (2 Kings 4:2–4).

The vessels were gathered, the door was shut, and the widow began to pour. As each empty vessel was brought, it was filled with the oil. When every borrowed vessel was filled, the widow asked her son to "bring me yet a vessel." And he said to her, "There is not a vessel more" (2 Kings 4:6). Clearly this woman of faith anticipated that the oil would last until every vessel was filled. Then the widow returned to Elisha, who told her, "Go, sell the oil, and pay thy debt, and live thou and thy children of the rest" (2 Kings 4:7).

The Lord often gives us more than we ask. The widow was concerned only with her payment to the creditor, but the Lord provided sufficient for her family to live on. There is hope and encouragement in this story for anyone in a similar situation. Elisha asked the widow first to provide what she had. The Lord then multiplied what she had until it was sufficient for her needs and beyond.

While serving as a bishop I saw this miracle repeated in the lives of several ward members. Some had children on missions. Some had suffered financial reverses. I saw it especially in the lives of faithful single sisters who were struggling to maintain their family. I remember my mother worrying about how she would find sufficient funds for our college and mission years. We did all we could to provide for ourselves, and then the Lord stepped in and the vessels began to be filled. When those years were ended, my sisters and I all had college degrees and I had finished my mission. Mother said, "Those were the easiest years of my life." Truly, the Lord filled our vessels.

Each of us is tested in different ways. I testify that if we live a life of faithfulness, a life of following the prophets in a world where few obey, and if we use what we have, the Lord will multiply it so that we will have sufficient and beyond.

Spiritual things as well can be miraculously multiplied. When we feel unable to fulfill our callings or face our challenges, if we are willing to pour out what we do have, the Lord will give us sufficient for our needs and beyond. When discouraging moments come, we can find hope and encouragement by returning to the portrait of the indebted widow and reflecting on the miracle that supplied what she lacked. With faith and faithfulness, we may anticipate the Lord will do as much for us.

THE SHUNAMMITE WOMAN: SERVICE THAT SEEKS NO REWARD

Immediately after the portrait of the indebted woman with her two sons is the portrait of the woman of Shunem. She is introduced as a "great woman." We see in her another unnamed woman of faith and compassion in an unbelieving and hostile world. Without being asked, she graciously saw to the needs and comfort of Elisha. "And it fell on a day, that Elisha passed to Shunem, where was a great woman; and she constrained him to eat bread. And so it was, that as oft as he passed by, he turned in thither to eat bread" (2 Kings 4:8).

Not satisfied with providing an occasional meal, the woman "said unto her husband, Behold now, I perceive that this is an holy man of God, which passeth by us continually. Let us make a little chamber, I pray thee, on the wall; and let us set for him there a bed, and a table, and a stool, and a candlestick: and it shall be, when he cometh to us, that he shall turn in thither" (2 Kings 4:9–10). The husband agreed with his wife's good counsel, and the chamber was made. This generosity was also extended to Gehazi, Elisha's servant.

I am impressed with her words, "I perceive that this is an holy man of God." In a society where most could not perceive men of God, she could. Our society, like hers, fails to recognize "holy men of God." The Doctrine and Covenants teaches that "intelligence cleaveth unto intelligence; wisdom receiveth wisdom; truth embraceth truth; virtue loveth virtue" (D&C 88:40). It takes the Spirit to recognize the Spirit in others. Her recognition of a man of God and her willingness to act on that knowledge produced great blessings in her life.

Elisha, grateful for the kindness of this "great woman" and sensing her desire to serve and be near a holy man of God, desired to reward her for her generosity. "He said to Gehazi his servant, Call this Shunammite. And when he had called her, she stood before him. And he said unto him, Say now unto her, Behold, thou hast been careful for us with all this care; what is to be done for thee?" (2 Kings 4:12–13). Several things were suggested that the woman might consider, but she replied, "I dwell among mine own people." The implication is that the woman expected no reward other than the natural joy such kindness produced.

WAS NOT THE GIVING ENOUGH?

Several years ago, I had a life-changing experience. This experience taught me the lesson I feel is reflected in the Shunammite woman's life. A woman about twenty-one years of age came into the institute of religion at the University of Utah in the last days of pregnancy. Starving and frightened, she had been sent to us from another religious group on campus. I took her home to my wife, and for several days my wife and another wonderful woman cared for and loved this young woman. In time we learned something of her past and the suffering she had endured. She wanted desperately for her unborn child to live in a loving home. Arrangements were made with LDS Social Services to place the baby in such a home when it was born. Other arrangements were made for the future happiness and security of this young woman.

Completely overcome by the love and kindness shown her and feeling unable to respond in kind, she went for a walk one day, boarded a bus, and left our lives as quickly as she had entered them. "All our plans were in vain," I thought. I became sullen and silently blamed the Lord for not stopping her departure. Could he not at least have kept her with us until the baby was born and placed in a good home? One night while I was tormented by these thoughts, it seemed the Spirit whispered to me, "That which you have done is not lost. Did you expect a reward for your love? Was not the giving enough?"

Part of the greatness I see in the Shunammite woman is her apparent understanding of that truth. Deep in her heart she knew that kindness, love, compassion, and charity need no reward. Therefore, she loved, served, and showed compassion. She knew that the giving is always enough.

THOU SHALT EMBRACE A SON

Still desirous to bless the woman with something that would show their appreciation, Elisha again asked his servant, "What then is to be done for her? And Gehazi answered, Verily she hath no child, and her husband is old" (2 Kings 4:14). Elisha called her and promised her she would embrace a son. Though she asked for nothing, the Lord, through his prophet, chose a suitable blessing. It is often best that way.

I have at times received my desires from the Lord only to discover they did not bring the fulfillment I had anticipated. Other times I have been denied what I wanted only to discover the Lord had chosen a better path for me. Like the Shunammite woman, let us serve for the joy of serving, allowing the Lord to choose those blessings that will result in our happiness.

After the promised son was born and had grown, he fell sick, was carried to his mother, and died in her lap. It must have seemed especially painful to have this son of promise taken away.

But the Shunammite woman laid her son in the little room prepared for Elisha and then went to Mount Carmel to find him. In her grief she refused to leave the prophet until he returned with her. Both her kindness and her faith were rewarded. After considerable prayer by Elisha, and surely by the son's mother, he was revived.

It was not only the faith of the mother at her time of need that resulted in this miracle but her past life of service and dedication. Her faithfulness had produced the necessary faith. Her kindness stirred the soul of Elisha. He joined his prayers to hers, and the Lord responded.

When we look at the portrait of the Shunammite woman, we see one who served without expectation of reward. We are reminded that the Lord will grant us the blessings that will bring us the greatest growth and joy. We see one who perceives when men are holy, desires their company, and goes to them for help with faith and confidence. Hers is a portrait we shall not forget.

NAAMAN'S LITTLE MAID: LOVE AND FAITH IN CAPTIVITY

The next portrait is a sketch of the maid to Naaman's wife. Were it not for the faith of this little maid, Naaman would have died a leper.

Naaman was a "great man with his master, and honourable, because by him the Lord had given deliverance unto Syria: he was also a mighty man in valour, but he was a leper. And the Syrians had gone out by companies, and had brought away captive out of the land of Israel a little maid; and she waited on Naaman's wife" (2 Kings 5:1–2).

A fair assumption would place this little maid between eight and twelve years of age. She was a captive, who surely would have preferred to be with her own people. Was she sullen, bitter, or angry at her masters? Did she doubt the Lord's love?

The words of faith she spoke to her mistress demonstrate the simple faith of a child and also her desire that healing come to her master. "And she said unto her mistress, Would God my lord were with the prophet that is in Samaria! for he would recover him of his leprosy" (2 Kings 5:3).

Her sincere wish to alleviate her master's and mistress' suffering make her an example of Paul's counsel: "Servants, be obedient to them that are your masters according to the flesh, with fear and trembling, in singleness of your heart, as unto Christ; not with eyeservice, as menpleasers; but as the servants of Christ, doing the will of God from the heart; with good will doing service, as to the Lord, and not to men: knowing that whatsoever good thing any man doeth, the same shall he receive of the Lord, whether he be bond or free" (Ephesians 6:5–8).

Her simple faith convinced those who heard her, and Naaman traveled to Samaria to be healed. When he arrived, he was angry over the manner Elisha chose, but there is no indication that he doubted Elisha could heal him. What was the foundation of his faith? It was the sweet testimony of a young girl.

The faith of this little maid contrasts with the lack of faith of the king of Israel who, when the king of Syria informed him he was sending Naaman to be healed, "rent his clothes, and said, Am I God, to kill and to make alive, that this man doth send unto me to recover a man of his leprosy?" (2 Kings 5:7). Yet a little maid, held captive in Syria, already knew that there was a prophet in Israel. Once again a woman, this time a very young one, was a touchstone of faith and goodness in a world of disbelief and apostasy.

HULDAH: VERIFYING THE SCRIPTURES

The last of the images framed in this room is that of Huldah the prophetess, who lived during the time of King Josiah and Jeremiah. Josiah was one of the most righteous kings of Judah. He tried very hard to eradicate the idolatrous practices of the past and turn the people completely back to God. He began his reign when he was eight years old.

When he was twenty-six, he set workers to repair the temple. There they discovered "a book of the law of the Lord given by Moses" (2 Chronicles 34:14). This book was probably a copy of

Deuteronomy. The priests took the book to the king, and "when the king had heard the words of the law, . . . he rent his clothes." The king commanded his scribes and priests to "go, enquire of the Lord for me, and for them that are left in Israel and in Judah, concerning the words of the book that is found: for great is the wrath of the Lord that is poured out upon us, because our fathers have not kept the word of the Lord, to do after all that is written in this book" (2 Chronicles 34:19–21).

The messengers "went to Huldah the prophetess, the wife of Shallum . . . and they spake to her to that effect" (2 Chronicles 34:22). Huldah not only verified the words of the book but added, "Thus saith the Lord, Behold, I will bring evil upon this place, and upon the inhabitants thereof, even all the curses that are written in the book which they have read before the king of Judah" (2 Chronicles 34:24).

Huldah gave a personal message of comfort to Josiah: "And as for the king of Judah, who sent you to enquire of the Lord, so shall ye say unto him, Thus saith the Lord God of Israel . . . Because thine heart was tender, and thou didst humble thyself before God, . . . I will gather thee to thy fathers, and thou shalt be gathered to thy grave in peace, neither shall thine eyes see all the evil that I will bring upon this place, and upon the inhabitants of the same" (2 Chronicles 34:26–28).

Josiah believed the words of Huldah. He gathered all the people together to read to them the words of the book. He then covenanted to keep the laws and worship only the God of Israel and caused his people to make the same covenant. Josiah died some time later in a battle with Pharaoh Necho at Megiddo, but he died in the peace that comes from righteousness, the peace that Jesus spoke of: "Peace I leave with you, my peace I give unto you: not as the world giveth, give I unto you" (John 14:27).

I have known many Huldahs, women who know the scriptures. One was an early morning seminary teacher, and another was a woman in France who taught the Gospel Doctrine class in her tiny branch. It was not just that these women knew the scriptures but they taught with the understanding they had received from the Holy Ghost. Once I had gained the assurance that their words about the scriptures were true through the clarity of their testimony, like Josiah, I could commit to my course of action, safe in the knowledge I had heard the truth.

Though the message Huldah gave Josiah was painful, she delivered it without equivocation. May she remind us to speak the Lord's truths without hesitation, to verify his scriptures, and to motivate others to more fully commit to keep the covenants of the Lord.

Though all these women endured hard circumstances, the fountain of charity within them continued to pour forth its sweetness. Neither famine nor captivity was sufficient to destroy their natural sympathy. No trial, even the death of their children, could destroy their faith in the Lord and his prophets.

The Lord prophesied of our day that "because iniquity shall abound, the love of men shall wax cold; but he that shall not be overcome, the same shall be saved" (Joseph Smith–Matthew 1:30). In such a world, we will return to this part of the gallery and ponder the strength of these women who trusted the Lord and his prophets amidst the evil of their time.

CHAPTER 15

CONTRASTING QUEENS

The next portrait we view in the halls of the Old Testament is that of a righteous and truly royal queen, the queen of Sheba. In stark and even shocking contrast to hers are the portraits of the ungodly wives of Solomon and the diabolical queens Jezebel and Athaliah.

THE QUEEN OF SHEBA: THE THIRST FOR KNOWLEDGE

Sheba is generally identified with Arabia. "When the queen of Sheba heard of the fame of Solomon concerning the name of the Lord, she came to prove him with hard questions" (1 Kings 10:1). There are many types of wisdom or learning, but this queen sought wisdom "concerning the name of the Lord."

"When she was come to Solomon, she communed with him of all that was in her heart" (1 Kings 10:2). We are told, "King Solomon gave unto the queen of Sheba all her desire, whatsoever she asked, beside that which Solomon gave her of his royal bounty" (1 Kings 10:13).

Solomon was known for his wealth and his wisdom. The queen of Sheba obtained both from Solomon, but her desire was for his wisdom. She is an example of the counsel the Lord gave to "seek not for riches, but for wisdom, and behold, the mysteries of

God shall be unfolded unto you, and then shall you be made rich. Behold, he that hath eternal life is rich" (D&C 6:7; see also 11:7).

There is a wisdom that teaches and a wisdom that desires to learn. Who is to say which is the greatest or most necessary? The wisdom of the queen of Sheba is repeated in the life of Mary, who sat at the feet of the Savior, and in the lives of other righteous women who desired the truth. Their wisdom is in their hunger to be taught and in their recognition of the source of truth. Such wisdom walks hand in hand with humility, which is a prerequisite to receiving the Spirit.

Jesus spoke of the visit of the queen of Sheba, saying, "The queen of the south shall rise up in the judgment with the men of this generation, and condemn them: for she came from the utmost parts of the earth to hear the wisdom of Solomon; and, behold, a greater than Solomon is here" (Luke 11:31). What lesson would the Savior have us receive from this queen of the south? It is to emulate her hunger for truth and wisdom.

Latter-day Saint women seek truth from many different sources. Like Emma Smith they are called to learn much (see D&C 25:8). They receive wisdom from prophets and apostles, from the scriptures, and from every other worthy source. The encouragement of the Lord that we "seek . . . out of the best books words of wisdom . . . even by study and also by faith" (D&C 88:118), is a guiding principle in their lives. I have seen this hunger for wisdom in the faces of the sisters who attend institute classes. I see it at Education Week where thousands of people, mainly women, gather to seek wisdom. I see it in Know Your Religion lectures. I see it in Gospel Doctrine and Relief Society classes. I see it in book clubs, where women gather to share ideas. I see it in the faces of busy young university women who find time to seek the wisdom associated with "the name of the Lord" at the institute of religion. These women understand why the queen of Sheba would travel a great distance to speak with Solomon.

The queen of Sheba told Solomon, "Happy are thy men, happy are these thy servants, which stand continually before thee, and that hear thy wisdom" (1 Kings 10:8). Perhaps this great woman would have loved to remain to hear daily the wisdom of the Lord that he possessed. She told Solomon, "Blessed be the Lord thy God, which delighted in thee" (1 Kings 10:9). The queen of Sheba realized that wisdom is a sign of the Lord's love and delight.

There is one more trait I admire in the portrait of the queen of Sheba. "When the queen of Sheba heard of the fame of Solomon concerning the name of the Lord, she came to prove him" (1 Kings 10:1). Paul encouraged the Thessalonians to "prove all things; hold fast that which is good" (1 Thessalonians 5:21). The queen of Sheba was not content merely to hear of Solomon; she wanted to know for herself.

After proving Solomon with hard questions and receiving answers, the queen of Sheba testified: "It was a true report that I heard in mine own land of thy acts and of thy wisdom. Howbeit I believed not the words, until I came, and mine eyes had seen it" (1 Kings 10:6–7). As Latter-day Saints we claim to have the gospel of Jesus Christ in its fulness. Many do not believe that claim and refuse to examine it. There are those, however, like this wonderful woman, who, when they hear the report, are determined to find out if it is true. Through study and faith women today prove for themselves that the gospel truths they have heard are true. Paul taught that faith is built on the solid foundation of evidence (see Hebrews 11:1). Like the queen of Sheba, latter-day women want that evidence and search for it.

Every ward and branch of the Church has such women. I taught and baptized them in the mission field. Like the queen of Sheba, they testified of what they had learned. When people have heard and seen, they must testify to the truths and wisdom they have received. There is no doubt in my mind that the queen of Sheba returned to her own land to affirm the truths she had learned.

We leave this royal portrait also determined to search for wisdom "concerning the name of the Lord," hoping to prove and examine all things and hold to that which is good, desiring to testify to the truths we have seen and heard. The portrait of the queen of Sheba reminds us that happiness is the natural result of living according to the wisdom of God. We, too, must continue the everyday business of our lives; we, too, must continue to take advantage of every opportunity to learn.

SOLOMON'S WIVES:
THERE WAS NOT AN HELP MEET FOR HIM

The next picture contains the many faces of the wives of Solomon. In Deuteronomy, Moses prophetically warned any future king of Israel not to "multiply wives to himself, that his heart turn not away" (Deuteronomy 17:17). Despite this wise counsel, "King Solomon loved many strange women, together with the daughter of Pharaoh, women of the Moabites, Ammonites, Edomites, Zidonians, and Hittites; of the nations concerning which the Lord said unto the children of Israel, Ye shall not go in to them, neither shall they come in unto you: for surely they will turn away your heart after their gods: Solomon clave unto these in love. . . . For it came to pass, when Solomon was old, that his wives turned away his heart after other gods: and his heart was not perfect with the Lord his God. . . . And Solomon did evil in the sight of the Lord, and went not fully after the Lord" (1 Kings 11:1–2, 4, 6).

The builder of the temple to Jehovah also built "an high place for Chemosh, the abomination of Moab, . . . and for Molech, the abomination of the children of Ammon. And likewise did he for all his strange wives, which burnt incense and sacrificed unto their gods" (1 Kings 11:7–8). Some of these gods demanded the sacrifice of infants. It is difficult to believe Solomon could permit such sacrifices and honor such gods, and yet it seems that he may have done so.

Rather than receive wisdom from Solomon, his wives "turned away his heart" from the very God who blessed him with that wisdom. Others may have recognized and learned from him, but his many wives held to their own wicked beliefs.

We have already seen portraits of women who learned to

worship the God of their husbands. Ruth, a Moabitess, a native of one of the countries specifically mentioned as the home of some of Solomon's wives, accepted the God of Israel. She affirmed to her mother-in-law, Naomi, "Thy God shall be my God." Rahab also made that choice, as did the wonderful Lamanite women in the Book of Mormon.

Turning Solomon away from the Lord had tragic consequences. Because he had allowed his wives to influence him unrighteously, the Lord told Solomon, "Forasmuch as this is done of thee, and thou hast not kept my covenant and my statutes, which I have commanded thee, I will surely rend the kingdom from thee, and will give it to thy servant. . . . Howbeit I will not rend away all the kingdom; but will give one tribe to thy son for David my servant's sake, and for Jerusalem's sake which I have chosen" (1 Kings 11:11, 13).

Before the death of Solomon, Ahijah the prophet anointed Solomon's son Jeroboam ruler over ten of the tribes of Israel. At the death of Solomon the kingdom fragmented into civil war. The wives of Solomon thus had a long-lasting and negative influence on the history of Israel. Solomon's downfall is further evidence of how important a true daughter of God can be as a help meet. It is also evidence of what may happen to even a wise and noble servant of God who does not have the companionship and counsel of a virtuous woman. Solomon himself wrote, "A virtuous woman is a crown to her husband" (Proverbs 12:4). Solomon wore a crown of gold, but among all his riches was not found the most precious crown of all, "a virtuous woman."

Solomon had all the gifts necessary to be truly great, but he unwisely allowed his unrighteous wives to influence him for evil. That made the difference. The portrait of Solomon's wives highlights the critical importance, indeed the necessity, of a virtuous woman standing beside a man of God.

JEZEBEL: THE AGGRESSIVE PURSUIT OF POWER

Ahab, king of Israel, was a wicked king, but his wife, Jezebel, surpassed him in wickedness and stirred him to even greater evil.

The first thing Jezebel did when she arrived in Israel was to introduce the worship of Baal and attempt to eradicate the worship of Jehovah. She "cut off the prophets of the Lord" and "slew the prophets of the Lord" (1 Kings 18:4, 13). The Lord sent Jehu to destroy the wicked house of Ahab, to "avenge the blood of my servants the prophets, . . . at the hand of Jezebel" (2 Kings 9:7).

Elijah decreed a famine to bring Israel to repentance. At the end of three years of famine he confronted and defeated "the prophets . . . which eat at Jezebel's table" at Mount Carmel (1 Kings 18:19). When Jezebel learned of the defeat of her "prophets" she threatened Elijah, saying, "So let the gods to me, and more also, if I make not thy life as the life of one of them by to morrow about this time" (1 Kings 19:2). Elijah fled, but the Lord sent him back. Again Elijah confronted Ahab for his and his wife's evil.

"Naboth the Jezreelite had a vineyard, which was in Jezreel, hard by the palace of Ahab king of Samaria" (1 Kings 21:1). When Naboth refused to sell the inheritance of his fathers, Ahab, like a spoiled child, "came into his house heavy and displeased. . . . And he laid him down upon his bed, and turned away his face, and would eat no bread" (1 Kings 21:4). Jezebel asked him why he was sad. He explained Naboth's refusal. Jezebel said, "Dost thou now govern the kingdom of Israel? arise, and eat bread, and let thine heart be merry: I will give thee the vineyard of Naboth the Jezreelite" (1 Kings 21:7). She arranged the murder of Naboth and told Ahab that the vineyard was his. When Elijah confronted Ahab walking in the vineyard, Ahab greeted Elijah with the words, "Hast thou found me, O mine enemy?" (1 Kings 21:20).

Ahab's actual enemy was "the wife of [his] bosom" (Deuteronomy 12:6). She encouraged him to both temporal and spiritual destruction. Jezebel gave Ahab whatever he wanted and spurred him to use his power selfishly. Elijah told Ahab the truth about himself and about his wife, but the truth is often hard. When we are blinded by the Jezebels of our lives, we may defend them against those who try to warn us against their negative influence. Paul once asked the Galatians, "Am I therefore become your enemy, because I tell you the truth?" (Galatians 4:16). The true friend will always encourage us to do good. There is no truer friend than a righteous woman. When a woman uses her intelligence, beauty, or any other attribute to persuade someone to do evil, she becomes not only his enemy but the enemy of God.

After Ahab was killed in battle, Jezebel continued to exert her authority through her son. In time, Jehu was selected by the Lord to overthrow the evil Jezebel. As he rode into Jezreel, "Jezebel heard of it; and she painted her face, and tired her head, and looked out at a window. And as Jehu entered in at the gate, she said, Had Zimri peace, who slew his master?" (2 Kings 9:30–31).

Years before, Zimri had assassinated the king and held power for seven days before being overthrown by Ahab's father, Omri. Jezebel was reminding Jehu of what often happens to usurpers. Her painted face and adorned head were an offer that they rule together. Jehu commanded that she be thrown down to her death.

Far too often we see Jezebels of both sexes today. I have seen many young people form friendships with others whose standards are much different from their own. Despite the counsel of loving parents and Church leaders, they have clung to these associations, regarding as an enemy anyone who tried to point out their detrimental effects. A Young Women president who saw the rapid spiritual deterioration of one of her Laurels said, "A temporary loss of judgment became a more lasting one when she considered every true friend an enemy."

It is well for us to reflect on the portrait of Jezebel and learn the lesson of forming righteous associations. That lesson is reinforced by the portrait of Athaliah, who repeated her mother's wicked influence and enlarged its scope.

ATHALIAH: LIKE MOTHER, LIKE DAUGHTER

Athaliah was the daughter of Jezebel and Ahab. In a sad lapse of wisdom, Jehoshaphat, a righteous king of Judah, arranged the marriage of his son Jehoram with Jezebel's daughter Athaliah (see

2 Chronicles 18:1). Perhaps he thought such a marriage would reunite the warring tribes. But the marriage and Athaliah proved disastrous to the Southern Kingdom of Judah and to the royal line of David. Her portrait teaches the very sobering lesson that evil will spread until it permeates the whole.

Like her mother, Athaliah was consumed with a lust for power that destroyed any vestige of compassion. At the death of Jehoshaphat, Jehoram "slew all his brethren with the sword, and divers also of the princes of Israel. . . . And he walked in the way of the kings of Israel, like as did the house of Ahab: for he had the daughter of Ahab to wife: and he wrought that which was evil in the eyes of the Lord" (2 Chronicles 21:4–6). As Jezebel had turned Ahab to greater evil, so did Athaliah encourage the evil aspirations of Jehoram.

Jehoram reigned only eight years and died "without being desired" (2 Chronicles 21:20), meaning, essentially, that nobody missed him. Ahaziah, son of Jehoram and Athaliah, became king. He, too, walked in the ways of the house of Ahab, for "his mother was his counsellor to do wickedly. Wherefore he did evil in the sight of the Lord like the house of Ahab: for they were his counsellors after the death of his father to his destruction" (2 Chronicles 22:3–5). These verses describe concisely the opposite of the good influence we have seen from so many women in the gallery. A mother must be her son's counselor to do righteously. She must counsel him in a manner that leads to his exaltation and happiness.

When Jehu destroyed Jezebel, he also killed Ahaziah, who was visiting her. Athaliah, upon hearing her son was dead and her own hold on power tenuous, "arose and destroyed all the seed royal of the house of Judah" (2 Chronicles 22:10). Only the quick thinking and compassion of a woman named Jehoshabeath saved the Davidic line. Jehoshabeath rescued and hid one infant boy named Joash. He was kept hidden for six years. In time Jehoida, the priest, Jehoshabeath's husband, overthrew Athaliah and executed her. This wicked queen had succeeded in bringing the kingdom of Judah to nearly the same state of evil found in the

Northern Kingdom of Israel. She undid many of the efforts of her father-in-law, Jehoshaphat, and his father, Asa, to maintain a people devoted to the service of Jehovah.

Evil seeks to destroy good. They cannot coexist. May the portrait of Athaliah lead us to have the foresight and wisdom to avoid the tragic mistake of Jehoshaphat and keep the Athaliahs of the world far from our homes and families.

CHAPTER 16

THREE QUEENS OF THE EAST

After the Babylonian captivity, many of the Jews returned to Israel to rebuild their land and their temple. Some, however, chose to remain in the east, where they had found a measure of acceptance under the Persians. The story of Esther takes place among those Jews who remained in Persia. Three queens play a role in the history of the Jews of this period, the Babylonian queen who counseled Belshazzar the night before Babylon fell, the Persian queen Vashti, and Esther.

THE QUEEN OF BABYLON: TESTIFYING OF A MAN OF GOD

Belshazzar was king of Babylon just before its destruction by the Persians. He and his lords forgot the service Daniel had rendered his father Nebuchadnezzar, but one in his kingdom had not forgotten the power of the Jewish prophet. In drunken revelry Belshazzar "commanded to bring the golden and silver vessels which his father Nebuchadnezzar had taken out of the temple which was in Jerusalem; that the king, and his princes, his wives, and his concubines, might drink therein. . . . In the same hour came forth fingers of a man's hand, and wrote over against the candlestick upon the plaister of the wall of the king's palace: and the king saw the part of the hand that wrote" (Daniel 5:2, 5).

Filled with fear, the king called for "the astrologers . . . and soothsayers" (Daniel 5:7) to come and interpret the handwriting on the wall. But they could not read it.

The queen heard of the problem and responded with wisdom. She remembered Daniel and knew what he could do. "The queen, by reason of the words of the king and his lords, came into the banquet house: and the queen spake and said, O king, live for ever: let not thy thoughts trouble thee, nor let thy countenance be changed" (Daniel 5:10).

She then gave one of the finest descriptions of a prophet found in scripture: "There is a man in thy kingdom, in whom is the spirit of the holy gods; and in the days of thy father light and understanding and wisdom, like the wisdom of the gods, was found in him; whom the king Nebuchadnezzar thy father, the king, I say, thy father, made master of the magicians, astrologers, Chaldeans, and soothsayers; forasmuch as an excellent spirit, and knowledge, and understanding, interpreting of dreams, and shewing of hard sentences, and dissolving of doubts, were found in the same Daniel, whom the king named Belteshazzar: now let Daniel be called, and he will shew the interpretation" (Daniel 5:11–12). The king sent for Daniel, who read the handwriting that predicted the downfall of Babylon and the rise of Persia.

Whether the queen of Babylon was righteous or not is hidden in history, but the sketch that is her portrait is worthy of contemplation. She recognized a prophet and trusted his ability to receive "light and understanding and wisdom." We have seen this recognition of prophetic qualities by other women in the scriptures. Righteous women recognize prophets, follow them, and, as did the queen of Babylon, teach others to seek out and receive instruction from one who possesses "the spirit of the holy gods."

Babylon has been a symbol for worldliness and rebellion since the days of the Old Testament. Yet the portrait of Babylon's last queen reminds us that she recognized a prophet of God. May we remember her and her description of a prophet when our own prophet speaks today.

VASHTI: REBELLION, OR VIRTUE DETHRONED?

Next we pause at the portrait of Vashti, a queen who was known for her beauty. As we study her features we ask ourselves, "Is this the face of a woman who rebelled against her husband, or did other factors lead her to remain outside the banquet hall?"

The book of Esther begins with feasts given by Ahasuerus and Vashti, king and queen of Persia. There was "royal wine in abundance" in the men's feast (Esther 1:7). On the seventh day, "when the heart of the king was merry with wine, he commanded" his seven chamberlains "to bring Vashti the queen before the king with the crown royal, to shew the people and the princes her beauty: for she was fair to look on" (Esther 1:10–11).

"But the queen Vashti refused to come at the king's commandment by his chamberlains: therefore was the king very wroth, and his anger burned in him" (Esther 1:12). The king sought counsel from some of his princes, who urged him to depose the queen, lest her example of disobedience spread to other wives in the kingdom. It may have been that the wives of some of these men were with the queen when she made her decision. They urged him to make a royal commandment, which could not be reversed, and send it throughout the kingdom. The commandment was written, and Vashti was removed.

The example Vashti set before the women attending her feast may have been an example of modesty and virtue, not a challenge to her husband's authority. Anyone acquainted with Middle Eastern customs knows the modesty of the women, both in dress and behavior. It is not hard to see Vashti as modest and humble, rather than defiant and rebellious. She knew the men were drinking. She also knew why the king had sent for her. Conscious that her refusal might anger the king, she made a decision of propriety and modesty.

Josephus attributes this motive to Vashti in his account of her refusal. "Now the king was desirous to shew her, who exceeded all other women in beauty, to those that feasted with him, and he sent some to command her to come to his feast. But she, out of regard to the laws of the Persians, which forbid the wives to be seen by strangers, did not go to the king, and though he often-times sent the eunuchs to her, she did nevertheless stay away, and refused to come, till the king was . . . much irritated" (*Antiquities of the Jews*, 237). Rather than admit he was at fault, the king became angry and interpreted her refusal as a challenge to his authority.

Vashti's behavior in this difficult situation makes her one of the exemplary women of the Bible, a woman who so valued virtue, propriety, and modesty she would not display her beauty to a room of drinking men despite great personal risk. Josephus described the king's second thoughts: "But the king having been fond of her, he did not well bear a separation, and yet by the law he could not admit of a reconciliation, so he was under trouble, as not having it in his power to do what he desired to do: but when his friends saw him so uneasy, they advised him to cast the memory of his wife, and his love for her, out of his mind, but to send abroad . . . and to search out for comely virgins, and to take her whom he should best like for his wife" (*Antiquities of the Jews*, 238).

Once sober, the king realized what he had done. It was too late, however, and the search for a replacement was suggested to distract him.

Like Vashti, the sisters of the Church today choose not to be placed in compromising environments. They have the courage to decide in favor of modesty, propriety, and decency. The portrait of Vashti reminds us that these qualities are pleasing to the Lord.

ESTHER: BORN TO SAVE HER PEOPLE

The portrait of Esther is one of the most beautiful in the gallery. In a variety of ways, Esther is a female counterpart to Joseph who was sold into Egypt. Like Joseph, Esther "obtained favour in the sight of all them that looked upon her" (Esther

2:15). While in the charge of Hegai, "keeper of the women," Esther "pleased him, and she obtained kindness of him . . . and he preferred her and her maids unto the best place of the house of the women" (Esther 2:8–9). Like Joseph, she found favor in the eyes of a king and was raised to a position of influence and power. Joseph saved his people from death by famine; Esther saved her people from death by the intrigues of Haman. Just as Joseph's descendants would save the world from a spiritual famine by teaching the truths of the Restoration, so may the spiritual descendants of Esther find in her a type for the women of today.

While Haman plotted the destruction of all the Jews in Persia and its provinces, Mordecai, Esther's relative, encouraged her to speak to the king on behalf of the Jews. Esther explained to Mordecai, "All the king's servants, and the people of the king's provinces, do know, that whosoever, whether man or woman, shall come unto the king into the inner court, who is not called, there is one law of his to put him to death, except such to whom the king shall hold out the golden sceptre, that he may live: but I have not been called to come in unto the king these thirty days" (Esther 4:11).

Esther had good cause for her concern. The reason for the king's law was that someone who came into the king's presence without having been summoned might have designs on the king's life.

Mordecai's answer reminded Esther of her opportunity and duty. "Think not with thyself that thou shalt escape in the king's house, more than all the Jews. For if thou altogether holdest thy peace at this time, then shall there enlargement and deliverance arise to the Jews from another place; but thou and thy father's house shall be destroyed: and who knoweth whether thou art come to the kingdom for such a time as this?" (Esther 4:13–14).

Occasionally Esther is criticized for marrying a Persian king. We do not know how much choice she had, but Mordecai believed the Lord had placed Esther in a position to save her entire people. With unselfish willingness to sacrifice her own life, Esther replied to Mordecai's letter with words that show her to be among the greatest women who have ever lived: "Go, gather together all the Jews that are present in Shushan, and fast ye for me . . . I also and my maidens will fast likewise; and so will I go in unto the king, which is not according to the law: and if I perish, I perish" (Esther 4:16).

Again we see the strength and loyalty that women often give one another in times of trial. For three days Esther was supported by her maidens. Then Esther entered the king's inner court and was allowed to make her request. Her plea for her people stopped Haman's plots, and the Jews were saved.

It is possible that Esther risked her life a second time in making a request of the king without having been called. After her two dinners and the execution of Haman, Esther approached the king a second time. "And Esther spake yet again before the king, and fell down at his feet, and besought him with tears to put away the mischief of Haman the Agagite, and his device that he had devised against the Jews. Then the king held out the golden sceptre toward Esther. So Esther arose, and stood before the king" (Esther 8:3–4). A new edict was issued, and the Jews in Persia were saved.

The courage of Esther has not been forgotten over the centuries. To this day, Jewish people celebrate Esther's victory over Haman at a holiday called Purim (see Esther 9:26). For the Jewish people, her story is a yearly reminder that God will save his people.

Many forces are arrayed against decency and goodness in our modern world. The family itself is besieged by the forces of the adversary. As the principles of righteousness and the value of the family are weakened and mocked, we see an increase of the social problems that cripple the world. Modern prophets have spoken eloquently in favor of the family, warning again and again that if the family no longer provides a foundation of morality, love, and security, societies and nations will fall. Recently the First Presidency and the Quorum of the Twelve Apostles issued to the world a proclamation on the family. Centered on the importance of maintaining the family, it ends with this strong statement: "We warn that the disintegration of the family will bring upon individuals, communities, and nations the calamities foretold by ancient and modern prophets" ("The Family," 102).

The Latter-day Saints face evils even more wicked than Haman, evils that seek not only the physical destruction of the children of God but their spiritual destruction as well. Paul described our more subtle opponent when he said, "We wrestle not against flesh and blood, but against principalities, against powers, against the rulers of the darkness of this world, against spiritual wickedness in high places" (Ephesians 6:12). Paul further described our day with these words: "In the last days perilous times shall come. For men shall be lovers of their own selves, covetous, boasters, proud, blasphemers, disobedient to parents, unthankful, unholy, without natural affection, trucebreakers, false accusers, incontinent, fierce, despisers of those that are good, traitors, heady, highminded, lovers of pleasures more than lovers of God" (2 Timothy 3:1–4).

The Lord has chosen, called, and sent modern Esthers who have come to earth for such a time as this. They have come to save the family, to save the principles of decency, righteousness, and honesty. They have come to save virtue, modesty, and respect. They have come to inspire hope through their courage and their sacrifice. They come supporting each other, as Esther's maids supported her. They also come fasting and praying, supplicating the Lord for his mercy, guidance, and direction.

Esther told Mordecai, "So will I go in unto the king, which is not according to the law" (Esther 4:16). Latter-day women often find themselves in a similar position. If they are to save the home, their families, and the foundations of society, they will find themselves increasingly believing and doing things that go against the customs and conventions of their day. They may face mockery, ridicule, and the cynical attitude of a sophisticated society. Their beliefs, decisions, and lifestyles will not be popular, but they will step forward with courage, focused on the critical duty that lies before them, knowing they, too, came into the world "for such a time as this."

Just as Esther was God's "enlargement and deliverance" (Esther 4:14) in Persia, so, armed with the truths of the Restoration and standing side by side with righteous men, Latter-day Saint women will be God's enlargement and deliverance now. Esther risked her life in going to the king without being commanded; Vashti risked her life in refusing to obey the king's command. Both stood for righteous causes. May their latter-day sisters consider their own situations and choices and return often to this room of the gallery to find inspiration in their royal sisters of old. They will maintain their modesty and integrity. They will strive to find favor in the sight of good people and to influence them in positive and noble ways. They, like Esther, will save their people. Like Esther's maidens, they will readily support, pray, and fast for each other. Their courage, faith, and sacrifices will be celebrated by a righteous posterity long into the Millennium.

ZERESH: COUNSEL WITHOUT PITY

The last portrait in this room is a sketch of Zeresh, the wife of Haman. Though not as overtly ambitious as Athaliah, she did anticipate rising with her husband's good fortunes. She knew of his plots against the Jews and of his hatred of Mordecai in particular. Zeresh is a dark foil to the bright example of women who counsel their husbands or sons in the ways of mercy, compassion and righteousness. When Haman was invited to attend Esther's banquet with the king, he "called for his friends, and Zeresh, his wife" (Esther 5:10). He related to them the good news of his invitation to Esther's banquet and added, "Yet all this availeth me nothing, so long as I see Mordecai the Jew sitting at the king's gate. Then said Zeresh his wife and all his friends unto him, Let a gallows be made of fifty cubits high, and tomorrow speak thou unto the king that Mordecai may be hanged thereon: then go thou merrily with the king unto the banquet. And the thing pleased Haman; and he caused the gallows to be made" (Esther 5:13–14).

When the king, wishing to honor Mordecai, chose Haman as the one to lead Mordecai through the streets, Haman realized his plots could be the undoing of all his ambitions. "Then said his wise men and Zeresh his wife unto him, If Mordecai be of the seed of the Jews, before whom thou hast begun to fall, thou shalt not prevail against him, but shalt surely fall before him" (Esther 6:13). Suddenly Zeresh, who had supported his plots and ambitions, became the voice of approaching doom. Haman's plot was discovered, and he died on the very gallows his wife had suggested he build.

Zeresh lacked the compassion natural to so many women. There is unfeeling hardness in her counsel to her husband, especially in the words, "then go thou merrily." The Lord's daughters should temper the passions of others, not fan them. Zeresh, however, counseled without pity, and her counsel condemned her husband to the very gallows she suggested he have constructed for Mordecai.

Though her portrait is only a sketch, the negative example of Zeresh and the consequences she helped bring about teach us to counsel in charity and forgiveness. Zeresh and her counsel without pity led to the death of her husband and sons. Her portrait contrasts sharply with that of Esther, whose influence brought salvation to her people.

———

CHAPTER 17

MORE PRECIOUS THAN RUBIES

Next we come to the portraits in the book of Proverbs. There we find that the portraits are composites, rather than of individuals, but though the portraits in Proverbs do not depict individuals, they give us much to think about.

Proverbs describes three types of women. One is a "strange woman," meaning the seductive woman who "forsaketh the guide of her youth, and forgetteth the covenant of her God" (Proverbs 2:16–17). The man who seeks this type of woman takes "fire in his bosom" and "destroyeth his own soul" (Proverbs 6:27, 32). Another type is "a brawling woman," "a contentious and an angry woman" (Proverbs 21:9, 19). "A continual dropping in a very rainy day and a contentious woman are alike" (Proverbs 27:15). "It is better to dwell in the corner of the housetop, than with a brawling woman and in a wide house" (Proverbs 25:24). "A virtuous woman" who "is a crown to her husband" (Proverbs 12:4) is described in detail. The man who can find this type of wife "findeth a good thing, and obtaineth favour of the Lord" (Proverbs 18:22). "House and riches are the inheritance of fathers: and a prudent wife is from the Lord" (Proverbs 19:14). Notice that a virtuous wife is a gift from God, a gift whose "price is far above rubies" (Proverbs 31:10).

HER HUSBAND DOTH SAFELY TRUST IN HER

Let us look more closely at the portrait of the virtuous woman of Proverbs. The first characteristic we notice is that of the woman's relationship with her husband. "The heart of her husband doth safely trust in her, so that he shall have no need of spoil. She will do him good and not evil all the days of her life" (Proverbs 31:11–12). *Spoil* in this verse is better translated "gain" or "value." The meaning is that the husband of a virtuous woman will lack nothing of value because she will wisely use their resources.

Priesthood holders are taught that their first and most important responsibility is toward their wives. It is therefore fitting that the virtuous woman's first responsibility is toward her husband, who trusts her judgment, her dependability, and her wisdom. She uses the resources of the family with wisdom. Her primary desire centers on doing good to her companion all the days of her life.

HER CANDLE GOETH NOT OUT BY NIGHT

The virtuous woman is industrious. "She . . . worketh willingly with her hands" (Proverbs 31:13). She serves her family out of her love and her selfless nature. We see this quality in wives and mothers who work nonstop to create a positive environment for their families.

The tasks of a virtuous woman are fatiguing and their repetitiveness tedious, but she performs them without complaint and often without the gratitude she deserves. She will often rise "while it is yet night" (Proverbs 31:15) and continue to serve well into the night when her "candle goeth not out" (Proverbs 31:18).

Like many other wives and mothers, my wife is often the first to rise in the morning and the last to retire at night. The "candle goeth not out by night" often, because that is the only time she has a moment to refresh her own spirit before she willingly faces the tasks of a new day.

SHE STRETCHETH OUT HER HAND

The virtuous woman is compassionate and charitable. "She stretcheth out her hand to the poor; yea, she reacheth forth her hands to the needy" (Proverbs 31:20). In the midst of caring for her family, she finds time and love to fill the needs of those who are around her. This is one of the guiding principles of the Relief Society, the one that led to its formation. I am frequently amazed at the concern women have for others and the distance their love can reach.

Stretcheth and *reacheth* are such beautiful words. They suggest the effort this type of compassion demands, and yet there is a yearning gentleness in the image they create in our minds. Her hands are held out in a gesture of empathy, mercy, and charity. Although her face is not described in the verse, surely it is filled with desire and compassion. This image is one of my favorites.

SHE IS NOT AFRAID OF THE SNOW

After reading of a virtuous woman's compassionate nature, we are told of her foresight and preparation. "She is not afraid of the snow for her household: for all her household are clothed with scarlet" (Proverbs 31:21). The virtuous woman anticipates the needs of her family and plans accordingly.

This planning could include such things as food storage and educational plans for herself or children. But this verse can also be applied to spiritual preparation. The Lord, speaking to Enoch, said of the people, "Their eyes cannot see afar off" (Moses 6:27), for their decisions were centered on immediate gratification. But the eyes of the virtuous woman do see afar off. Her day-to-day decisions take into consideration the future of herself and family. She sees to it that she and her family are physically and spiritually prepared for the storms of life. Her preparations produce a calming influence on her family, for they see she is not afraid.

STRENGTH AND HONOR ARE HER CLOTHING

Although the writer of Proverbs indicates that the virtuous woman is dressed in "silk and purple" (Proverbs 31:22), "strength and honour are her clothing" and will lead her to "rejoice in time to come" (Proverbs 31:25). "She girdeth her loins with strength" (Proverbs 31:17). The word translated *strength* here means majesty and dignity. Her bearing and dignity enhance her natural beauty. Fashions come and go, but modesty, dignity, and honor are always right.

WISDOM AND KINDNESS

The speech of the virtuous woman, as well as her bearing and dignity, recommend her to the world.

Proverbs is full of sayings dealing with the tongue, many of them with the fool's tongue: "A fool uttereth all his mind: but a wise man keepeth it in till afterwards" (Proverbs 29:11). Some deal with gossip: "The words of a talebearer are as wounds" (Proverbs 18:8). Some teach that our true character shows quickly in speech: "The heart of the righteous studieth to answer: but the mouth of the wicked poureth out evil things" (Proverbs 15:28).

Likewise, the words of the virtuous woman reveal her heart. "She openeth her mouth with wisdom; and in her tongue is the law of kindness" (Proverbs 31:26). The phrase "law of kindness" indicates, among other things, the type of discipline she uses. Notice the balance indicated by the words *wisdom* and *kindness*. Her words are not only wise, indicating the nature of her mind, but also kind, revealing the nature of her heart. Her word is law, but it is obeyed because it is kind, not angry, threatening, or nagging. Her word is followed because it is wise.

SHE EATETH NOT THE BREAD OF IDLENESS

"She looketh well to the ways of her household, and eateth not the bread of idleness" (Proverbs 31:27). Care and solicitude toward family and its resources are mentioned more than once in the description of the virtuous woman. The "bread of idleness" is bread one has not earned. It suggests an irresponsible, wasteful lifestyle.

In the Doctrine and Covenants the Lord warned against

eating the bread of idleness: "Thou shalt not be idle; for he that is idle shall not eat the bread nor wear the garments of the laborer" (D&C 42:42). This verse is often applied to the idle poor who wish to live off the laborer, but it also refers to the idle rich who live off the labors of others. The virtuous woman does not live at the expense of others.

HER CHILDREN CALL HER BLESSED
AND HER HUSBAND PRAISETH HER

The virtuous woman serves those outside her family, but her children and husband are the main recipients of her virtue. They realize that their lives are profoundly blessed by her love and example. "Her children arise up, and call her blessed; her husband also, and he praiseth her. Many daughters have done virtuously, but thou excellest them all" (Proverbs 31:28–29). Though other women are also virtuous, her husband feels she is the most virtuous woman of all. Her children share in that belief.

That is the way I feel about both my wife and my mother. My mother's commitment to the gospel was the foundation of my life. Her example of generosity and kindness has mellowed my own more selfish nature. Her faith has sustained me, and her unquestioned love has helped me see worth in myself. She taught me to read and introduced me to the beauty of the scriptures and the sacredness of life. I feel about her the way President Joseph F. Smith felt about his mother: "I learned in my childhood . . . that no love in all the world can equal the love of a true mother. I did not think in those days, and still I am at a loss to know, how it would be possible for anyone to love her children more truly than did my mother. I have felt sometimes, how could even the Father love his children more than my mother loved her children? It was life to me; it was strength; it was encouragement; it was love that begat love or liking in myself. I knew she loved me with all her heart" (*Gospel Doctrine*, 314).

I was counseled in my youth to spend my life seeking to fulfill the prayer that would always be in the heart of my mother. That is perhaps the most precious gift a mother could receive from her child. As her son, I am indeed honored to "arise up, and call her blessed."

THOU EXCELLEST THEM ALL

I also echo the husband's words of praise. "Many daughters have done virtuously, but thou excellest them all" (Proverbs 31:29). In my eyes no woman is more beautiful than my wife. She is the soul and heart of our home, and her spirit touches and refines all I love. Her gentleness and compassion have guided our children through every crisis and taught them dignity and worth. Her belief in me inspires me to higher levels of achievement. Her reaching out to others has fanned the coals of my own compassion. Her counsel and the intuitive goodness of her wisdom have steadied our course and calmed my overanxious soul. I believe of my wife, as I hope all husbands believe of theirs, that she "excellest them all."

A WOMAN THAT FEARETH THE LORD

The last characteristic mentioned in Proverbs 31 is the crowning quality of the virtuous woman. "Favour is deceitful, and beauty is vain: but a woman that feareth the Lord, she shall be praised" (Proverbs 31:30). Fear of the Lord is reverence, profound love mingled with deep respect. The virtuous woman loves and respects her Father in Heaven. It is his favor she seeks. It is his praise she longs to hear. Popularity, fame, and position are all deceitful, for they cannot last. Physical beauty is vain, for it fades with time, but reverence for the Lord creates a beauty of the soul that increases.

This beauty of soul endears the virtuous woman of Proverbs to us. We sense her reverence for the Lord, for his prophets, and for his gospel. She understands the importance of her role in fulfilling the great plan of happiness for all the Father's children. She accepts the challenges and sacrifices that role demands with faith that her efforts will be pleasing to the Lord, who will exalt her one day in his eternal kingdom.

Proverbs ends with a prayer that the virtuous woman will

receive "the fruit of her hands" and a blessing that "her own works praise her in the gates" (Proverbs 31:31). When we are called to render an accounting of our stewardship, her fruits and her works will announce to all that she is worthy of exaltation and eternal life.

CHAPTER 18

SURVIVING THE CRUCIBLE
OF SUFFERING

The sketch of Job's wife reveals the face of a woman who has seen much suffering. Her face is lined with the memory of the trials of her husband, Job, for she shared his suffering.

She seems to have passed the tests of the first round of suffering, but the second onslaught of the adversary against her husband was too much for her to bear. With that in mind, we can learn some important lessons from her experience.

The story of Job began when the Lord pointed out to Satan the righteousness of Job. Satan replied: "Doth Job fear God for nought? Hast not thou made an hedge about him, and about his house, and about all that he hath on every side? . . . But put forth thine hand now, and touch all that he hath, and he will curse thee to thy face" (Job 1:9–11). The Lord then allowed Satan to try Job in all areas except his physical health. In rapid succession, Satan destroyed all that Job and his wife had, including their children. The death of even one child is trial enough, but the death of all one's children is a trial almost beyond comprehension.

How faithful would we be to the Lord if we suffered such severe losses? Would we trust in God when he seemed indifferent to our devastating pain? "Naked came I out of my mother's womb," Job cried out, "and naked shall I return thither: the Lord gave, and the Lord hath taken away; blessed be the name of the Lord" (Job 1:21).

Unable to conquer the faith of Job and turn him against God, Satan tried another tactic. The Lord allowed Satan to test Job further, with the provision that he not kill him. "So went Satan forth . . . and smote Job with sore boils from the sole of his foot unto [the] crown" of his head (Job 2:7).

CURSE GOD AND DIE

Job's wife reached her breaking point. Their former prosperity and possessions were gone, their children were dead, and now her husband was covered with excruciatingly painful boils. Seeing her husband's deep suffering finally brought forth her anguished cry to "curse God, and die" (Job 2:9). Most of us would rather suffer ourselves than see the suffering of those we love. It seems that Job's physical suffering, added to his emotional torment, was more than his wife could bear.

"How can you still remain righteous and believing," his wife asked, "when obviously God has abandoned us?" Surely she had prayed for her husband. Could not the Lord at least heal him of the boils?

It is very difficult to continue to believe when everything crashes around us and we cry out to God but hear only silence. Often in these moments we are tempted to blame God for our suffering. We may not exactly "curse God," but we doubt his love. Yet, as Job affirmed, God is the same God from whom we received good things (see Job 2:10).

If we view Job as a man who was tried to the greatest degree through the things he suffered, we must surely view his wife as one of the most tried of women. If we reflect for a moment, we can understand why she would say to Job, "Curse God and die." God has all power and can, therefore, remove our pains. If he does not, it is difficult not to cry out in desperation. Our knocking on heaven's door for answers may turn to poundings of anger.

An older couple I knew had served God most of their lives. Then the husband was diagnosed with cancer. Despite prayers, fasting, and blessings, he continued to fail. He lived in constant pain. His wife suffered with him, pleading with the Lord to heal him or end his misery. The pain increased as the husband lingered. Finally, after many months, he died. Though the wife did not outwardly "curse God," she could not rid herself of her bitterness over the Lord's apparent indifference. Eventually she drifted from the Church.

We cannot judge such people, especially if we have not felt the tremendous weight of their suffering. We can only empathize, offer comfort, and encourage those who face such pain to trust in a loving God. We leave Job's wife in the hands of the Savior, knowing that he, above all others, truly does understand such burdens.

But the sketch of Job's wife is important for us to ponder. All of us will face trials and pain. We will cry out to God in our sufferings and, like Joseph Smith, we will wonder, "O God, where art thou? And where is the pavilion that covereth thy hiding place?" (D&C 121:1). When it would be easy to accuse God or doubt his wisdom and love, let us recall the portrait of Job's wife and draw upon our last reserves of trust and faith to endure. Many women have carried tremendous burdens of sorrow and pain and yet continued to love, believe, and serve God when every sign of his presence seemed to have vanished. Their courage and patience witness that Satan's assertion that we love God only when things are going well is not true.

When Job's trial was at last over, he and his wife were given "twice as much as he had before" (Job 42:10). A description of their blessings follows. Chief among those blessings are daughters, whose names have all been recorded: "And he called the name of the first, Jemima; and the name of the second, Kezia; and the name of the third, Keren-happuch. And in all the land were no women found so fair as the daughters of Job: and their father gave them inheritance among their brethren" (Job 42:14–15).

CHAPTER 19

THE DAUGHTERS OF ZION

Near the end of the halls of the Old Testament is a portrait that is not the image of any particular woman. Yet it is a detailed portrait, painted with Isaiah's words of condemnation of the worldly women of his age. Its relevance is not hard to detect.

Isaiah began his exhortation to the women with the following words: "Moreover the Lord saith, . . . the daughters of Zion are haughty, and walk with stretched forth necks and wanton eyes, walking and mincing as they go, and making a tinkling with their feet" (Isaiah 3:16). A stretched-forth neck is an arrogant neck. Wanton eyes are sensual eyes. Mincing is walking "with short, rapid steps in an affected manner" (Isaiah 3:16, e). Tiny bells were sometimes placed on the hems of women's clothing or around their ankles to make a noise and draw attention to the women when they walked.

The Lord spoke of the "bravery" of the beauty aids the women of ancient Israel used to produce the look they desired (see Isaiah 3:18–23). *Bravery* is a wonderful word to describe the false sense of security and self-importance that physical attractiveness may create. If Isaiah were writing today, he would list different items of clothing, jewelry, makeup, or hairstyling, but the meaning would be the same.

Isaiah also revealed other aspects of the women's "bravery." He spoke of the "sweet smell" of perfume, "well set hair," a "stomacher" (robe), and the overall impression of "beauty" created by all of these things (see Isaiah 3:24). This list is followed by images of the poverty and slavery into which the women would go when the Assyrian and Babylonian captivity came.

Isaiah was warning against the illusion of pride and overemphasis on the physical at the expense of more substantial characteristics. Talents can grow. Character can improve with age and is eternal. Personality can be developed and refined. Spirituality can be constant and thrive, but physical beauty of the type Isaiah described is fleeting. Women who heed the Spirit know that, and though they pay attention to their outward appearance, they find their "bravery" in more lasting areas.

Unlike the women of ancient Israel, members of the Church in Alma's time "did not wear costly apparel, yet they were neat and comely" (Alma 1:27). Costly apparel in the scriptures is always indicative of pride. The vain portrait of the "daughters of Zion" reminds women how important it is to distinguish by the Spirit between "neat and comely" and the fashions of the day.

OUR OWN BEAUTY

The Lord counseled the early Saints, "Thou shalt not be proud in thy heart; let all thy garments be plain, and their beauty the beauty of the work of thine own hands" (D&C 42:40). The beauty of the Latter-day Saints is not the beauty of the world. We must establish our own standard rather than borrow the standard of the world.

Brigham Young counseled the Saints, "Beauty must be sought in the expression of the countenance, combined with neatness and cleanliness and graceful manners" (*Journal of Discourses*, 18:75). He also said, "The daughters of Israel should understand what fashions they should have, without borrowing from the impure and unrighteous" (*Journal of Discourses*, 12:220). The beauty of Latter-day Saint women is created by their adherence to the standards of the Church, the dictates of modesty, the refining influence of the Spirit, and some good common sense.

We are often told that the great women in the scriptures were "fair to look upon." It is hardly conceivable that their fairness depended upon the bravery Isaiah described. When we reflect on the beauty and spirituality of these sisters, may we be reminded that theirs was a beauty that did not need the excesses of Isaiah's day.

CHAPTER 20

FAIR AS THE MOON, CLEAR AS THE SUN

Not all of the portraits in the gallery of the scriptures are of actual women. Some of the portraits are metaphorical. Often in the scriptures the Lord draws on the natural qualities of women to teach symbolic truths. Various qualities of the soul, such as charity, are personified as women. Most of these metaphorical portraits are first used in the Old Testament.

THE BRIDE OF CHRIST

One of the most beautiful of the portraits of women in the scriptures is the metaphorical bride of Christ. When the Lord chose an image to describe his Church or his people, he chose the image of a bride. Phrases from the Old Testament Song of Solomon, a poem of love between a husband and wife, are echoed in modern-day revelation, the Doctrine and Covenants, to describe the Church, or bride, of Christ. Filled with love, the husband describes his bride: "Who is she that looketh forth as the morning, fair as the moon, clear as the sun, and terrible [awe-inspiring] as an army with banners?" (Song of Solomon 6:10).

Later we see the bride coming up "from the wilderness, leaning upon her beloved" (Song of Solomon 8:5).

Early in the Restoration the Lord described his Church in similar words: The Church will come forth "out of the wilderness—clear as the moon, and fair as the sun, and terrible as an army with banners" (D&C 5:14). *Wilderness* in this verse could mean the frontier wilderness of the time in America when this revelation was given, but a truer meaning is the untamed, disobedient wilderness of apostasy. Despite his love for her, the Savior's bride, his people, have left him. Instead of being obedient, cultivated, domesticated, and productive, his people are wild and untamed. But in the latter days, according to the Old Testament prophet Hosea, the Lord "will allure her, and bring her into the wilderness, and speak comfortably unto her" (Hosea 2:14). In the latter days, the Church has indeed risen out of the wilderness, leaning lovingly upon her husband, the Savior, who speaks comfortably to her and wins her love.

The bride of Christ, or the Church, is "fair as the moon" (Song of Solomon 6:10). We all know the beauty and softness of moonlight, especially when it is full. As the Church grows, its light, like the increasing light of the moon progressing through its phases, will spread and grow. Like the brilliant full moon against the black night sky, the Church will stand out against the darkness of a world steeped in sin and apostasy.

Likewise, the bride, or the Church, is "clear as the sun" (Song of Solomon 6:10), sending her warmth and radiance upon all. Just as the sun brings life and growth, the Church brings life to all who come under her influence. As the sun enlightens the dark world, allowing us to see clearly, so too will the doctrine and teachings of the gospel enlighten.

Finally, the bride of Christ is "terrible as an army with banners" (Song of Solomon 6:10). As she marches forth, she inspires awe in all who see her. Nothing will stand in the way of the progress of the Lord's kingdom. Like an army with banners, the Lord's work is unstoppable. The inspiration the Church creates as she marches forth sweeps up spectators who desire to join in her victories. Speaking of the growth of the Church in the latter days, the Lord said, "First let my army become very great, and let it be sanctified before me, that it may become fair as the sun, and clear as the moon, and that her banners may be terrible unto all nations; that the kingdoms of this world may be constrained to acknowledge that the kingdom of Zion is in very deed the kingdom of our God and his Christ; therefore, let us become subject unto her laws" (D&C 105:31–32).

In the dedicatory prayer of the Kirtland Temple, the Lord again referred to the Church as his bride, using words from the Song of Solomon. This time, however, he added the image of a bride adorned in her wedding finery. "Remember all thy church, O Lord, . . . ; that thy church may come forth out of the wilderness of darkness, and shine forth fair as the moon, clear as the sun, and terrible as an army with banners; and be adorned as a bride for that day when thou shalt unveil the heavens . . . ; that thy glory may fill the earth" (D&C 109:72–74). The image of the bride beautifully arrayed for her wedding is seen in both the Old Testament and the New. "As the bridegroom rejoiceth over the bride," Isaiah taught, "so shall thy God rejoice over thee" (Isaiah 62:5).

Hosea spoke tenderly of the sweet relationship between the Lord as the husband and the people as his bride: "I will betroth thee unto me for ever; yea, I will betroth thee unto me in righteousness, and in judgment, and in lovingkindness, and in mercies. I will even betroth thee unto me in faithfulness: and thou shalt know the Lord. . . . And I will say . . . , Thou art my people; and they shall say, Thou art my God" (Hosea 2:19–20, 23).

The Lord uses the image of the bride to help us understand the extent of his love for us and the love he desires from us in return. Just as a bride longs to be one with her husband and looks forward to her wedding day, so too does the Church long to be one with the Savior and longs for his coming. "And the Spirit and the bride say, Come" (Revelation 22:17).

But even as the bride looks forward to her wedding day, she prepares for it fervently: "Let us be glad and rejoice, and give honor to him: for the marriage of the Lamb is come, and his wife hath made herself ready. And to her was granted that she should be arrayed in fine linen, clean and white: for the fine linen is the righteousness of saints" (Revelation 19:7–8). The wife is "a woman clothed with the sun, and the moon under her feet, and upon her head a crown of twelve stars" (Revelation 12:1).

I particularly love the phrase "and his wife hath made herself ready" (Revelation 19:7). As I observed the many preparations my daughter made for her marriage, one of the most critical was the wedding dress. Few things in the world are as beautiful as a virtuous bride arrayed in her wedding dress. Of all the images the Lord could have chosen to depict his Church in her glory, he chose this one. The dress itself symbolizes the righteousness of his Saints. The Lord's people, like a bride, desire to be beautiful for him. They array themselves in layer upon layer of righteousness. How wonderful it would be if every member of the Church felt toward the Savior the way a bride feels toward her bridegroom on the day they are united for eternity. And how wonderful it would be if every member of the Church realized the Lord loves his people the way a bridegroom loves and cherishes his bride.

BE DANDLED UPON HER KNEES

The image of the cherished, beloved bride is not the only feminine image the Lord employs in the scriptures to describe his people or his Church. He also uses the image of a mother's love in describing his own love for his people: "As one whom his mother comforteth, so will I comfort you" (Isaiah 66:13). The Lord's poignant lament over his fallen people adds to the image of a mother's love: "How oft have I gathered you as a hen gathereth her chickens under her wings, and have nourished you. And again, how oft would I have gathered you as a hen gathereth her chickens under her wings, yea, O ye people of the house of Israel, who have fallen; . . . yea, how oft would I have gathered you as a hen gathereth her chickens, and ye would not" (3 Nephi 10:4–5).

The Savior uses the metaphor of the deep desire a woman has

to bring forth children to describe the desire of the Church to spread the gospel throughout all the world: "Lift up thine eyes round about, and see," the husband tells his bride, "all they gather themselves together, they come to thee: thy sons shall come from far, and thy daughters shall be nursed at thy side" (Isaiah 60:4). As the children gather in the last days, the husband tells his bride to "break forth into singing. . . . Enlarge the place of thy tent, and let them stretch forth the curtains of thine habitations: spare not, lengthen thy cords, and strengthen thy stakes" (Isaiah 54:1–2).

As the Church grows there must be more room in the family tent for the additional children. Within the safe environment of home the mother's greatest desire is fulfilled: "All thy children shall be taught of the Lord; and great shall be the peace of thy children" (Isaiah 54:13; see also 3 Nephi 22:13). Further, the Lord promises the children that their mother will nourish them and care for them: "Ye shall be borne upon her sides, and be dandled upon her knees" (Isaiah 66:12). We have all seen mothers carry children on their hip or play with a child upon their knees. These tender images were chosen by the Lord as images for his Church in the last days. As a loving mother nourishes and cares for each child, so too will each member be nourished by the Savior's gospel truths.

WISDOM

In Proverbs, wisdom is depicted as a woman. She is even described in the same terms as the virtuous woman in the last chapter of Proverbs. Both have a value far above that of rubies: "Happy is the man that findeth wisdom, and the man that getteth understanding. . . . She is more precious than rubies: and all the things thou canst desire are not to be compared unto her. . . . Her ways are ways of pleasantness, and all her paths are peace. She is a tree of life to them that lay hold upon her: and happy is every one that retaineth her. . . . Take fast hold of instruction; let her not go: keep her; for she is thy life" (Proverbs 3:13, 15, 17–18; 4:13). As a woman gives life, so, too, will wisdom grant life to those who hold fast to her.

THE MOTHER OF MEN

The earth itself is portrayed in the scriptures as the "mother of men" (Moses 7:48). Just as women are characteristically generous and giving, so, too, does the "earth yield her increase" (Psalm 67:6; see also Ezekiel 34:27; Helaman 11:13). "Yea all things which come of the earth . . . are made for the benefit and the use of man, both to please the eye and to gladden the heart; yea, for food and for raiment, for taste and for smell, to strengthen the body and to enliven the soul" (D&C 59:18–19). The earth bounteously yields not only the things necessary for survival but also the beautiful things which make that survival enjoyable. The Doctrine and Covenants depicts the earth as yielding spiritual nourishment: "The earth hath travailed and brought forth her strength; and truth is established in her bowels; and the heavens have smiled upon her; and she is clothed with the glory of her God" (D&C 84:101).

A most poignant personification of the earth as a woman is found in the Pearl of Great Price. Before the Flood, "Enoch looked upon the earth; and he heard a voice from the bowels thereof, saying: Wo, wo is me, the mother of men; I am pained, I am weary, because of the wickedness of my children. When shall I rest, and be cleansed from the filthiness which is gone forth out of me? When will my Creator sanctify me, that I may rest, and righteousness for a season abide upon my face?" (Moses 7:48). In this verse the anguish expressed by a mother over a rebellious child conveys understanding to Enoch as he views the wickedness that covers the earth.

These few portraits show how the Lord draws upon the natural qualities of his daughters to teach powerful truths about his relationship with us and our relationship with him. Although some metaphorical women in the scriptures portray negative qualities (the faithless wife or harlot, for example), most represent desirable characteristics. These personifications strengthen and add dignity to our image of the daughters of God and their contributions to the Lord's great plan of salvation.

THE HALLS OF THE NEW TESTAMENT

CHAPTER 21

———

MARY, THE CHOSEN AND
PRECIOUS VESSEL

Mary is the supreme example, the centerpiece, of the Lord's scriptural gallery. Two Book of Mormon prophets saw her in vision and described her in words that expressed their admiration. Nephi was shown "a virgin, most beautiful and fair above all other virgins," one who was "exceedingly fair and white" (1 Nephi 11:13, 15). Alma told his people that Mary was "a virgin, a precious and chosen vessel" who would "bring forth a son, yea, even the Son of God" (Alma 7:10). Nephi and Alma spoke not only of the physical beauty of Mary but also of the beauty of her character and commission. What can we learn about womanhood from this precious and chosen daughter of God who was beautiful and fair above all other women?

The precious beauty seen by Nephi and Alma is revealed when we examine what she says and what is said to and about her.

THE LORD IS WITH THEE

We are introduced to Mary in the book of Luke when the angel Gabriel revealed to her she was to be the mother of the Savior. "Hail, thou that art highly favoured," he greeted her, "the

Lord is with thee: blessed art thou among women" (Luke 1:28). The word *blessed* means to be fortunate or happy. There are many different images of the highly favored and happy woman in the world. Is the highly favored and blessed woman one with physical beauty? Is she one with great talent? Is she one with personality, intelligence, and friends?

Undoubtedly, Mary had been blessed with many of these attributes, but Gabriel told Mary she was favored because the Lord was with her and she had been chosen to do his work. That is the deepest meaning of the words *favored* and *blessed*. When a woman lives in such a way that the Lord's Spirit and influence are with her and she can be called to further the Lord's work, then she is truly highly favored and blessed.

Mary was surprised by the salutation of the angel. Luke tells us that "when she saw him, she was troubled at his saying, and cast in her mind what manner of salutation this should be" (Luke 1:29). Mary was troubled not by the appearance of the angel Gabriel, as Zacharias was, but by the angel's salutation. In her meekness, she wondered how she could be such a highly favored and blessed woman. Her humility is striking. While serving in priesthood callings I have seen this humble attitude almost every time a sister has been called to a position of responsibility. It is a response most pleasing to the Lord.

Because of Mary's thoughts concerning the greeting he had just given her, Gabriel reaffirmed his original words: "Fear not, Mary: for thou hast found favour with God" (Luke 1:30). Mary was favored to be the mother of the Redeemer. In that she was doubly blessed and highly favored.

I KNOW NOT A MAN

Yet Mary wondered at the angel's message, asking, "How shall this be, seeing I know not a man?" (Luke 1:34). Nephi said Mary was "a virgin, most beautiful and fair above all other virgins" (1 Nephi 11:15). Mormon affirmed that "chastity and virtue" are "most dear and precious above all things" (Moroni 9:9). Virtue was a principal aspect of Mary's beauty, a beauty all women can possess. Elder David O. McKay testified of this truth: "There is a beauty every girl has,—a gift from God, as pure as the sunlight, and as sacred as life. It is a beauty that all men love, a virtue that wins all men's souls. That beauty is *chastity*. Chastity without skin beauty may enkindle the soul; skin beauty without chastity can kindle only the eye.

"Chastity enshrined in the mould of true womanhood will hold true love eternally" ("True Beauty," 360).

BEHOLD THE HANDMAIDEN OF THE LORD

Gabriel's answer to Mary's question, "How shall this be, seeing I know not a man?" (Luke 1:34), was simply, "The Holy Ghost shall come upon thee, and the power of the Highest shall overshadow thee: therefore also that holy thing which shall be born of thee shall be called the Son of God" (Luke 1:35). Mary's response shows the sweet, submissive obedience that marks the great women and men of the scriptures: "Behold the handmaid of the Lord; be it unto me according to thy word" (Luke 1:38).

MARY AROSE WITH HASTE

Gabriel explained to Mary that her "cousin Elisabeth, she hath also conceived a son in her old age: and this is the sixth month with her, who was called barren" (Luke 1:36). This news caused Mary to arise "with haste" and go into the "hill country . . . of Juda," where she "entered into the house of Zacharias, and saluted Elisabeth" (Luke 1:39–40).

Mary may have gone to Elisabeth because she wanted to share her own marvelous secret with someone who would understand, but I believe Mary also went "with haste" to share in the happiness of Elisabeth. Elisabeth shared in Mary's joy and proclaimed, "Blessed art thou among women, and blessed is the fruit of thy womb" (Luke 1:42). Added to their natural joy over the anticipated birth of their sons was the knowledge that the long-awaited Messiah soon would redeem his people.

Many women have a natural capacity to be as thrilled over their sisters' blessings as over their own. This is a godly quality—

one we would all do well to emulate. It is a quality that destroys envy, jealousy, and pride. Such women also feel the pains of others as if they were their own.

A short time after the birth of Jesus, Mary and Joseph traveled to Jerusalem to fulfill the requirements of the law of Moses. There Simeon met them and, taking the infant Jesus into his arms, pronounced a blessing upon him. Then he warned Mary, "Yea, a sword shall pierce through thy own soul also" (Luke 2:35). Mary felt deeply the pains of her Son many times throughout her life but none more strongly than when she stood at the foot of the cross. "For God so loved the world, that he gave his only begotten Son" (John 3:16). Mary, too, gave her Son, a gift that caused a sword to pierce her soul. When Jesus was on the cross he cried out, "My God, my God, why hast thou forsaken me?" (Matthew 27:46). For the Son to fulfill his great atoning sacrifice, the Father had to withdraw his Spirit. Nevertheless, Mary, Jesus' mother, remained with him during his long hours on the cross.

BLESSED IS SHE THAT BELIEVED

Elisabeth told Mary, "Blessed is she that believed: for there shall be a performance of those things which were told her from the Lord" (Luke 1:45). Mary showed great faith. In contrast, the silence of Elisabeth's husband, Zacharias, was a daily reminder of his inability to believe Gabriel without a sign (see Luke 1:20). Mary's faithful response to Gabriel's announcement was much different. Is it more difficult to believe that an old couple can have a son, or that a young virgin "who know[s] not a man" can give birth to a son? There were precedents for what Zacharias was asked to believe. There were none for Mary.

When Mary returned from her three-month visit with Elisabeth, she must have told Joseph of her condition. I imagine that was a difficult conversation. Joseph pondered his course, for he did not want to "make her a publick example" and "was minded to put her away privily" (Matthew 1:19). Then the angel appeared to him in a dream to verify Mary's story: "Fear not to take unto thee Mary thy wife: for that which is conceived in her is of the Holy Ghost" (Matthew 1:20). In other words, "Mary has told you the truth." This was a sacred, beautiful, and private thing.

MY SOUL DOTH MAGNIFY THE LORD

Mary chose to turn the lens of her soul upon the Lord and make him large in her life. I believe Jesus learned at Mary's feet many wonderful things that grew out of her love for her Father in Heaven, for children generally see God first through the eyes and the soul of their mother. Mary's own words might indicate what the child Jesus saw through his mother's soul: "My soul doth magnify the Lord. . . . For he that is mighty hath done to me great things; and holy is his name" (Luke 1:46, 49). Through the centuries mothers have repeated these words of Mary in their own way to their children, who then could carry throughout their lives the enlarged vision of God first shown to them by their mother, who magnified the Lord.

MY SPIRIT HATH REJOICED IN GOD MY SAVIOR

Mary not only magnified the Lord but rejoiced in him: "My spirit hath rejoiced in God my Saviour" (Luke 1:47). The purpose of our existence is to be happy. Some try to find happiness without God. Others find only secondary joy in the gospel. Mary rejoiced in the Lord and in his work. She rejoiced in her contribution to it. We, too, are invited to rejoice in the Lord, in his great compassion and mercy, and in our contribution to it. We can teach our children the joys our Father has prepared for those who love him both now and in eternity.

My second daughter taught me the meaning of "rejoic[ing] in God my Saviour" (Luke 1:47) when she was only three. We were visiting the North Visitors' Center on Temple Square. As we climbed the circular ramp that leads to the *Christus*, my daughter was holding my hand and looking wide-eyed at the painting of the universe on the walls and the ceiling. Suddenly she saw the back of the beautiful statue of the Savior. Her eyes filled with a love, happiness, and delight I have rarely seen even in children. With intense eagerness she said, "Oh, Daddy! It's Jesus!" She dropped my hand and ran up the ramp to the foot of the statue. As I watched, I pictured the real Savior greeting her when she reached the top.

I have seen many women reflect in a more subdued and reverent manner that same eagerness, love, and delight in the Savior, in his words, in his Church, and in the great truths of his gospel. One woman in particular comes to mind. She is a young woman from Vienna, Austria, who has debilitating medical problems. Yet despite her many physical challenges, she constantly rejoices in the Lord and in the wonders of his gospel. When she was touring Israel with us, she instantly became the soul of the group because of the wonder and gratitude she felt in everything she saw. Whenever I think of her I think of the words of testimony written by Habakkuk so many years ago: "Although the fig tree shall not blossom, neither shall fruit be in the vines; the labour of the olive shall fail, and the fields shall yield no meat; the flock shall be cut off from the fold, and there shall be no herd in the stalls: yet I will rejoice in the Lord, I will joy in the God of my salvation" (Habakkuk 3:17–18).

MARY PONDERED ALL THESE THINGS IN HER HEART

When spiritual experiences took place in Mary's life, such as the visit of the shepherds or Jesus teaching in the temple, we read the words, "Mary kept all these things, and pondered them in her heart" (Luke 2:19; see also v. 51). Mary is a great example of the Lord's counsel to "treasure these things up in your hearts, and let the solemnities of eternity rest upon your minds" (D&C 43:34).

Each of my daughters received from her grandmother a beautiful cedar chest in which to keep the important things they have gathered. Occasionally my daughters have permitted me to look inside their cedar chests to see the things they treasure. There are objects that bring back memories: corsages, pictures, souvenirs from trips, and gifts from friends. There are also things for their future in their own families. I have watched my daughters open the lid of their cedar chests to sort through, straighten, and reflect on what is inside.

As with my daughters' cedar chests, the Lord wants us to treasure our own sacred memories of experiences with the Spirit and reflect on them frequently. When we ponder on them, their ability to bless and teach grows. A spiritual experience is like a living thing: the more we nourish it by reflection, meditation, and pondering, the more it can give back to us. As we cherish these moments and ponder them, the Spirit will teach us ever increasing truths.

Jesus himself taught, "Therefore every scribe which is instructed unto the kingdom of heaven is like unto a man that is an householder, which bringeth forth out of his treasure things new and old" (Matthew 13:52). Many women, like Mary, learn new truths while pondering the treasures of the Spirit they already have.

HE AROSE AND TOOK THE YOUNG CHILD AND HIS MOTHER

Mary was not alone in carrying the great responsibility of protecting and guiding the Savior as he prepared for his mission; she had Joseph to aid her. The scriptures show Joseph was a compassionate man in tune with the Spirit. In Matthew we are told of four dreams he received. The first instructed him to "fear not to take unto thee Mary thy wife: for that which is conceived in her is of the Holy Ghost" (Matthew 1:20). The second dream warned Joseph to "take the young child and his mother, and flee into Egypt" (Matthew 2:13). The third instructed Joseph to "take the young child and his mother, and go into the land of Israel: for they are dead which sought the young child's life" (Matthew 2:20). The last warned Joseph to "[turn] aside into the parts of Galilee" (Matthew 2:22).

Mary followed the revelation of her husband as it came to him in his dreams. But the last we hear of Joseph is at the temple when the Savior was twelve. It may be that Joseph had died by the time the Savior began his ministry. If so, the wonderful relationship Mary enjoyed with her Son would have deepened as she relied more and more on his strength. We see this reliance in the account of the marriage at Cana.

When there was no wine, Mary went to Jesus and said, "They have no wine" (JST John 2:3). Mary did not make a demand but simply presented a problem. Jesus replied, "Woman, what wilt thou have me to do for thee? that will I do; for mine hour is not yet come" (JST John 2:4). Mary turned to the servants and said: "Whatsoever he saith unto you, do it" (John 2:5). This is but one example of their relationship. Mary knew Jesus would bless and help her. Mary's simple instruction to the servants shows her complete trust in his ability to handle the problem properly.

In essence, Jesus was saying to his mother, "Whatever you want me to do for you, I will do, until my atonement is at hand." Jesus continued to treat his mother in this manner up to and including the hour of his atoning sacrifice. How wonderful it would be if all children, regardless of age, respected their wives, their sisters, and their mothers in this manner.

Mary had at least four other sons and also daughters. At Jesus' rejection in Nazareth, his fellow townsmen had said: "Is not this the carpenter's son? is not his mother called Mary? and his brethren, James, and Joses, and Simon, and Judas? And his sisters, are they not all with us?" (Matthew 13:55–56). James and Jude later wrote epistles that are included in the New Testament. Yet from the cross Jesus counseled his mother, "Woman, behold thy son!" Then he said to John the Beloved, "Behold thy mother! And from that hour that disciple took her unto his own home" (John 19:26–27). We do not know why the Savior placed his mother in John's care, but Mary followed his counsel. She trusted the guidance of those righteous men, who loved her.

I was the youngest child in our family of four, both my sisters being older. I recall distinctly the words of my mother on the day I received the priesthood at age twelve. After the ordination she said to me: "Now you are the priesthood bearer in our family, and we will all honor the priesthood you hold." Notice she said not "We will honor you" but rather "We will honor the priesthood you hold."

From that day forward my mother had me call on members of the family to offer our daily prayers. This act alone produced in me a deep sense of responsibility towards the priesthood and the members of my family. I was reminded of it each time I asked my mother or one of my sisters to offer the prayers in our home. As I advanced in the priesthood, other responsibilities and opportunities have come, but I do not think I have ever functioned in the priesthood with a greater sense of awe and humility than I did as a twelve-year-old boy asking my mother or sisters to offer the prayers and knowing from my mother of her desire to honor the priesthood held by her son.

ALL THINGS ACCORDING TO THE LAW OF THE LORD

There were numerous rituals, ordinances, and observances associated with the law of Moses, and Mary observed them faithfully. She accomplished the "days of her purification according to the law of Moses," and she offered "a sacrifice according to that which is said in the law of the Lord" (Luke 2:22, 24). While at the temple Mary "performed all things according to the law of the Lord" (Luke 2:39). During the years of Jesus' youth, "his parents went to Jerusalem every year at the feast of the passover" (Luke 2:41).

Mary's example teaches us to hold sacred the ordinances required by our Father in Heaven. She teaches us to teach our children the ordinances of salvation, as she did Jesus. If Mary had been born in our time, she would have been baptized, partaken of the sacrament, and attended the temple. Mary testifies to us of the need to remain worthy of every ordinance and to share our conviction with our children so they too will seek the ordinances of salvation.

Some sisters, through no fault of their own, may be denied the privilege of participating in some priesthood ordinances. The Lord knows the soul of each of his daughters and will bless them according to their opportunities and circumstances. The Lord rewards those who desire to live according to his laws. The desire to worthily receive the ordinances of the gospel will always distinguish the faithful Latter-day Saint woman.

THE YEARS OF SILENCE

There is a sort of wonder in the silence of the New Testament about the first thirty years of Jesus' mortal life. In this silence I find a tremendous lesson. Countless Marys quietly and without attention—and too often without hearing expressions of gratitude—teach, guide, direct, comfort, weep with, and pray for their children, who then grow to live lives of service and dignity. Next to his own Father in Heaven, no one had a greater effect on Jesus than his mother. Often the child is noticed and remembered, while the mother remains in relative obscurity. Her recompense will surely come from a Father in Heaven who knows the power of the silent years in the formation of his noblest sons and daughters.

THESE ALL CONTINUED WITH ONE ACCORD

The last reference in the Bible to Mary is found in the first chapter of Acts. After the Savior's postresurrection ministry, he ascended into heaven. Then, under the leadership of Peter, the apostles and disciples continued to meet in Jerusalem. In Acts 1:14 we read that the apostles "continued with one accord in prayer and supplication, with the women, and Mary the mother of Jesus, and with his brethren."

Mary remained faithful to the Church. Her other sons also remained faithful. One of them, James, led the Church in Jerusalem, wrote the epistle of James, and met with Paul and the other apostles (see Matthew 13:55; Acts 12:17; 15:13; Galatians 1:19). Another of Mary's sons, Judas, wrote the epistle of Jude and was also a leader in the early Church (see Jude 1:1). Mary's continuing loyalty to the leaders chosen by her Son undoubtedly strengthened the commitment of her other children.

Latter-day Saint women who follow the counsel of the Lord's chosen leaders bless their children because of their example. They continue with "one accord" with their leaders. When present leaders die or are released, such women have no difficulty following and sustaining the leaders who are called to replace them. Both they and their children are blessed because of their constancy and example of faith in the Lord's chosen leadership.

Though Mary was chosen and precious because of her unique calling, many women share her type of beauty. They are women who seek favor with God and know what it means to be highly favored and blessed. They are humble and live lives of chastity and virtue. They willingly submit to the will of the Lord. They rejoice in the joys and blessings of others and mourn with them. They have believing hearts and magnify the Lord, thus creating through the purity of their own souls a lens through which others may see God. They rejoice in the Savior and in his gospel, and they recognize his gifts and mercies. They treasure in their souls the sacred experiences of their lives. They also trust and follow the guidance of righteous priesthood leaders. When new leaders are called they sustain them and follow their counsels. They hunger to participate in the exalting ordinances of the temple. The portrait of Mary reminds them always that they, too, are chosen and precious.

CHAPTER 22

ELISABETH AND ANNA, AGED WOMEN OF GOD

The portrait of Elisabeth is next to that of Mary, and nearby is that of the prophetess Anna. The faces of both Elisabeth and Anna show the lines of age and wisdom. Their portraits may have been painted from Mary's memory, for it seems likely that Luke obtained his information from her.

ELISABETH:
SHE WALKED IN ALL THE COMMANDMENTS

Like Sarah, Elisabeth bore a chosen son when she was "well stricken in years" (Luke 1:7) and past childbearing age. Unlike Sarah, however, Elisabeth seems to have had no promise she would one day be a mother. Might Elisabeth have cried out, as did her predecessor Rachel, "Give me children, or else I die"? (Genesis 30:1). Might she have asked her husband to entreat the Lord in her behalf, as had her ancestor Rebekah? We know Zacharias prayed for a child because the angel told him, "Thy prayer is heard; and thy wife Elisabeth shall bear thee a son, and thou shalt call his name John" (Luke 1:13).

Luke tells us that Elisabeth and Zacharias "were both righteous before God, walking in all the commandments and ordinances of the Lord blameless" (Luke 1:6). It is one thing to be righteous when everything is going right. It is quite another to do so when the greatest desire of your life is denied, when your prayers are not answered even after years of pleading.

I have known people who have allowed trials to blind them to the love of God. A dear friend believed God did not love mankind because of the sorrows he had experienced in Vietnam. Many feel they have sinned so grievously that the Lord cannot possibly forgive them. "Surely," they reason, "if God is loving and has all power, he would bless me. Since he hasn't, either he does not exist or he does not care about me." Their eyes become blind, and their hearts are hardened.

Yet Elisabeth, though she was denied the joy of having children and undoubtedly wondered why the Lord would not remove her reproach, lived a blameless life and walked in all the commandments and ordinances of the Lord.

I have a very vivid memory of a modern Elisabeth who lived in my ward while I was growing up. She had an incurable cancer that slowly and painfully destroyed her body. Many prayers and blessings were offered in her behalf, but the cancer grew and the pain increased. She served in her calling with the young women of the ward as long as she was able and then continued to attend church even though the pain was tremendous. Wisdom might have suggested she remain at home, but every Sunday she was there, sitting in the last row on the side of the chapel so she would not disturb anyone. One Sunday morning shortly before she died I passed the sacrament to her. Her fists were clenched, and she was digging her fingernails into the palms of her hands. Yet through it all she continually expressed gratitude for her blessings. She walked blameless before the face of heaven that seemed to many of us heedless of her prayers or her pain. But her grip on the iron rod was as tight as her fists that Sunday morning.

ELISABETH HID HERSELF FIVE MONTHS

Zacharias returned from the temple to tell Elisabeth the words of the angel. After she conceived, "Elisabeth . . . hid herself five months, saying, Thus hath the Lord dealt with me in the days wherein he looked on me, to take away my reproach among men" (Luke 1:24–25).

Why did she do that? It was not customary. Perhaps Elisabeth desired to "devote herself entirely to prayer and thanksgiving for so signal a mercy" (Dummelow, *Bible Commentary*, 738). In the scriptures, men called to perform great missions for the Lord retired into seclusion to prepare. Jesus withdrew into the wilderness for forty days. Paul retired to Arabia. Moses was in the wilderness. It is not difficult to imagine that Elisabeth, knowing she was to give birth to the foreordained prophet who would prepare the way for the Messiah himself, retired into seclusion to express gratitude and seek guidance from the Lord.

ELISABETH WAS FILLED WITH THE HOLY GHOST

In her sixth month Elisabeth was visited by Mary. It is recorded in Luke 1:41 that when Elisabeth heard Mary's greeting "the babe leaped in her womb." Elisabeth, "filled with the Holy Ghost," interpreted this as a leap of joy and knew that Mary was the chosen mother of her Lord. Mary does not seem to have told Elisabeth about her own pregnancy before her visit, and Mary herself did not know of Elisabeth's condition until the angel informed her: "This is the sixth month with her, who was called barren" (Luke 1:36). Elisabeth learned through inspiration that Mary was to be the mother of the chosen Messiah.

Elisabeth's words were surely a strength and a comfort to Mary: "Blessed art thou who believed, for those things which were told thee by the angel of the Lord, shall be fulfilled" (JST Luke 1:44). These words were said in the humility of an older woman strengthening and comforting a young girl. Imagine Mary's relief when she knew that another human being knew what she knew, believed, and bore a confirming witness. Perhaps her feelings were like those of the Prophet Joseph Smith, who said to his parents when the Three Witnesses had been shown the plates, "I feel as if I was relieved of a burden which was almost too heavy for me to bear, and it rejoices my soul, that I am not any longer to be entirely alone in the world" (Smith, *History of Joseph Smith by His Mother*, 152).

For three months Elisabeth and Mary strengthened each other. Soon Elisabeth would flee into the wilderness and Mary into Egypt, but they were given a short time to share love and wonder at the sons they carried, free of the dangers that would soon change their lives forever.

We know from the writings of Joseph Smith that Zacharias was killed when the children of Bethlehem were slaughtered at the command of Herod the Great. Zacharias had sent Elisabeth and John into the wilderness for safety and refused to reveal their hiding place. He paid for his silence with his life (see Smith, *Teachings of the Prophet Joseph Smith*, 261). Elisabeth was left to rear their son alone. John remained "in the deserts till the day of his shewing unto Israel" (Luke 1:80). In the desert he "grew, and waxed strong in spirit" (Luke 1:80). Would not his mother have played a critical role in that growth?

Let us take one more look at Elisabeth, the woman who bore John the Baptist and strengthened the young mother of the Savior. When our desires and prayers are not immediately granted, when the love of God is obscured by the mists of life, let us remember the portrait of Elisabeth, who continued to walk blameless through the years of barrenness and hid herself for five months to express gratitude and to seek guidance when she knew she was to bear a child. Filled with the Holy Ghost, Elisabeth in humility then strengthened the faith of Mary with her own testimony. Like the portraits of Ruth and Naomi, the portraits of Mary and Elisabeth are a most pleasing and tender combination of two women selflessly blessing each others' lives.

ANNA: A LONG LIFE OF SERVICE

The portrait of Anna is painted in just three verses. Like Elisabeth, she provided strength to the young Mary. We are fortunate that Luke gave us not only her words but also her name.

Anna was "a prophetess, the daughter of Phanuel, of the tribe of Aser" (Luke 2:36). Because Anna, being a prophetess, was filled with the testimony of Jesus (see Revelation 19:10), it is understandable that she would recognize the Savior in the temple. Anna "had lived with an husband seven years from her virginity" and may have lived alone about eighty-four years, for she was "a widow of about fourscore and four years" (Luke 2:36–37). If Anna had married as early as twelve or thirteen, she might have been more than one hundred years old when she saw Mary and Joseph and the infant Jesus in the temple.

ANNA SERVED GOD NIGHT AND DAY

What did Anna choose to do during her years of widowhood? Luke tells us she "departed not from the temple, but served God with fastings and prayers night and day" (Luke 2:37). Anna's life was a life of service. She chose the temple for her fasting and prayers, but perhaps earlier in her life she had chosen other forms of service.

I have met dozens of faithful Annas in the Jordan River Temple, where I too have the privilege of serving. One such Anna is of a great age. Her research has resulted in thousands of ordinances being performed for the dead. When my son received his endowment, she spoke to him in the celestial room and helped make his first temple experience more meaningful. Then, with a twinkle in her eyes, she said, "I don't really look this way, all wrinkled and shriveled. This is just a disguise I put on so the men will leave me alone to do the Lord's important work here in the temple."

Other single sisters have chosen other ways of serving the Lord. I am deeply indebted to a professor of English at Brigham Young University who made the students her family. I was one of her "children." In class after class she taught me how to see the themes, the beauty, and the power in the words of great works of literature. She gave me the key to many treasures in the scriptures. I will be forever grateful for the loving, dedicated service of this wonderful modern Anna.

Some may be Anna at age twenty-five, others at age thirty-eight or sixty-eight or in their eighties or nineties. They serve their fellowmen and in this way, as King Benjamin taught, they serve God (see Mosiah 2:17). To Mary, who went to the temple bearing the Savior of the world, Anna gave encouragement and testimony. Were Anna's years of service and dedication an inspiration to Mary? If Mary was indeed the source of Luke's information about Anna, then Mary remembered not only Anna's testimony about the infant Jesus but also her name and the dedicated service of her life.

ANNA GAVE THANKS AND SPAKE OF HIM TO ALL

Anna teaches us other important lessons about the influence of dedicated women. Luke records, "She coming in that instant gave thanks likewise unto the Lord, and spake of him to all them that looked for redemption in Jerusalem" (Luke 2:38). Anna gave thanks for the coming of the Savior, for the privilege she had of seeing him, and for the redemption he would bring.

Her example reminds us to express gratitude for the Savior. Her words echo Simeon's: "Lord, now lettest thou thy servant depart in peace . . . for mine eyes have seen thy salvation" (Luke 2:29–30). Anna probably died long before Jesus reached manhood, but she expressed her gratitude for his promise of salvation, a salvation she would share because she had spent her life in service. She, like others, "died in faith, not having received the promises, but having seen them afar off" (Hebrews 11:13).

Anna did not keep her joy and gratitude to herself. She "spake of him to all them that looked for redemption in Jerusalem" (Luke 2:38). She fulfilled Peter's admonition to be "ready always to give an answer to every man that asketh you a reason of the hope that is in you with meekness and fear" (1 Peter 3:15). We find Annas of today in the mission field. We find them sharing the gospel with their neighbors, their friends, and their families. We find them in the organizations of the Church. And when these women pass through the gallery where the portrait of Anna hangs, may they see the tender face of Anna smiling back at them.

TEACHERS OF GOOD THINGS

Anna and Elisabeth remind me of the words of Paul to Titus when he spoke of the aged women of the ancient Church: "The aged women likewise, that they be in behaviour as becometh holiness, . . . teachers of good things; that they may teach the young women to be sober, to love their husbands, to love their children, to be discreet, chaste, keepers at home, good, obedient to their own husbands, that the word of God be not blasphemed" (Titus 2:3–5).

When I was a deacon, I was assigned to pass the sacrament to the last bench in the chapel. That was the bench where all the older sisters and widows sat. Most of the areas in the chapel were assigned a number by the deacons, but the last bench of the chapel we simply called "widow's row." Those sisters were kind and generous to me. I did yard work for several of them, and they became good friends. I never knew what callings these women had in the ward, because the more demanding callings were filled by younger women. It took me years to understand the tremendous power their presence added to the ward.

That realization first hit me when I met my wife's Grandmother Elsie. Her face radiated the inner strength she had built through her life, for she was a woman of great love and gentleness. She had a happy face. Looking at the wrinkles of her face, I found it difficult to imagine they could ever turn into the lines of a frown. Long years of laughter and joy had molded them into patterns of happiness. When we visited her home, I enjoyed watching her talk with her children, grandchildren, and great-grandchildren. She brought such peace into all of our lives.

One day when we were visiting Grandma Elsie, I looked at the lines of joy in her face, and the Spirit whispered, "This is what a lifetime of living the gospel creates." I was looking at the fruits of a life of gospel service and faith. I remembered "widow's row" and realized the testimony the presence of those wonderful women imparted to the ward every Sunday. I believe that Anna and Elisabeth looked like them.

We frequently hear the Brethren calling for more older couples to serve in the mission field. I wonder if these older brothers and sisters realize the power of their missions. Those who hunger for truth will see in their faces and in the sweetness of their love for each other the fruits of the gospel. They are their own testimony, their own evidence of truth, their own witness for the Lord.

We see in Anna a single woman who through a long life served God day and night, expressing gratitude and testifying of the Savior's redeeming love. May we return often to that part of the gallery where Anna's portrait hangs next to Mary's and Elisabeth's. May the older sisters of the Church learn from her that their years of service have made them God's witnesses to the power and truth of his gospel.

CHAPTER 23

THREE WOMEN WHO
LOVED JESUS

On the wall opposite the portraits of Mary, Elisabeth, and Anna hang the portraits of three younger women who figured in the ministry of Jesus: Mary and Martha of Bethany and Mary Magdalene. If these three devoted disciples whose portraits we now view were married and had children, there is no mention of their families in the Gospels. Perhaps they were single during the ministry of the Savior.

Many of the women in the New Testament were widowed or unmarried. In an apostate world of unbelief and hostility, their mildness, love, and devotion served as a calm in the midst of the storm encircling Jesus. Their sacrifice and dedication inspire us all and set standards of true discipleship.

MARTHA AND MARY:
A MEMORIAL OF SERVICE AND LOVE

John introduces us to Martha and Mary with these tender words: "Now Jesus loved Martha, and her sister" (John 11:5). Perhaps no greater tribute could be given to a woman than John's simple and moving words, for in their solicitous care for the

Savior we learn wonderful lessons about our own relationship with the King of kings. There are three main stories that include Mary and Martha: the dinner in Bethany, the raising of Lazarus, and the anointing of Jesus before his death.

ONE THING IS NEEDFUL

There is much discussion about the five short verses that recount the dinner in Bethany. "Martha received him into her house. And she had a sister called Mary, which also sat at Jesus' feet, and heard his word. But Martha was cumbered about much serving" (Luke 10:38–40).

Martha was "cumbered about much serving" when she asked the Savior to have Mary help her. I believe Martha was anxious about preparing a meal for more people than her sister and Jesus. With tenderness, Jesus answered her, "Martha, Martha, thou art careful and troubled about many things: but one thing is needful: and Mary hath chosen that good part, which shall not be taken away from her" (Luke 10:41–42). The second "Martha" sounds so gentle and full of understanding. Jesus loved this woman. Martha was not doing anything wrong in serving her Lord, for we have all been asked to serve him. We remember the Shunammite woman to whom Elisha said tenderly, "Behold, thou hast been careful for us with all this care; what is to be done for thee?" (2 Kings 4:13).

Through years of teaching I have discovered that many women believe the Savior said not that Mary chose "that good part" but that she chose "the better part." Yet that is not what the scriptures say. Mary had certainly chosen a good part, but I see no suggestion in the story that Martha had chosen a lesser part.

Martha's home was a haven of peace for Jesus in a troubled world. He often visited to rest. Just over the hill from Bethany lay Jerusalem, an environment of jealousy, plotting, and opposition. Martha's priorities were exactly right. Service to the Lord is commendable.

Many of us feel "cumbered" and "careful and troubled about many things." The many things are almost always good things.

I watch the good women in my ward, for example, who are so careful that relationships, feelings, programs, and their own performance are the best they can be. They want everyone to be edified and happy. They often worry that they will not measure up. The continual weight of these responsibilities is often cumbersome not because they are unessential, menial, or unimportant but because there are so many of them and because they want to perform them just right.

Perhaps Jesus understood these feelings from observing his own mother. Was not Mary careful and troubled over the wine at the marriage feast? Jesus' words to Martha, however, were these: "But one thing is needful." *Needful* is the key word. Jesus' words impart counsel to all the Marthas of the world—and I suspect there is a Martha in every Latter-day Saint woman. In their cumbered, careful, troubled world of service they also need to sit quietly at the feet of the Savior and be nourished. He invites them to rest and to receive the things of the Spirit. This too is a good part, acceptable in the sight of God and necessary for their spiritual well-being.

It is a good part for a woman to sit quietly in the temple, to attend a scripture class or have lunch with a friend and share feelings and thoughts. It is a good part to pray and to enjoy nature. That is also true for men. How many times in my own cumbered life have I felt the Spirit whisper, "Michael, Michael, thou art careful and troubled about many things, but one thing is needful."

Jesus understood this need better than anyone. It was needful for him to rest occasionally from the heavy responsibilities of his continual service. Jesus also sought solitude, communion with his Father, and rest. We read in the Gospels how the people thronged him. "Come ye yourselves apart into a desert place, and rest a while," he said to his apostles, "for there were many coming and going, and they had no leisure so much as to eat" (Mark 6:31). How many wives and mothers serve a meal and somehow never find time to sit down and eat because so many are "coming and going"?

Jesus "departed into a desert place by ship privately. And the people saw them departing, and many knew him, and ran afoot thither out of all cities, and outwent them, and came together unto him. And Jesus, when he came out, saw much people, and was moved with compassion toward them, because they were as sheep not having a shepherd: and he began to teach them many things" (Mark 6:32–34).

Many sisters can see their own situations in that of the Savior. How many times I have seen my wife try to take a nap, talk on the telephone to a friend, quietly read a book, or plan time to go to the temple only to be interrupted by the thousand and one cumbering demands that, like the people who outwent Jesus, seek her service. Yet she and other wonderful Marthas are, like Jesus, moved with compassion.

"One thing is needful." If a woman chooses the needful, good part of rest, leisure, spiritual rejuvenation, and prayer, she chooses wisely. She also chooses wisely when she serves. Neither Mary nor Martha displeased the Savior. Jesus loved them both, and certainly Mary also ministered of her substance and Martha sat at his feet and listened.

The portraits of Mary and Martha remind us of the need for balance in our lives. We are invited both to serve and to search out the opportunities to rest at the Savior's feet. That may be difficult, but when we do take the time to rest and refresh ourselves at the Savior's feet, we find our spirits rejuvenated to serve.

THOU ART THE CHRIST, THE SON OF GOD

Martha's great faith, a faith that must have been born as she sat at Christ's feet to hear his teachings, was demonstrated at the raising of her brother Lazarus.

When Lazarus became sick, Jesus was east of the Jordan River because the Jews had "sought again to take him" (John 10:39). Martha and Mary sent word that "he whom thou lovest is sick" (John 11:3). This was not a direct request, but the sisters certainly must have desired Jesus to come immediately and heal their brother. Yet Jesus deliberately delayed until Lazarus had been buried. What must have been the thoughts and anxiety of the sisters as Jesus delayed?

When Jesus finally arrived, Lazarus had been dead four days. Perhaps there was a tiny, questioning rebuke in both Martha's and Mary's words: "Lord, if thou hadst been here, my brother had not died" (John 11:21, 32). Some commentators on the Bible, including Frederic W. Farrar, have felt Martha's and Mary's words were spoken "in tones gently reproachful" (*Life of Christ*, 478). Elder Bruce R. McConkie indicated that the Savior "tested the faith of Mary and Martha to the utmost" when Lazarus died (*Doctrinal New Testament Commentary*, 1:530).

Yet in spite of his delay, Martha's faith and devotion did not change. Notice the three separate testimonies she bore on this occasion: "But I know, that even now, whatsoever thou wilt ask of God, God will give it thee" (John 11:22). "I know that he shall rise again in the resurrection at the last day" (John 11:24). "I believe that thou art the Christ, the Son of God, which should come into the world" (John 11:27).

Jesus had delayed coming to save her brother and had not healed him from a distance, as he had done for others on occasion, but Martha's faith remained strong. If there was slight questioning in her first words of anguish, it quickly changed to belief and testimony. In this trait she reflects the character of Sarah and Elisabeth, who, though denied the desire of their hearts, still believed. Though Jesus had not saved her brother from death, Martha's faith was unaltered, her love for her Savior uncompromised.

Martha's faith can be contrasted with that of some of Jesus' disciples, who "went back, and walked no more with him" (John 6:66) when he refused to perform the miracles they desired. They wanted him to continue to feed them bread; he wanted to give them the bread of life. They were offended and murmured at his refusal to measure up to their expectations (see John 6:61).

After confessing her belief in the Savior, Martha went to Mary and told her the Master wanted to see her. Mary fell at his feet, weeping, and repeated Martha's first words, "Lord, if thou hadst been here, my brother had not died" (John 11:32). The sorrow of these women over the death of their brother and their unfailing faith in Jesus moved the Savior deeply. "He groaned in the spirit, and was troubled, and said, Where have ye laid him? They said unto him, Lord, come and see. Jesus wept" (John 11:33–35).

He wept for Martha and Mary and for all who suffer or cry out in anguish, "Lord if thou hadst been here!" He wept for all who long for the Lord to heal their sorrows, to wipe away their tears, to reward their faith in him. He wept for all whose brothers would not return from the grave until the resurrection, whose sufferings he was not invited to alleviate. He wept for all the innocent, trusting, faithful Saints who would always say, no matter what happened, "I believe that thou art the Christ, the Son of God, which should come into the world" (John 11:27). The Savior knows that in time he will "wipe away all tears from their eyes" (Revelation 7:17), but, as in the case of Mary and Martha, that time may not come as quickly as desired.

Such faithful women may also find great comfort in the words of Elder James E. Talmage, who said: "When the frailties and imperfections of mortality are left behind, in the glorified state of the blessed hereafter, . . . [t]hen shall woman be recompensed in rich measure for all the injustice that womanhood has endured in mortality. Then shall woman reign by Divine right, a queen in the resplendent realm of her glorified state. . . . Mortal eye cannot see nor mind comprehend the beauty, glory, and majesty of a righteous woman made perfect in the celestial kingdom of God" ("Eternity of Sex," 602–3).

A MEMORIAL OF MARY

Immediately after relating the raising of Lazarus, which focused so dramatically on the faith of Martha, John described the anointing of Jesus by Mary. These two stories are a fitting portrait of these sisters whom Jesus loved. "Six days before the passover," Jesus "came to Bethany. . . . There they made him a supper; and Martha served" (John 12:1–2). It is wonderful to read that Martha was still serving.

"Then took Mary a pound of ointment of spikenard, very costly, and anointed the feet of Jesus, and wiped his feet with her hair: and the house was filled with the odour of the ointment" (John 12:3). Judas and others complained, saying, "Why was not this ointment sold for three hundred pence, and given to the poor?" (John 12:5; see also Mark 14:3–5). Three hundred pence would have been the wage for three hundred days' labor, one penny being the wage for a day's labor of twelve hours. The oil was thus an offering of considerable value.

There is no question Mary's anointing of Jesus was a sign of her love and devotion. It may also be an indication that she knew he was soon to die. Mary "brake the [alabaster] box and poured it on his head" (Mark 14:3) and then anointed his feet with the ointment as John described.

Jesus protected Mary from criticism by saying to all, "Let her alone; why trouble ye her? For she hath wrought a good work on me. . . . She has done what she could, and this which she has done unto me, shall be had in remembrance in generations to come, wheresoever my gospel shall be preached; for verily she has come beforehand to anoint my body to the burying" (JST Mark 14:6–8). Matthew affirmed that "wheresoever this gospel shall be preached in the whole world, there shall also this, that this woman hath done, be told for a memorial of her" (Matthew 26:13).

How long had she kept that alabaster box of ointment? It was a gift of great expense, and yet to Mary, I am sure, it was not sufficient to show her love for the Master. The very best she had to offer belonged to the Savior, and she poured out that offering willingly, grateful to show her devotion. This was her act of love for the coming atonement and sacrifice of her Lord. It expressed her gratitude in a manner worthy of the dignity of him who would perform it. The Savior recognized that and, therefore, told everyone present that her act would be remembered. It is a supreme example of the true disciple's devotion. Matthew, Mark, and John all record it.

This virtuous woman of Bethany demonstrated what all disciples need to do. Willingly, gratefully, lovingly we must offer our very best. It must be said of us also that we have done what we could. We must freely break the box of our hearts and "offer [our] whole souls as an offering unto him" (Omni 1:26). Some of the disciples felt the gift was too much; Mary knew it was not sufficient, for none of us can do too much for the Lord. Did not Benjamin teach "if [we] should render all the thanks and praise which [our] whole soul has power to possess, . . . if [we] should serve him with all [our] whole souls yet [we] would be unprofitable servants"? (Mosiah 2:20–21).

Not only is it proper to pour out our love to the Savior but it is needful, and Jesus recognized Mary's need to show her love. Such expressions of love are necessary to create oneness with the Savior. Unity with others is created and strengthened when we give to others and when we allow them to give to us. Both actions are necessary, and neither the giver nor the receiver is more important. Jesus allowed Mary the privilege of offering her gift, just as he allowed another woman to wash his feet with her tears.

True enough, the ointment could have been sold to benefit the poor, but there are times when we need to give openly and freely to those we love. My children have demonstrated this many times. I have been touched by their gifts and their desire to serve. Their gifts bind our souls. Perhaps no disciple had ever been at one with the Savior as deeply as Mary was at this time. Jesus invites us all to share this oneness, but it requires us to offer all we have, as did Mary.

Jesus often spoke of his oneness with the Father. Was not that oneness created by the Son's desire to do all he could for the Father, even to the laying down of his life? In Gethsemane did he not break the alabaster box of his own body and pour out his soul to the Father? As much as his sacrifice was his gift of love to us, it was also his gift of love to the Father.

We sometimes say, "Oh, you shouldn't have done that," when someone expresses love in service or sacrifice. Jesus and Mary knew better. They knew that it is important to allow others to express their love, even lavishly at times. The alabaster boxes of ointment, broken and poured, sanctify and purify and make two souls one, as Mary and Jesus became one that afternoon in the house at Bethany while the odor of spikenard filled the room (see John 12:3).

We now leave the portraits of Mary and Martha. When we think of them, we will remember to serve continually while also recognizing the need to rest at the feet of the Savior, hungering to be taught. We will testify, "I believe that thou art the Christ, the Son of God," even as we cry, "Lord, if thou hadst been here." We will strive to give all we can, to pour out our love, devotion, and gratitude to our Savior, who atoned for our sins. With Mary's memorial fixed in our minds, we will break our own alabaster boxes, fill our own homes with the odor of spikenard, and in so doing obtain our own oneness with the Savior.

WOMAN, WHY WEEPEST THOU?

The sketch of Mary Magdalene is contained in a few short verses. No other woman in the scriptures except Mary, the mother of Jesus, is so closely associated with the Master. Mary, Jesus' mother, opened the doors to the Savior's life in mortality. Mary Magdalene was the first to witness him open the door to eternal life. Both these devoted and virtuous women shared the pain at the cross; both shared the joy of the Resurrection.

Luke tells us early in his Gospel that "certain women, which had been healed of evil spirits and infirmities, Mary called Magdalene, out of whom went seven devils, . . . ministered unto him of their substance" (Luke 8:2–3). Mary followed the Savior and listened to him as he traveled throughout Galilee. She was present at the foot of the cross and followed Joseph of Arimathea to see where he laid the body of Jesus. Other than this, our knowledge of her is confined to a few verses in the twentieth chapter of John. The power of those verses, however, has immortalized and elevated Mary Magdalene. Speaking of all the "remarkable women of God," Elder Neal A. Maxwell said, "Greatness is not measured by coverage in column inches, either in newspapers or in the scriptures" (Conference Report, April 1978, 13).

GOD SHALL WIPE AWAY ALL TEARS FROM THEIR EYES

The story of Mary is a story of hope for all of us. The depth of her sorrow changed instantly to the heights of joy by the Savior's gentle call foreshadows what is promised to everyone who loves and worships the Savior. That promise is recorded three times in the Bible: once in Isaiah and twice in Revelation.

Speaking of the Savior, Isaiah prophesied, "He will swallow up death in victory; and the Lord God will wipe away tears from off all faces" (Isaiah 25:8). As Mary sat at the tomb weeping, the angels and then the Savior asked her, "Woman, why weepest thou? whom seekest thou?" She answered, "they have taken away my Lord, and I know not where they have laid him" (John 20:13–15). At that moment, Jesus had already "swallow[ed] up death in victory," and he would soon "wipe away tears" from the face of Mary. He called her name. Recognizing his voice, she turned and whispered, "Rabboni" (John 20:16).

Joseph Smith changed the Savior's next words from "Touch me not," as they are given in John 20:17, to "Hold me not" (JST John 20:17). Mary was not forbidden to touch Jesus. I believe that she, like the other women, "came and held him by the feet" (Matthew 28:9). She certainly "held," or embraced, Jesus. Her joy, rising out of the ashes of grief, would naturally have caused her to hold him as long as she could. He gently reminded her, "I am not yet ascended to my Father: but go to my brethren, and say unto them, I ascend unto my Father, and your Father" (John 20:17). Thus in this passage of scripture, "Hold me not" means "detain me not."

With what joy Mary must have run to give the news to the disciples. Her tears had been wiped away. In Revelation the Lord promises us he will wipe away our tears just as he wiped away Mary's. "The Lamb . . . shall feed them, and shall lead them unto living fountains of waters: and God shall wipe away all tears from their eyes" (Revelation 7:17). This was such an important source of hope that John repeated those comforting words: "And God shall wipe away all tears from their eyes; and there shall be no more death, neither sorrow, nor crying, neither shall there be any more pain: for the former things are passed away" (Revelation 21:4).

As a bishop, I saw many tears. I saw tears of sorrow over beloved children who returned to their Father in Heaven in tragic ways. I saw tears of anguish over children who were dying spiritually. I saw tears of grief over inactive spouses and tears of pain brought on by divorce or unfaithfulness. I saw tears of longing from the aged, yearning for reunion with loved ones beyond the veil. I saw tears of guilt over broken commandments.

I listened to those who wept and handed them a handkerchief or a tissue from my pocket. They wiped away the tears I could see, but often their souls were still weeping. I was troubled by my inability to provide more comfort, to find the word that would turn pain to joy. During one of those moments I discovered the promise of the Lord in Isaiah and Revelation.

Though I could not always wipe away the tears there is One who can. What Jesus did for Mary at the tomb he will one day do for all. As we return often to her portrait, may that truth be a constant, sustaining element in our lives.

THE BEGINNING AND THE END

Jesus has many titles. The one I love best is "I am . . . the beginning and the end" (Revelation 21:6). He is the end of crying. He is the end of death. He is the end of sorrow. He is the end of pain. He is the end of guilt. He is the end of tears. By contrast, he is the beginning of life. He is the beginning of happiness. He is the beginning of peace. He is the beginning of mercy and forgiveness. He is the beginning of tears of joy. There is such sweetness in the words, "God shall wipe away all tears from their eyes" (Revelation 7:17). One day a wonderful sister pointed something out to me. "The Savior will wipe the tears away," she said. "He will not just hand us a tissue." Suddenly the image became much more intimate. Only my mother and my wife have ever actually wiped tears from my eyes, and I have wiped tears only from the eyes of my children and my wife. I would not presume to wipe the tears from the eyes of anyone else. I have watched my wife gently sweep tears from the cheeks of our children. It is a gesture of love and tenderness, a gesture of the Savior himself.

IT IS FINISHED

Mary sat at the foot of the cross during the long hours of the Savior's torment. Undoubtedly Mary Magdalene, like Mary, Jesus' mother, felt the "sword . . . pierce through [her] own soul also" (Luke 2:35). She watched Jesus hang in agony, denied even the comfort of a drink of water. No mortal being ever suffered more than he did. No grief was greater, no sorrow darker, no pain more intense. Yet, there came a time when the supreme sacrifice was completed, and Jesus said, "It is finished" (John 19:30). He had fulfilled his Father's will. And "it is finished" was also true of his pain. The agony, the betrayal, the grief of Gethsemane and the thorns of Calvary were over.

Mary's grief may have been at its fullest when he died, but when he returned to wipe away her tears, she too could say, "It is finished." All of us, no matter what our pain, sorrow, or grief, no matter what our trial, will one day be able to say, "It is finished." There is an end to suffering. Jesus is that end. There is a beginning to joy. Christ is that beginning. Mary of Magdala, a tiny village near the Sea of Galilee, was chosen to witness both the end of suffering at Calvary and the beginning of joy at the tomb.

THEY RAN TO BRING HIS DISCIPLES WORD

Matthew tells us that Mary and the other women "departed quickly from the sepulchre with . . . great joy; and did run to bring his disciples word" (Matthew 28:8). With peace and truth burning in her heart, Mary ran to share her joy. I can see Mary in my mind's eye, running from the tomb and through the streets of Jerusalem, almost bursting with the joy she carried. It is an image of womanhood in the scriptures most dear to my heart. With the utmost assurance that Christ lives, with the knowledge that tears can be wiped away forever, with the joy of truth burning in their hearts, Latter-day Saint women continue to run, spreading the good news.

Isaiah wrote: "How beautiful upon the mountains are the feet of him that bringeth good tidings, that publisheth peace; that bringeth good tidings of good, that publisheth salvation; that saith unto Zion, Thy God reigneth!" (Isaiah 52:7). In the ancient world, the "good tidings" of victory were sent by runners. The joy of their message caused them to run all the more quickly and steadily. Their feet were beautiful because of the wonderful tidings they bore.

Isaiah knew no runners would ever carry a more marvelous message than that of the victory won by the Savior's atoning sacrifice. Though others had prophesied of this great event, Mary Magdalene was the first to see its reality. She ran swiftly to proclaim Christ's victory. How beautiful upon the mountains were her feet. How beautiful upon the mountains are the feet of all the sisters who have ever run with the tidings of the Savior's life and victory. How beautiful are the feet of the sister missionaries who run to the far corners of the world, bearing Mary's message of joy. How beautiful upon the mountains are the feet of all the sisters who testify of the Savior. May the portrait of Mary Magdalene be a constant affirmation of their own fulfillment of Isaiah's prophecy.

CHAPTER 24

SEEKING THE BLESSINGS
OF THE SAVIOR

With the beauty of the last portraits fixed solidly in our memory, we quietly move into the next room of the gallery. Here we see a number of portraits. Though none is as complete as those we have just left, and few are named, each is of a woman touched by the Savior.

SALOME: MOURNING WITH THOSE WHO MOURN

One of these women was named Salome, who watched at the Crucifixion. Mark records, "There were also women looking on afar off: among whom was Mary Magdalene, and Mary the mother of James the less and of Joses, and Salome" (Mark 15:40). Matthew, too, lists several women who were present at the Crucifixion: "And many women were there beholding afar off, which followed Jesus from Galilee, ministering unto him: among which was Mary Magdalene, and Mary the mother of James and Joses, and the mother of Zebedee's children" (Matthew 27:55–56). Mark indicates that Salome was also present at the tomb when the women had "bought sweet spices, that they might come and anoint him" (Mark 16:1). Most biblical scholars believe Salome was Zebedee's wife and therefore the mother of

James and John, two of Jesus' apostles (see Bible Dictionary, s.v. "Salome"). John's list of women at the cross includes "his [Jesus'] mother, and his mother's sister, Mary the wife of Cleophas, and Mary Magdalene" (John 19:25). This verse has caused some to believe that Salome was Mary's sister. If so, that would make James and John cousins to Jesus.

Regardless of the relationship, Salome supported and sustained Mary in her grief and pain. The image of these women, comforting and sustaining each other in mutual grief, is one of the most beautiful in the scriptures. The image is repeated as we read that Mary Magdalene went with other women, including Salome, "when it was yet dark" (John 20:1) to the tomb on resurrection morning so as to be there "at the rising of the sun" (Mark 16:1–2).

Our baptismal covenant includes the willingness to "bear one another's burdens, that they may be light; . . . to mourn with those that mourn; yea, and comfort those that stand in need of comfort" (Mosiah 18:8–9). This willingness is shown powerfully and beautifully by Salome and the other women as they mourn with Mary at the cross and at the tomb, bearing her burden and comforting her and each other.

This quality of empathy is particularly associated with the Savior and was often demonstrated during his ministry. Isaiah prophesied of this quality of the Savior: "Surely he hath borne our griefs, and carried our sorrows" (Isaiah 53:4). Isaiah prophesied that Jesus would "speak a word in season to him that is weary" (Isaiah 50:4). This endearing quality of the Savior is a quality given to many women, who seem to naturally carry others' sorrows, to know how to speak a word in season to him that is weary. In these moments they are closer to the Savior than they may realize. Perhaps that is one reason that charity and mercy are personified as women in the scriptures.

LET HIM BE YOUR SERVANT

Salome ministered of her substance, reared two sons who served in the First Presidency of the ancient Church, comforted Mary and shared her burden, and was one of the earliest witnesses of the resurrected Savior. What a legacy of faith she left in the few verses that mention her.

Yet she was not perfect, and we are shown one of her moments of weakness when the Savior gently taught her a better way: "Then came to him the mother of Zebedee's children with her sons, worshipping him, and desiring a certain thing of him. And he said unto her, What wilt thou? She saith unto him, Grant that these my two sons may sit, the one on thy right hand, and the other on the left, in thy kingdom" (Matthew 20:20–21).

It is natural for a mother to want her children to succeed. It is also common to equate success with position. So Jesus used her request to teach his followers not to measure themselves by the importance of positions they might hold. The Savior said: "Ye know that the princes of the Gentiles exercise dominion over them, and they that are great exercise authority upon them. But it shall not be so among you: but whosoever will be great among you, let him be your minister; and whosoever will be chief among you, let him be your servant: even as the Son of man came not to be ministered unto, but to minister, and to give his life a ransom for many" (Matthew 20:25–28). Even the mother of James and John needed to be reminded of that important truth: In the Lord's kingdom, the one most esteemed is the servant of all.

From time to time even righteous and noble women need to be corrected. We all need to be reminded not to seek for power or authority over others, not to measure the success of our children by positions they hold in the kingdom. We all must learn to seek, and teach our children to seek, the glory of God and the eternal welfare of others. In time James, John, and Salome learned to seek only the glory of God and the eternal welfare of their brothers and sisters. Those who do so are great in the eyes of God. Salome's portrait bears witness to these truths.

SUFFER LITTLE CHILDREN

Perhaps it is due to the many wonderful paintings of the story of Jesus blessing the children, or perhaps it is just my own imagination, but I had always believed that mothers took their children to Jesus. Then, as I studied these portraits and the lessons they teach, I discovered that all three accounts of this story say simply: "And *they* brought unto him also infants, that he would touch them" (Luke 18:15; emphasis added). Mark records the incident in this manner: "And *they* brought young children to him, that he should touch them" (Mark 10:13; emphasis added). Matthew's version varies only slightly from this pattern: "Then were there brought unto him little children, that he should put his hands on them, and pray" (Matthew 19:13).

I had always pictured this scene with the mothers standing in the background. Yet though the accounts do not specify mothers, I do not think it necessary to abandon that traditional picture. After all, mothers have always had the primary responsibility of caring for the children.

Matthew's version tells us that Jesus was asked not only to touch the little children but also to pray for them. Mark says that Jesus was "much displeased" at his apostles' rebuke of those who brought the children, saying, "Suffer the little children to come unto me, and forbid them not: for of such is the kingdom of God." Jesus then "took them up in his arms, put his hands upon them, and blessed them" (Mark 10:14, 16).

LITTLE CHILDREN ARE IMPORTANT, TOO

I like to think that the mothers of these children recognized the importance of little children and the great love the Lord had for them. When I was a new bishop, I was told to focus my efforts on the youth. Eager to do everything I could for the youth, I planned to put the best teachers in the ward in the Young Men, Young Women, and youth Sunday School programs. When the Primary president was told that another one of her teachers was going to be taken from the Primary, she came to see me in my office. With deep emotion she said, "Bishop, *little* children are important, too!" The Spirit bore strong testimony to me of the truth of her words.

I love that Primary president for the lesson she taught me. From that time forward, a member of the bishopric went to

Primary each Sunday to tell scripture stories to the children. Some of my choicest memories are of those visits. I also spent more time in my interviews with the children when they were baptized or received awards. We allowed the littlest children, who sometimes wandered away from their parents during sacrament meeting, to sit on the laps of members of the bishopric.

Occasionally members of the ward complimented one of the bishopric on our attention to the little children, but the praise and the gratitude really belonged to a wonderful Primary president. I am sure she would have been among the mothers who took their little children to Jesus had she lived when he was on the earth. Her words echo again in my mind every time I am invited to stand with other priesthood bearers to give a name and a blessing to a baby. Each time I pass by a room in which a Primary class is being taught, I think of her conviction. When I am asked to teach in Primary, I feel honored. And I know there are thousands upon thousands more Latter-day Saint women like her.

ONE BY ONE

In the Book of Mormon, Jesus asked for the little children to be brought to him. Surrounded by the little children, he prayed and wept. Then "he took their little children, one by one, and blessed them, and prayed unto the Father for them" (3 Nephi 17:21). How those words strike chords in our hearts. They tell us that God is concerned about every individual. We know there were twenty-five hundred people in the multitude at Bountiful that day. How many little children did Jesus bless and pray for one by one?

Whenever I read that story, I am reminded of the Savior's answer to Moses' question about worlds without number. The Lord said, "Innumerable are they unto man; but all things are numbered unto me, for they are mine and I know them" (Moses 1:35). We are all the Father's children, and he knows us individually.

One of my daughters went through a very difficult time in the seventh grade. Junior high school children can be quite cruel. She felt unloved and friendless. Because our children receive their patriarchal blessings when they turn thirteen, she knew this experience was coming and she, like Rebekah of old, "went to enquire of the Lord" (Genesis 25:22). She told her Father in Heaven she wanted to know that he loved her, and she asked him to tell her so in her blessing. She kept this matter between herself and the Lord.

The night of her blessing finally came. When the blessing was over and we were driving home, she related to her mother and me her desire to know of her Father in Heaven's love. The first sentence in my daughter's blessing assured her that her Heavenly Father was pleased at her desire to know of his love for her. What an effect that statement had on a thirteen-year-old girl.

I am grateful for the mothers who took their children to Jesus. I am grateful for all the virtuous women who have taught me, in so many ways, that we are all numbered to the Lord, for we are his, and he knows us. He wants us to come unto him to be touched, to be prayed for, to be blessed. Though the lines and features are faint, and the image small, the sketch of these women is one we treasure for the beauty of the truth it conveys.

A WOMAN HAVING AN ISSUE OF BLOOD

The next portrait is that of the woman with "an issue of blood" (Matthew 9:20). As Jesus was on his way to heal the daughter of Jairus, "a certain woman, which had an issue of blood twelve years, and had suffered many things of many physicians, and had spent all that she had, and was nothing bettered, but rather grew worse, when she had heard of Jesus, came in the press behind, and touched his garment. For she said, If I may touch but his clothes, I shall be whole. And straightway the fountain of her blood was dried up; and she felt in her body that she was healed of that plague" (Mark 5:25–29).

Those twelve years had been a terrible ordeal for this woman, for not only were there the physical problems related to her condition but also the condition made her ceremonially unclean and severely limited her contact with others (see Leviticus 15:19–30).

Furthermore, she had suffered from the treatments of the physicians and they had taken all her money without any results.

With the assurance in her heart that Jesus could heal her, she
reached through the crowd and touched his garment. Perhaps she
sought healing in this manner because she did not want contact
with her disease to render the Savior unclean. Her faith was
rewarded by her Father in Heaven, who granted her relief.

This woman is an example of great faith. Jesus told her, "Thy
faith hath made thee whole" (Matthew 9:22). Her portrait
teaches us that when all other efforts to find help and healing fail,
we can go to the Savior, who will reward us according to our
faith, in accordance with his divine purposes.

FEARING AND TREMBLING

When the woman touched him, "Jesus, immediately knowing in himself that virtue had gone out of him, turned . . . and
said, Who touched my clothes?" (Mark 5:30)

What thoughts went through this woman's mind? What fears
gripped her heart? She knew her quiet act of faith was now
known. Jesus had felt her unclean touch and was searching the
crowd for her.

"When all denied, Peter and they that were with him said,
Master, the multitude throng thee and press thee, and sayest
thou, Who touched me? And Jesus said, Somebody hath touched
me: for I perceive that virtue is gone out of me" (Luke 8:45–46).

I do not think her denial was overt; rather, I think she hoped
to hide in silence. But Jesus persisted: "And he looked round
about to see her that had done this thing. But the woman fearing
and trembling, knowing what was done in her, came and fell
down before him, and told him all the truth" (Mark 5:32–33).

She feared she had done wrong. She had gone against the traditions of her people and the law of Moses, and yet her faith had
produced healing. How sweet the Savior's next words must have
been, for he said, "Daughter, be of good comfort: thy faith hath
made thee whole; go in peace" (Luke 8:48).

Many times we fear we will be chastised when we have acted

in faith. After serving for only nine months as a stake mission president, I was called to go to Haiti and begin seminary and institute classes in the Caribbean. It had been years since I had spoken French, and I knew nothing of Creole. I was given about six months to prepare.

I enrolled in French classes and ordered correspondence courses in Creole. After three or four months, I began to panic. How could I establish the Church programs in the Caribbean if I could not communicate? Because the stake mission work left me no time to study, I went to the stake president and asked to be released. He was understanding and released me, but I felt guilty.

If the Savior had come at that time and asked, "Who in this room asked to be released from his calling?" I would have slipped to the back, hoping he was talking about someone else. If he persisted, I would have come forward, fearing and trembling. I believe he would have said, "Be of good comfort. Go in peace."

A wonderful sister in an institute class asked rather hesitatingly, "We have been told to read the Book of Mormon, and I try to read it as much as I can, but this year we are studying the New Testament in Gospel Doctrine, and I just don't seem to find the time to read both. If I read the Book of Mormon, I don't read the New Testament, and I know I should, but if I read the New Testament, I don't read the Book of Mormon. I don't want to be guilty of not following counsel. What should I do?"

When she asked the question, I imagined the Savior turning and saying, "Who has been reading the New Testament instead of the Book of Mormon?" This dedicated sister would have slipped into the background and hoped he was not talking about her. But if he had singled her out, I believe he would have said, "Be of good comfort: thy faith is accepted; go in peace."

A last glance at the portrait of the woman with the issue of blood reminds us that although we may approach the throne of grace with fear and trembling, we can trust in the Savior. He will see our faith, not our uncleanness, and as long as we reach out to receive his healing power, we will hear the words, "Daughter, be of good comfort: thy faith hath made thee whole; go in peace" (see Matthew 9:22; Mark 5:34; Luke 8:48).

A CERTAIN POOR WIDOW

The next portrait is of a "certain poor widow" who walked one day into the temple courtyard to give her offering to the Lord (Mark 12:42). Her image, however, has instructed prophets, and her example has been a light to the entire Church.

"Jesus sat over against the treasury, and beheld how the people cast money into the treasury: and many that were rich cast in much. And there came a certain poor widow, and she threw in two mites, which make a farthing" (Mark 12:41–42).

This widow's action has become a symbol for gifts offered to the Lord through sacrifice and faith. The Savior told his disciples, "Verily I say unto you, That this poor widow hath cast more in, than all they which have cast into the treasury: for all they did cast in of their abundance; but she of her want did cast in all that she had, even all her living" (Mark 12:43–44).

Ancient Israel offered to the Lord the firstlings of the flocks and the firstfruits of the field. *Firstlings* and *firstfruits* suggest that obligations to the Lord should be fulfilled first. Likewise, our tithes and offerings should be paid first. This widow is one of the finest examples of fulfilling obligations to the Lord above every other consideration. I believe she did so, trusting that the Lord would "open [her] the windows of heaven, and pour [her] out a blessing, that there shall not be room enough to receive it" (Malachi 3:10).

President Gordon B. Hinckley expressed the influence of this widow's life on his own: "I keep on the credenza behind my desk a widow's mite that was given me in Jerusalem many years ago as a reminder, a constant reminder, of the sanctity of the funds with which we have to deal. They come from the widow; they are her offering as well as the tithe of the rich man, and they are to be used with care and discretion for the purposes of the Lord. We treat them carefully and safeguard them and try in every way that we can to see that they are used as we feel the Lord would have them used for the upbuilding of His work and the betterment of people" (Conference Report, October 1996, 69).

The Doctrine and Covenants teaches, "Out of small things proceedeth that which is great" (D&C 64:33). We never know how the simplest actions of our lives may influence others. Like the ripples in a pond, the circles of our influence continue to expand.

As a brand-new deacon, I was asked to give the opening prayer in stake conference. I remember standing behind the pulpit, barely able to see over it, staring at the hundreds of people, and then closing my eyes and offering the prayer. I didn't say anything special—I just said a prayer. Ten years later a sister from another ward said to me, "I need to thank you for changing my life. When you were a new deacon, you gave the opening prayer at stake conference. I was struggling with some problems and having difficulty believing God heard my prayers. Then I heard a young boy, barely able to see over the pulpit, offer a prayer. There was nothing significant in what the boy said, but hearing a young deacon pray softened my heart, and I remembered my own childhood prayers. I thought, *If a child can believe there is a God who listens to him, so can I.* That was a turning point for me. Thank you."

There is no act of service in the Church more common than offering a prayer in behalf of others, yet we do not know who is watching us and how they will be influenced.

The poor widow could not have known how significant her act would be. Let us learn from her portrait that we are never insignificant to the Lord's work or to each other. I do not think she even knew the Savior was watching her. I wonder how she would feel to see the widow's mite sitting on the desk of the President of the Church?

I hope that every woman who has placed her offerings in the hands of the Lord will remember this certain widow and receive the assurance that the Lord does watch and that others may be profoundly influenced for good. Though small, this sketch is one of the treasures of the Lord's gallery.

A WOMAN OF CANAAN:
CRUMBS FROM THE MASTER'S TABLE

The last portrait in this group is that of a Canaanite woman from the "coasts of Tyre and Sidon." During his ministry Jesus sometimes sought rest from the multitudes by going into the mountains or onto the Sea of Galilee or to other places of solitude. On one such occasion he "departed into the coasts of Tyre and Sidon. And, behold, a woman of Canaan came out of the same coasts, and cried unto him, saying, Have mercy on me, O Lord, thou Son of David; my daughter is grievously vexed with a devil. But he answered her not a word. And his disciples came and besought him, saying, Send her away; for she crieth after us" (Matthew 15:21–23).

What must this woman have felt as the Savior ignored her, answering her pleas with silence? What must she have thought when she heard his apostles tell him to "send her away"? Finally the Savior explained his silence: "I am not sent but unto the lost sheep of the house of Israel" (Matthew 15:24). Could the Lord of compassion refuse her request because she was not a woman of Israel? Had not Jesus once used a woman of Sidon as an example of faith to shame his own city of Nazareth? (see Luke 4:26).

Rather than take offense, however, "came she and worshipped him, saying, Lord, help me" (Matthew 15:25). Mark adds that the woman "came and fell at his feet" (Mark 7:25). But Jesus still did not heal her daughter. He "said unto her, Let the children of the kingdom first be filled: for it is not meet to take the children's bread, and to cast it unto the dogs" (JST Mark 7:26).

The Savior's reply sounds extremely harsh. But this woman did not question his reasons nor take offense. She did not leave to tell her neighbors how poorly she had been treated by the Jewish Messiah. Elder James E. Talmage said: "The words, harsh as they may sound to us, were understood by her in the spirit of the Lord's intent. . . . Certainly the woman took no offense at the comparison, and found therein no objectionable epithet" (*Jesus the Christ*, 355).

"And she said, Truth, Lord: yet the dogs eat of the crumbs which fall from their master's table. Then Jesus answered and said unto her, O woman, great is thy faith: be it unto thee even as thou wilt" (Matthew 15:27–28).

I cannot adequately express how much admiration I have for this woman of Canaan who refused to be offended either by Jesus' silence or by his words. She simply chose not to take offense. How many of us, if we had endured the Savior's silence or heard his reference to dogs, would have walked away, never to return?

YOU CAN CHOOSE NOT TO BE OFFENDED

The bishop of a ward my family once lived in related the following experience: "A brother who was struggling with paying his tithing approached me one Sunday morning with his tithing envelope. I did not see him coming and turned to talk to another member just as he approached. He thought I was turning my back on him to speak to another member who was more important. He took offense and left the church angry. At home he told his wife the bishop had shunned him. If she had not called to tell me what had happened, I would never have understood his sudden coldness to me. I was able to speak with him and straighten everything out, but only because his wife made me aware of the situation."

We must learn not to take offense, especially when none was intended. And even when offense is intended, we can choose not to be offended. A fellow seminary teacher learned this truth early in his career: "I had difficulty dealing with the son of one of the prominent families of the small community in which I was teaching. The young man's attitude and discipline in class deteriorated so much that I finally asked him to leave. That afternoon I received a telephone call from his mother. I have never had a conversation that was more offensive to me. The aspersions that were cast upon me and others of my profession were so odious that I have never repeated them to anyone. I held my temper until she hung up, and then I exploded. When I finally calmed down somewhat, the Spirit whispered words I will never forget.

'You can choose not to be offended.' I could not accept this truth immediately. How could I possibly choose not to be offended? She had said terrible, insulting words. Anyone would have been offended. Once again the Spirit repeated the words, 'You can choose not to be offended.' When I finally accepted the truth of these words, the bitterness left me, and I could actually laugh about the situation and my own anger."

How deeply offended the woman of Canaan could have been. Yet she chose not to be offended, and her choice resulted in the healing of her daughter. Many women of the Church share the attitude of this woman of Canaan. Though words are said or deeds done that could give them reason to be offended, become inactive, or break relationships, they choose not to take offense. With forgiveness and understanding, they do what they can to promote unity within their families and their wards.

Many times I have returned to admire the portrait of this woman of Canaan and found inspiration in her example. How grateful we all can be that the writers of the Gospels chose to include her portrait in the gallery of the scriptures.

CHAPTER 25

HOPE FOR THE PENITENT

The Savior said, "Come unto me, all ye that labour and are heavy laden, and I will give you rest. Take my yoke upon you, and learn of me; for I am meek and lowly in heart: and ye shall find rest unto your souls. For my yoke is easy, and my burden is light" (Matthew 11:28–30). There is no weight heavier than sin, and no yoke more cumbersome than a violated conscience.

The three women at whose portraits we now pause give hope to those pressed down under the weight of past or present transgression. The women are not named, but together they provide a study in penitence, forgiveness, and hope. One sought out the Savior in the house of Simon the Pharisee, desiring the peace he promised. One met him as she drew water from Jacob's well. One was brought before him in humiliation as he taught in the crowded courts of the temple. They are the feminine counterparts of Alma the Younger, Corianton, the four sons of Mosiah, and others who learned to "sing the song of redeeming love" (Alma 5:26). Each woman teaches us that if we are willing to throw off the yoke of sin, we will find the promised rest. They did not come to the Savior virtuous women, but they left him renewed and determined to become such.

A WOMAN IN THE CITY: THE SOUL OF REPENTANCE

The woman who sought out Jesus while he dined at the house of Simon the Pharisee may have heard the Savior's invitation to take his yoke. Sensing his compassion, this "woman in the city, which was a sinner, when she knew that Jesus sat at meat in the Pharisee's house, brought an alabaster box of ointment, and stood at his feet behind him weeping, and began to wash his feet with tears, and did wipe them with the hairs of her head, and kissed his feet, and anointed them with the ointment" (Luke 7:37–38).

Here was a woman laden with many sins (see Luke 7:47). In spite of the condemnation she faced in the Pharisee's house, she poured out her remorse, love, and gratitude. Knowing that it is important to allow those suffering under the burden of guilt to show their deepest feelings, the Savior silently allowed her to offer her gift. Then turning to Simon, the Savior related a parable. "There was a certain creditor which had two debtors: the one owed five hundred pence, and the other fifty. And when they had nothing to pay, he frankly forgave them both. Tell me therefore, which of them will love him most?" (Luke 7:41–42).

The key words of this parable are "when they had nothing to pay, he frankly forgave them both." This woman gave what she could. She laid her sins at the Savior's feet and then showed her gratitude by washing his feet with her tears, wiping them with her hair, and anointing them with ointment.

Jesus knew her heart and "turned to the woman, and said unto Simon, Seest thou this woman? I entered into thine house, thou gavest me no water for my feet: but she hath washed my feet with tears, and wiped them with the hairs of her head. Thou gavest me no kiss: but this woman since the time I came in hath not ceased to kiss my feet. My head with oil thou didst not anoint: but this woman hath anointed my feet with ointment. Wherefore I say unto thee, Her sins, which are many, are forgiven; for she loved much. . . . And he said unto her, Thy sins are forgiven" (Luke 7:44–48).

THY SINS ARE FORGIVEN

There is no more beautiful picture than that of a penitent person doing what she can do to have the stains of her sins taken away. We feel her repentance. Washing his feet with water was not enough: She washed them with tears. Wiping them with a towel was not sufficient: She wiped them with her hair. Kissing his cheek would not show the depth of her humility: She kissed his feet without ceasing. Anointing his head with oil was not good enough for her Lord: He was worthy of ointment for his feet.

While serving as a bishop, I listened to many confessions. Some individuals were deeply repentant, ready to lay their burden at the feet of the Savior. Like the debtors in the parable, they had nothing to pay, but they were willing to do whatever was necessary to go in peace. Others desired to lay the burden down but hesitated to do whatever was necessary. They too had nothing to pay but they seemed to hope that a little water, a quick kiss on the cheek, and a little oil would be sufficient.

During those sessions, I frequently turned to the seventh chapter of Luke and together we would read the episode at the house of Simon. The truly penitent recognized themselves in the weeping woman and received hope. The others were softened by her example. Defensive attitudes would break down, and healing could begin.

In the simple humility of this unnamed woman, we are invited to feel repentance; we are invited to feel forgiveness. She awakens both the longing to be clean and the desire to forgive. Because we feel the remorse of her penitent heart, we are strengthened in our desire to lay our burdens down and anoint the feet of our Lord. We feel the Savior's acceptance of her gift, our own faith increases, and we know he will accept all we have to offer.

Jesus repeated to this woman three times the assurance that her faith had saved her and her sins were forgiven (see Luke 7:47–48, 50). He placed his own light yoke of obedience upon her and bade her go in peace.

THE WOMAN AT THE WELL:
THE LIVING WATER OF LOVE

John testified, "There are also many other things which Jesus did, the which, if they should be written every one, I suppose that even the world itself could not contain the books that should be written" (John 21:25). Obviously, then, John must have considered the events he included to be particularly significant. He wrote of the raising of Lazarus—emphasizing the faith and grief of Mary and Martha. He testified of the resurrection—giving Mary Magdalene's encounter with Jesus the primary position. With these points in mind, Jesus' conversation with the Samaritan woman at Jacob's well takes on added significance. Why did John feel this conversation was so important?

Perhaps the positioning of this story in relation to another gives us a key. John 3 records the conversation between Nicodemus and Jesus. Nicodemus came in the night, probably fearing the Pharisees who opposed Jesus. "A ruler of the Jews" (John 3:1), Nicodemus was learned, respected, part of the elite of the Jerusalem community. Yet Nicodemus did not understand the spiritual nature or symbolic language the Savior used in speaking of being born again. The Savior gently rebuked Nicodemus for not receiving His witness (see John 3:11).

The very next chapter of John contains the portrait of the Samaritan woman at the well. In contrast to Jesus' conversation with Nicodemus, this one took place in broad daylight with a woman who was the lowest of the low in Israel. Her past had been less than wholesome, for she had had five husbands and was now with a man who was not her husband (see John 4:18). Moreover, she was a Samaritan, and the "Jews have no dealings with the Samaritans" (v. 9). The apostles openly "marvelled that he talked with the woman" (v. 27). The Samaritan woman, who was not learned, had difficulty understanding the symbolic language of the Savior when he promised her "living water" (John 4:10), yet she believed the Savior and openly proclaimed his Messiahship. She was one of the first to whom he openly declared himself the Christ.

The very juxtaposition of these stories conveys to us the message that neither birth nor position establishes us as citizens in the kingdom of God but rather humility, faith, and a willingness to declare and testify. The highest of the high may never enter; the lowest of the low need not fear exclusion. Nothing will keep us from the desired blessings if we accept Jesus with faith and a willingness to change.

As Jesus sat by the well, weary from his journey, the Samaritan woman approached with her water pot. She was surprised he asked her for a drink. Often those who are sinful or who occupy a lower position in their society feel uncomfortable. "If thou knewest the gift of God," Jesus responded, "and who it is that saith to thee, Give me to drink; thou wouldest have asked of him, and he would have given thee living water" (John 4:10).

This verse inspires hope in us all. If we ask of him, he will give us the living water, no matter who we are. Even though she did not understand all his words, the Savior perceived her spiritual thirst and gave her living water.

The living water Jesus offers symbolizes the truths of his gospel as it also symbolizes his love. When Nephi saw in vision the tree of life, he saw a fountain next to it. "I beheld that the rod of iron, which my father had seen, was the word of God, which led to the fountain of living waters, . . . which waters are a representation of the love of God" (1 Nephi 11:25). The Savior offered not only truth to the Samaritan woman but his love and the full benefits of his atoning mercy. This love and mercy can become "a well of water springing up into everlasting life" (John 4:14).

For those who struggle with feelings of unworthiness—those who, like the Samaritan woman, are surprised that the Savior would speak to them, let alone invite them to drink the living waters—the events at Jacob's well inspire hope. He will not refuse our requests for love, for forgiveness, for inclusion in his kingdom. We must simply ask.

THE WOMAN THEN LEFT HER WATERPOT

As the apostles approached the well, the woman "left her waterpot, and went her way into the city, and saith to the men, Come, see a man, which told me all things that ever I did: is not this the Christ?" (John 4:28–29). The waterpot was forgotten. It was time to testify.

Every day, thousands of dedicated Latter-day Saint women, like the woman at the well, leave their daily obligations to testify and invite. Some do that through a formal mission call. Some do it day by day as they serve in their Church callings, speak with their neighbors, and teach their children. As the world grows more wicked, there is an increasing need for those who have received the living water to run to others, crying, "Come, see a man . . . is not this the Christ?"

A WOMAN TAKEN IN ADULTERY: LEARNING TO SIN NO MORE

The portrait of the woman taken in adultery is one of the more familiar portraits of the New Testament.

Jesus was teaching in the most public place in Jerusalem, the temple mount, when "the scribes and Pharisees brought unto him a woman taken in adultery." When they had "set her in the midst, they say unto him, Master, this woman was taken in adultery, in the very act. Now Moses in the law commanded us, that such should be stoned: but what sayest thou?" (John 8:3–5). The self-righteousness and lack of compassion these men showed by setting her in their midst must have offended the Savior deeply. This was not a matter for public scrutiny.

Stooping down, Jesus began to write on the ground, "as though he heard them not." His action announced to all that he did not wish to judge this woman. Then he said, "He that is without sin among you, let him first cast a stone at her" (John 8:6–7). Since they were so eager to judge, he gave them someone to judge: themselves. One by one they walked away. They did not want their sins paraded before the multitudes that crowded the temple mount. The woman remained in the presence of the Savior, waiting for his judgment.

"When Jesus had lifted up himself, and saw none but the woman, he said unto her, Woman, where are those thine accusers? hath no man condemned thee? She said, No man, Lord. And Jesus said unto her, Neither do I condemn thee: go, and sin no more" (John 8:10–11).

There is hope for all in knowing that the Savior does not wish our sins to be paraded before the world. He judges privately, and when real repentance is offered, then, as Ezekiel said, "all his transgressions that he hath committed, they shall not be mentioned unto him" (Ezekiel 18:22).

When we are tempted to condemn others, we must learn to do as Jesus did. We must remember our own weaknesses. And when judgment is required, we must judge without condemnation. Even to those who have sinned as seriously as did this woman, the Savior says, "Neither do I condemn thee; go, and sin no more." The Joseph Smith Translation adds one final and important sentence to this story: "And the woman glorified God from that hour, and believed on his name" (JST John 8:11).

All of us sin, and none of us desires to have our transgressions paraded before the world. All of us hope that others, like Jesus, will act "as though [they] heard them not" when our own weaknesses are exposed. All of us pray the Savior will not condemn us. But do all of us, like this woman, go and sin no more? When we have been forgiven, do our lives glorify God from that hour? The woman taken in adultery teaches something we would do well to remember. A newly forgiven person sins no more but glorifies God and believes on his name.

GO IN PEACE

Bishops listen to the confessions of some who have made the mistakes these three women had made. Some, like the woman taken in adultery, do not go to the bishop willingly. But even in those circumstances the mercy of the Savior is abundant.

One woman I became acquainted with was guilty of serious

sin. She repented deeply and grieved for many months. Like Alma the Younger and the sons of Mosiah, she worked zealously to repair all the injuries she had done to those who loved her. Like the woman who entered Simon's house, she poured out her love at the Savior's feet. Like the woman at the temple mount, she sinned no more and spent her life glorifying God. Like the Samaritan woman, she spoke freely to everyone about the Savior's love, for she knew he was the Christ.

When I think of her I am reminded of the power of the Atonement to change and purify a soul. It has been many years since her sin, and I have often heard others say, "I wish I were like that sister. She exemplifies all that is good in women."

HERODIAS AND HER DAUGHTER: SILENCING THE VOICE IN THE WILDERNESS

In sharp contrast to the portraits of these penitent women hangs the portrait of Herodias, who, when confronted with the call to repentance issued by John the Baptist, not only refused to abandon her sins but sought to silence his voice. Her inclusion in the gallery testifies of the necessity of heeding the call to repentance and warns that our refusal may well lead us deeper into sin.

The New Testament includes few examples of wicked women, but one of them, Herodias, let ambition draw her into committing terrible deeds. She also spurred a weak husband to commit evil. She desired to hold onto power, and John the Baptist's condemnation of her marriage to Herod Antipas threatened her. How dare he challenge her or her husband? How dare he call them to repentance?

Brooding over the insolence of John's cries, she awaited her opportunity. "Therefore Herodias had a quarrel against him, and would have killed him; but she could not: for Herod feared John, knowing that he was a just man and a holy man, and one who feared God and observed to worship him; and when he heard him he did many things for him, and heard him gladly" (JST Mark 6:20–21). Herodias knew her husband's weaknesses, however, and bided her time.

Herodias found the perfect occasion on the birthday of her husband. "Herod . . . made a supper to his lords, high captains, and chief estates of Galilee; and when the daughter of the said Herodias came in, and danced, and pleased Herod and them that sat with him, the king said unto the damsel, Ask of me whatsoever thou wilt, and I will give it thee" (Mark 6:21–22).

Mark's version of the beheading of John the Baptist indicates that at this point Herodias' daughter ran to her mother to ask what she should ask of Herod. Being instructed of her mother, she then returned to Herod: "I will that thou give me by and by in a charger the head of John the Baptist" (Mark 6:25). Matthew's account, however, states that "she, being before instructed of her mother, said, Give me here John Baptist's head in a charger" (Matthew 14:8).

In any case, Herodias had known her husband would grant her daughter a request if her dance pleased him. Both mother and daughter demonstrate the same calculating disposition as Jezebel and Athaliah in the Old Testament and the daughter of Jared in the Book of Mormon.

Herodias suspected her husband would be sorry and wish to spare John's life. She had devised a plan, however, that ensnared him into doing her will: "Nevertheless for the oath's sake, and them which sat with him at meat, he commanded it to be given her. . . . And his head was brought in a charger, and given to the damsel: and she brought it to her mother" (Matthew 14:9–11). The macabre request to receive John's head ensured Herod's compliance with Herodias' evil plan.

The scriptures do not tell what became of Herodias, but Josephus informs us that she later prompted her husband to ask the emperor Caligula to make him a king. Caligula not only refused the ambitious couple's request but angrily stripped them of power and banished them to Gaul in A.D. 39.

BECOMING VIRTUOUS WOMEN

How different was Herodias' end from that of the three penitent women who share with her this room in the gallery. The portraits of these righteous women give us great reason to rejoice. I believe they spent the rest of their lives in dignity and purity. I believe that from their contact with the Savior, they began to acquire, trait by trait, the beautiful characteristics of the numerous exemplary women in the scriptures. Although they did not begin as virtuous women, they became such, through the mercy and goodness of the Lord Jesus Christ. They heeded the call to repentance rather than silencing it. Though we do not now know their names, if we meet them in the Lord's kingdom, we will know them as women of virtue who "glorified God . . . and believed on his name" (JST John 8:11). There is no need to know any more than that about them, or about any other woman who may have committed errors, found mercy at the feet of the Savior, and heard the sweet words, "Thy faith hath saved thee; go in peace" (Luke 7:50).

CHAPTER 26

NAMES WRITTEN IN
THE BOOK OF LIFE

We leave the hall of the penitent and enter a hall that is different from all the others we have visited because here there are no substantial portraits at all. Nevertheless, a number of sketches combine to portray the devoted sisters who labored with the apostles in the early Christian church. Speaking of the account of Tabitha, one of these women, President Thomas S. Monson asked: "Are these sacred and moving accounts recorded only for our uplift and enlightenment? Can we not apply such mighty lessons to our daily lives?" (Conference Report, October 1989, 85–86).

WOMEN WHO LABORED IN THE GOSPEL

As the gospel began to spread after the ascension of the Savior, many women embraced it and contributed greatly to the growth of the Church. In his Epistle to the Philippians, Paul spoke of "those women which laboured with me in the gospel, . . . whose names are in the book of life" (Philippians 4:3). Many of those women are mentioned by name, and though we do not know much about their lives, there is truth to be discovered even in the sketchiest of their portraits.

TABITHA (DORCAS): GOOD WORKS PRECEDE THE MIRACLE

Tabitha was a disciple who dwelt at Joppa, on the coast of Israel. It is recorded in Acts that "there was at Joppa a certain disciple named Tabitha, which by interpretation is called Dorcas: this woman was full of good works and almsdeeds which she did" (Acts 9:36). Tabitha demonstrated her faith by her works. "And it came to pass in those days, that she was sick, and died: whom when they had washed, they laid her in an upper chamber." Hearing that Peter was a short distance away, they sent for him. "When he was come, they brought him into the upper chamber: and all the widows stood by him weeping, and shewing the coats and garments which Dorcas made, while she was with them" (Acts 9:37–39). She was mourned by those who knew of her charity. One of her good works, that of sewing clothes, perhaps for the poor and perhaps for the very widows who mourned her passing, is spoken of here.

Then "Peter put them all forth, and kneeled down, and prayed; and turning him to the body said, Tabitha, arise. And she opened her eyes: and when she saw Peter, she sat up" (Acts 9:40).

Miracles are produced by the great faith of those who receive their benefits. How many times did Jesus say, "Thy faith hath made thee whole"? Miracles are also granted through the prayers and faith of others.

Faith precedes miracles, and faithfulness also precedes them. Peter "gave her his hand, and lifted her up, and when he had called the saints and widows, presented her alive" (Acts 9:41). Peter gave Tabitha back to those faithful people who loved her, to those she had faithfully served. This was not only a presentation testifying to the power of God but a presentation of love.

In every case in which the Bible tells of raising the dead, women were significant participants in the miracle. This is true of the widow of Zarephath, the Shunnamite woman, Jairus' daughter, the widow of Nain, Mary and Martha and Lazarus, and Tabitha. There is power in the faith and faithfulness of women, and it is demonstrated by their good works.

RHODA: JOY IN THE PROPHET

We cannot help but smile as we view the sketch of Rhoda. Hers is an endearing portrait, painted in only one humorous incident in her life. When Peter was released from prison by an angel, "He came to the house of Mary the mother of John, whose surname was Mark; where many were gathered together praying. And as Peter knocked at the door of the gate, a damsel came to hearken, named Rhoda. And when she knew Peter's voice, she opened not the gate for gladness, but ran in, and told how Peter stood before the gate. And they said unto her, Thou art mad. But she constantly affirmed that it was even so" (Acts 12:12–15).

When Peter had been arrested, "prayer was made without ceasing of the church unto God for him" (Acts 12:5). Perhaps the gathering at Mary's house was a special gathering to fast and pray for the release of Peter. What joy met Rhoda's ears as she heard his voice on the other side of the gate. The news that their prayers had been answered was too great, too wonderful, for delay. She forgot, however, to open the gate. Peter was left standing outside.

President Spencer W. Kimball admired Rhoda's persistent affirmation of the truth she knew even in the face of those who said she was mad. "I like the story of Rhoda in the Book of Acts who answered when the prophet Peter stood before the gate. Rhoda took the glad news of the presence of this prophet to others, yet they disbelieved her. 'But she constantly affirmed that it was even so' (Acts 12:15). Let us likewise constantly affirm the reality of the presence of living prophets who are among us in this dispensation, even when others doubt and even when others mock. To 'affirm constantly' the truthfulness of the gospel is a wonderful thing for all to do as leaders and as followers. Please note the word *constantly*" ("The Uttermost Parts of the Earth," 2–3).

Joseph Smith, speaking of the First Vision, and the persecution it generated, said, "I continued to affirm that I had seen a vision" (Joseph Smith–History 1:27). Throughout the Church are women who continually affirm the truth of what they know despite opposition and mockery. The joy and gladness of knowing they are led by living prophets outweigh the pain and sorrow of being mocked by those who do not believe their testimony.

LYDIA: A BELIEVING HEART

While Paul was teaching in Asia Minor, he had a "vision in the night; there stood a man of Macedonia, and prayed him, saying, Come over into Macedonia and help us." Immediately Paul and his companions responded, and they arrived a few days later at Philippi. "And on the sabbath we went out of the city by a river side, where prayer was wont to be made; and we sat down, and spake unto the women which resorted thither. And a certain woman named Lydia, a seller of purple, of the city of Thyatira, which worshipped God, heard us: whose heart the Lord opened, that she attended unto the things which were spoken of Paul. And when she was baptized, and her household, she besought us, saying, If ye have judged me to be faithful to the Lord, come into my house, and abide there. And she constrained us" (Acts 16:13–15).

The sketch of Lydia, as drawn by these verses, is representative of many of the women of the Church. President Joseph F. Smith testified of the predisposition of women to believe and remain firm: "They are always more willing to make sacrifices, and are the peers of men in stability, Godliness, morality and faith" (*Gospel Doctrine*, 352).

When Lydia heard the gospel, she believed immediately and was baptized. Her eagerness for the truths of the gospel brought her household into the Church. Once a member, she invited the apostles and missionaries to live at her house, for she felt it a privilege to care for them. Lydia's house became a gathering place for the Church in Philippi.

When Paul and Silas were arrested, beaten, imprisoned, and

then released the next morning with the request to leave Philippi, they "entered into the house of Lydia: and when they had seen the brethren, they comforted them, and departed" (Acts 16:40).

Paul organized and visited churches in many cities, but the one at Philippi remained close to his heart. That tenderness is evidenced in his epistles and in the care that the Philippian Saints extended to him. "Now ye Philippians," he wrote, "know also, that in the beginning of the gospel, when I departed from Macedonia, no church communicated with me as concerning giving and receiving, but ye only. For even in Thessalonica ye sent once and again unto my necessity" (Philippians 4:15–16).

Undoubtedly, Lydia contributed to the faithfulness of the church at Philippi and was one of the Philippian Saints of whom Paul wrote: "I thank my God upon every remembrance of you, always in every prayer of mine for you all making request with joy, for your fellowship in the gospel from the first day until now" (Philippians 1:3–5). Lydia, we remember, met Paul and believed his message "from the first day."

There are Lydias all over the Church. We meet them as missionaries and are amazed at their believing hearts and their generosity. We teach their friends and families and watch the power of their testimony convince the more reluctant members of their family. Women have often been the first in a family to open their hearts to the truth and have proved most stalwart in trials. Past or present, these are women who, like Lydia, open their hearts to the words of truth.

PRISCILLA AND AQUILA: INSEPARABLE AND EQUAL

The next portrait is of a woman and a man. Every time we read of Priscilla, her husband, Aquila, is mentioned also. Sometimes the scriptures record the names as "Aquila and Priscilla," and sometimes they record them as "Priscilla and Aquila." This seems to confirm their unity and suggest their equality.

These two Saints show the power a couple can wield for good

when they work together. They remind me of all the wonderful older couples serving together in the mission field and strengthening the Church. They remind me, too, of the many younger couples whose devotion to each other and mutual strengths bless their wards and stakes.

Our knowledge of Priscilla and Aquila comes from bits and pieces gathered from Acts and the Epistles of Paul. We first read of this admirable couple in Acts: "After . . . Paul departed from Athens, and came to Corinth; and found a certain Jew named Aquila, born in Pontus, lately come from Italy, with his wife Priscilla; (because that Claudius had commanded all Jews to depart from Rome:) and came unto them. And because he was of the same craft, he abode with them, and wrought: for by their occupation they were tentmakers" (Acts 18:1–3).

Priscilla and Aquila had resettled in Corinth, where they worked together making tents. We do not know whether Paul had converted them, but they invited him to work and live with them. Paul stayed with them for eighteen months while he preached in Corinth. The Savior had instructed his apostles, "Into whatsoever city or town ye shall enter, enquire who in it is worthy; and there abide till ye go thence" (Matthew 10:11). Obviously Paul found this couple worthy. Finally he "took his leave of the brethren, and sailed thence into Syria, and with him Priscilla and Aquila; . . . and he came to Ephesus, and left them there" (Acts 18:18–19).

While Paul was preaching "over all the country . . . a certain Jew named Apollos, born at Alexandria, an eloquent man, and mighty in the scriptures, came to Ephesus. This man was instructed in the way of the Lord; and being fervent in the spirit, he spake and taught diligently the things of the Lord, knowing only the baptism of John. And he began to speak boldly in the synagogue: whom when Aquila and Priscilla had heard, they took him unto them, and expounded unto him the way of God more perfectly" (Acts 18:23–26). Like Priscilla, many of the Lord's daughters know and can expound the great truths of the gospel from the pages of the scriptures. Apollos later became an apostle and a great missionary.

MY HELPERS IN CHRIST

In his epistle to the Romans, Paul sent greetings to Priscilla and Aquila, through which we learn of other contributions of this remarkable couple. "Greet Priscilla and Aquila my helpers in Christ Jesus: who have for my life laid down their own necks: unto whom not only I give thanks, but also all the churches of the Gentiles. Likewise greet the church that is in their house" (Romans 16:3–5). Apparently they were willing to sacrifice themselves in Paul's behalf. Perhaps in the eternities we will learn the events behind Paul's gratitude.

The strengthening service of Priscilla and Aquila merited the thanks of "all the churches of the Gentiles" (Romans 16:4). We do not know the specifics behind this comment, but it must be considered in light of the fact that Priscilla and Aquila were Jews. In the early Church the rift between Jewish and Gentile converts eventually split the Church and contributed greatly to the Apostasy. It was difficult to rise above centuries-old prejudices. The issue even precipitated a confrontation between Peter and Paul (see Galatians 2:11–14). Apparently, like Paul, Priscilla and Aquila loved and accepted the Gentiles.

The home of Priscilla and Aquila was a center of the Church, and meetings were held there. That would have necessitated some labor, especially on the part of Priscilla. Church members must have gravitated to them and received strength from their testimonies. Paul wrote from Philippi to the Saints in Corinth: "The churches of Asia salute you. Aquila and Priscilla salute you much in the Lord, with the church that is in their house" (1 Corinthians 16:19). The word *much* in this greeting suggests an enthusiastic greeting from Priscilla and Aquila, one filled with love.

ENDURING TO THE END

The last epistle Paul wrote was his personal letter to Timothy, which adds another valuable detail to the portrait of this righteous couple. This letter was written after Paul had been taken before Nero the second time, and he knew he would soon be put to death. In this epistle Paul penned these stirring words of farewell: "I have fought a good fight, I have finished my course, I have kept the faith" (2 Timothy 4:7).

By this time apostasy was already tearing at the fabric of the early Church. With resignation and sadness Paul told Timothy of a number of brethren who had already turned against him and the truth (see 2 Timothy 1:15; 4:10, 14–16). Yet in this epistle, so filled with betrayal and apostasy, Paul concluded with thoughts of his old and faithful friends: "Salute Prisc[ill]a and Aquila" (2 Timothy 4:19). Priscilla and Aquila were still enduring faithful to the end, still Paul's "fellowlabourers, whose names are in the book of life" (Philippians 4:3). We learn much from their portraits sketched in the details recorded of their lives.

SAPPHIRA: LESS THAN FULL CONSECRATION

Contrast in works of art is often used to highlight the important aspects in a picture. The portrait of the weak and sinful Sapphira and her equally weak and sinful husband Ananias teaches us valuable lessons as it contrasts sharply with the portraits of Priscilla and Aquila and other faithful and righteous members of the early Church.

"A certain man named Ananias, with Sapphira his wife, sold a possession, and kept back part of the price, his wife also being privy to it, and brought a certain part, and laid it at the apostles' feet" (Acts 5:1–2). When Peter exposed his deception and hypocrisy, Ananias "gave up the ghost." Three hours later Sapphira came to Peter, who asked her, "Tell me whether ye sold the land for so much? And she said, Yea, for so much. Then Peter said unto her, How is it that ye have agreed together to tempt the Spirit of the Lord? . . . Then fell she down straightway at his feet and yielded up the ghost" (Acts 5:8–10).

Although the punishment laid upon Ananias and Sapphira may seem extreme, undoubtedly the Lord wanted us to see the lessons in it. First, they kept back part of their consecrated property. Consecration in the early Church was voluntary, just as it is today. Faithful Saints, recognizing that all things belong to God, fully consecrate their time, talents, and material blessings. The failure of Sapphira and Ananias to consecrate fully their possessions reminds us that our own consecration must be voluntary and total. Our desire to see the kingdom of God established on the earth is what motivates us to use our surplus to build up the kingdom and to help the poor.

Our individual circumstances determine what we can consecrate. Some give time, some give talents, some give money, and some give every combination. King Benjamin indicated that our consecrations may be spiritual or temporal (see Mosiah 4:26). Each of us blesses and builds how and where we can. Sapphira contributed to the Church but not with faith or a full heart. She contrasts starkly with the widow who cast two mites into the treasury and with Mary, who with a heart full of love, poured precious and expensive ointment over the Savior as an offering of full consecration.

Again in contrast to Aquila and Priscilla, Ananias and Sapphira lied to the Lord's chosen leaders. They not only kept back part of the money but tried to deceive the Lord's chosen leaders. Peter makes it clear that when they lied to him, their priesthood leader, they lied to the Holy Ghost and to God. Their lying was also hypocrisy. They wanted to appear to be fully consecrating members without fully sacrificing.

Those who wish to avoid the sin of Sapphira and Ananias do not tell their bishop they are full-tithe payers if they have kept back part. They do not lie to obtain a temple recommend. They recognize the Lord's representatives on earth and are as open with them as they would be with the Lord himself.

The deaths of Ananias and Sapphira are a sober warning about the seriousness of hypocrisy and of lying to the Lord's servants. This type of immediate punishment is rare in both the Old Testament and the New. Occasionally, however, examples are set to teach us the serious nature of various offenses. Latter-day Saint women understand the seriousness of such offenses. They hold nothing back from the Lord, neither consecrated offerings nor the truth. With relief, we return to considering the many faithful sisters this gallery contains.

EUNICE AND LOIS: THE LEGACY OF FAITH

Two faces, one of an older woman and another of a younger woman, fill the next frame in the portrait gallery of the New Testament. They are the faces of Lois and Eunice. In his final epistle to Timothy, Paul spoke of these two sisters of the ancient Church by name. Eunice was the mother of Timothy, and Lois was his grandmother. Paul attributed much of Timothy's faith to these two faithful women: "I call to remembrance the unfeigned faith that is in thee, which dwelt first in thy grandmother Lois, and thy mother Eunice; and I am persuaded that in thee also" (2 Timothy 1:5).

Like the faith of the stripling warriors in the Book of Mormon, Timothy's faith rested upon the legacy of belief and righteousness bestowed by his mother and grandmother. We know nothing more of Lois, but the scriptures do reveal some beautiful truths about Timothy's mother, Eunice.

"Then came [Paul] to Derbe and Lystra: and, behold, a certain disciple was there, named Timotheus, the son of a certain woman, which was a Jewess, and believed; but his father was a Greek" (Acts 16:1). Whether Timothy's Greek father ever joined the early Church we are left to surmise, but his mother believed. Even before accepting the truths of Christ, Eunice and perhaps her mother, Lois, had seen that Timothy was schooled in the scriptures. This we know from Paul's epistle to Timothy, in which Paul described the "perilous times" that would come in the last days and reminded Timothy to "continue thou in the things which thou hast learned and hast been assured of, knowing of whom thou hast learned them; and that from a child thou hast known the holy scriptures, which are able to make thee wise unto salvation through faith which is in Christ Jesus" (2 Timothy 3:1, 14–15).

The teachings of Lois and Eunice and their continual application in his life enabled Timothy to become a "man of God," one "throughly furnished unto all good works" (2 Timothy 3:17). They followed the counsel of Moses: "Thou shalt teach them [the scriptures] diligently unto thy children, and shalt talk of them when thou sittest in thine house, and when thou walkest by the way, and when thou liest down, and when thou risest up" (Deuteronomy 6:6–7). Jewish boys received education in the synagogue, but they were also taught of the scriptures in their homes. Surely Timothy received scriptural tutorials from his mother and grandmother. He continued to build upon the foundation given him by those righteous women.

Eunice and Lois provide a wonderful example for all who must rear their children in perilous times. We must help our children see the power of the scriptures early, so they will have the defenses they need against worldliness and temptation. Particularly if Timothy's father did not believe as his mother did, then the portrait of Eunice provides particular inspiration and hope to thousands of women in the Church who are striving to rear righteous children without a father who is an active member of the Church.

The Lord has frequently described the scriptures as a sword and life as a battle for which we must "put on the whole armour of God" if we hope to survive (Ephesians 6:11). Eunice prepared her son, and he in turn helped prepare others to put on the armor of the Lord.

PHEBE, MARY, PERSIS, CLAUDIA: NAMES FROM THE BOOK OF LIFE

Paul greeted other women in his letters and reminded his readers of the labor these women had contributed in building up the kingdom. We have only the faintest outlines of these good sisters. Phebe was one of them. She was trusted by Paul to carry the epistle to the Romans from Corinth for him. Speaking of her, Paul said, "I commend unto you Phebe our sister, which is a servant of the church which is at Cenchrea: that ye receive her in the Lord, as becometh saints, and that ye assist her in whatsoever business she hath need of you: for she hath been a succourer of many, and of myself also" (Romans 16:1–2).

Paul also spoke of "Mary, who bestowed much labour on us," and the "beloved Persis, which laboured much in the Lord" (Romans 16:6, 12). In 2 Timothy 4:21, Paul mentioned Claudia. He called these women "beloved," as he called Apphia in his epistle to Philemon (Philemon 1:2). Paul was grateful for their service. These sisters and others like them contributed to the success of the early Church, and Paul acknowledged their labor, sacrifice, and love. Perhaps the greatest tribute he could give to them is contained in Philippians, in which he indicated that the names of the wonderful women "which laboured with [him] in the gospel" were written "in the book of life" (Philippians 4:3).

The images of sisters painted in Acts and the Epistles remind us of the images of the sisters of today. The beautiful characteristics and attributes of righteous women have not changed. Latter-day women, too, have believing hearts. They bless and convert their households. They care for the messengers of truth. Their houses are often filled with Saints, who gather to support and strengthen each other. They are filled with "good works and alms-deeds" (Acts 9:36). They rejoice in their prophet and affirm the things they know to be true. Their unity with their husbands and their willingness to sacrifice for the spread of the gospel proclaim their devotion. They love and teach the scriptures, arming others in the Church and, most important, their own children, for the perilous times in which we live. May these latter-day laborers in the gospel receive the assurance that their names also are written in the book of life.

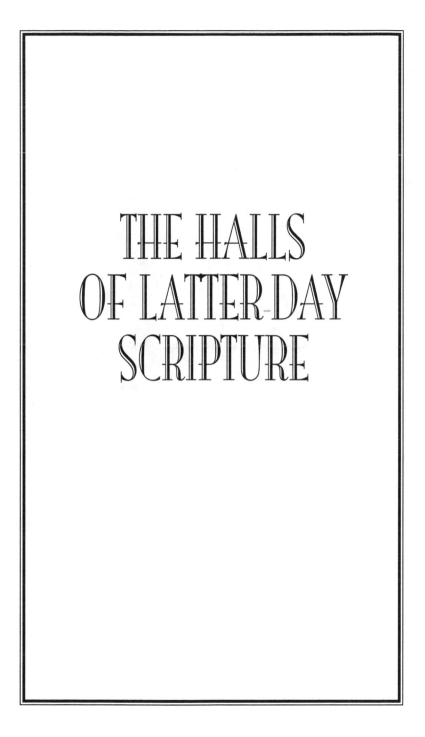

THE HALLS
OF LATTER-DAY
SCRIPTURE

CHAPTER 27

COURAGE IN THE WILDERNESS

We now enter the third wing of the gallery. It is smaller than the others because the Book of Mormon and the Doctrine and Covenants, unlike the Bible, are more doctrinal than narrative in nature. Perhaps because there are fewer of them, the portraits in this part of the gallery become even more precious to us. As with the portraits in the other halls of the gallery, some of these women were not worthy of emulation, but others accomplished wonderful things and moved the Lord's work forward.

The women of the scriptures struggled with human frailties, as we do, but we can still see their most noble selves, as we must learn to see our own nobility. The portrait of Sariah and the portrait of one of the daughters of Ishmael exemplify this principle.

HAVING BEEN BORN OF GOODLY PARENTS

Nephi introduced his mother with the words, "I, Nephi, having been born of goodly parents" (1 Nephi 1:1). Sariah was a good mother who taught her children. Her faith in her husband is demonstrated by her leaving her home and its comforts to share a hard life with her husband in the wilderness. She bore at least two children, Jacob and Joseph, while in the wilderness and suffered extreme trials while journeying to the promised land. Her sons

Nephi and Jacob became great prophets, whose writings have edified millions. Sariah presents an image of successful motherhood and devoted support to a visionary husband.

Yet the portrait of Sariah painted by the scriptures shows us also her humanity. With all her devoted commitment to her husband and the Lord, when her four sons returned to Jerusalem for the brass plates, her faith weakened, and she complained against her husband. "Behold," Sariah said, "thou hast led us forth from the land of our inheritance, and my sons are no more, and we perish in the wilderness" (1 Nephi 5:2). Lehi attempted to comfort her, but her faith was not fully restored until her sons returned. Then she said, "Now I know of a surety that the Lord hath commanded my husband to flee into the wilderness; yea, and I also know of a surety that the Lord hath protected my sons" (1 Nephi 5:8).

WE MUST PERISH IN THE WILDERNESS

The portraits of both Sariah and the daughters of Ishmael show us another very human characteristic. Just as Sariah mourned for her sons, certain that they were no more until they returned alive, when Ishmael died, his daughters "mourn[ed] exceedingly" (1 Nephi 16:35). One of those daughters was Nephi's wife, who must have been noble and righteous. Their mourning for a present trouble extended to encompass both the past and the future: "Our father is dead [the present trial]; yea, and we have wandered much in the wilderness, and we have suffered much affliction, hunger, thirst, and fatigue; [past trials] and after all these sufferings we must perish in the wilderness with hunger [anticipated future sufferings]" (1 Nephi 16:35). They did not "perish in the wilderness with hunger"; on the contrary, they won a promised land. But like Sariah, the daughters of Ishmael feared the worst: "And thus they did murmur against my father, and also against me; and they were desirous to return again to Jerusalem" (1 Nephi 16:36).

It is a human tendency to magnify our trials. Instead of focusing only on the present grief, we remember all our past sorrows.

Then, not content to bear the present and past sorrows, we project the worst case future scenario. Both Sariah and the daughters of Ishmael fell into this pattern. When we do that, we begin to murmur and eventually may give up.

Missionaries may experience this phenomenon during a crisis such as losing a golden investigator, receiving a "Dear John" letter, being assigned a difficult companion, or struggling with a foreign language. Before long they may begin to think about past problems and then project those problems into the future. They will never learn the language, they will never get along with their companion, they will never meet another person like the one who wrote the "Dear John," they will never baptize. The natural consequence of these feelings is to murmur and want to go home.

Bishops witness this phenomenon in counseling with married couples. The couple face a present disagreement or crisis. Before long they begin to detail all the past problems and then project them into the future. If they are not careful, they may conclude that their partner will never change. They begin to murmur, and the desire to give up on the marriage grows. Divorce too often follows.

This pattern is also found in college students who face difficulties mastering certain classes or fulfilling requirements, and missionaries faced with setbacks or disappointments. It is a common pattern for suicide—the most tragic example of desiring to "return to Jerusalem." If we become aware of this pattern, we can work to overcome it.

One can be an exemplary woman, worthy of exaltation and admiration, and still have occasional doubts or complain against a visionary husband. Even Lehi murmured against the Lord when Nephi broke his bow, yet the Lord honored him with tremendous knowledge and wisdom. One can be a noble and devoted mother and struggle with rebellious children. One can project the worst, want to return to Jerusalem, and yet, in time, see the promised land.

We remember, too, that one of the daughters of Ishmael and her mother pleaded so eloquently for Nephi's life that they brought Laman and Lemuel to their knees, asking Nephi to for-give them. In their pleading they reveal the power a woman can wield in softening a hardened heart (see 1 Nephi 7:19).

The portraits of Sariah and the daughters of Ishmael remind us to take comfort, hope, and encouragement from their human-ity. Despite their weaknesses, they rose to meet their challenges and accomplished much good. Our lives may be made better because of them.

CHAPTER 28

REVIVING OLD SECRETS

The oldest historical account in the Book of Mormon gives us the portrait of the daughter of Jared. Though she is certainly one of the most evil women in the scriptures, she is relatively unknown. In some ways, she is a combination of both Jezebel and Delilah, for she seeks power and uses her sensuality and beauty to obtain it. Her portrait is a reminder of the great warning of the Book of Mormon against the evils of pride and of secret combinations.

Omer, a righteous king, was overthrown by his ambitious son, Jared, who was not particularly anxious to wait for his inheritance. He was later defeated by his brothers, who restored the kingdom to their father. "And now Jared became exceedingly sorrowful because of the loss of the kingdom, for he had set his heart upon the kingdom and upon the glory of the world. Now the daughter of Jared being exceedingly expert, and seeing the sorrows of her father, thought to devise a plan whereby she could redeem the kingdom unto her father" (Ether 8:7–8). The phrase "exceedingly expert" is exactly the same phrase used to describe Gadianton in Helaman 2:4. Like Gadianton, the daughter of Jared introduced secret combinations among her people.

"Now the daughter of Jared was exceedingly fair. And it came to pass that she did talk with her father, and said unto him: Whereby hath my father so much sorrow? Hath he not read the record which our fathers brought across the great deep? Behold, is there not an account concerning them of old, that they by their secret plans did obtain kingdoms and great glory?" (Ether 8:9). Of all that she could have learned from the records, she was attracted to and remembered the accounts of the great secret combinations before the Flood. Perhaps her example inspired the instructions Alma the Younger gave Helaman when he transferred the plates of Ether to him: "And now, my son, I command you that ye retain all their oaths, and their covenants, and their agreements in their secret abominations; yea, and all their signs and their wonders ye shall keep from this people, that they know them not, lest peradventure they should fall into darkness also and be destroyed" (Alma 37:27).

The daughter of Jared continued to unfold her plan to her father. "And now, therefore, let my father send for Akish, the son of Kimnor; and behold, I am fair, and I will dance before him, and I will please him, that he will desire me to wife; wherefore if he shall desire of thee that ye shall give unto him me to wife, then shall ye say: I will give her if ye will bring unto me the head of my father, the king. And now Omer was a friend to Akish" (Ether 8:10–11).

Trusting completely in her beauty and sensuality, the daughter of Jared was confident that her plan would work. Her words are calculating and cold. She would use any means, including her natural beauty, to obtain her objective. Marriage could be used to secure power. Lust could stimulate Akish to murder his friend the king.

"When Jared had sent for Akish, the daughter of Jared danced before him that she pleased him, insomuch that he desired her to wife. And it came to pass that he said unto Jared: Give her unto me to wife. And Jared said unto him: I will give her unto you, if ye will bring unto me the head of my father, the king" (Ether 8:11–12). Akish gathered his family and friends and "they formed a secret combination, even as they of old; which combination is most abominable and wicked above all, in the sight of God" (Ether 8:18).

Moroni observed, "And it was the daughter of Jared who put it into his heart to search up these things of old; and Jared put it into the heart of Akish" (Ether 8:17).

The Lord warned Omer to flee. Jared then became king, and "he gave unto Akish his daughter to wife" (Ether 9:4). But Jared had already set in motion a secret combination dedicated to seeking power through assassination. In an ironic twist of events, "Akish sought the life of his father-in-law . . . and they obtained the head of his father-in-law, as he sat upon his throne" (Ether 9:5). If the daughter of Jared could plot to kill her grandfather without hesitation, it is not difficult to believe she could also plot to kill her own father. Plots and counterplots continued until the people destroyed themselves in civil war and Omer and those who fled with him returned to take back the kingdom.

ADAH AND ZILLAH

The evil of the daughter of Jared contrasts sharply with the righteousness of two other women in the scriptures, Adah and Zillah. They were the wives of Lamech, a descendant of Cain and "Master Mahan" of the secret combination of his day. Lamech murdered Irad for having revealed some of their secrets (see Moses 5:47–49). Lamech's wives were horrified by his actions and revealed them. "Their works were abominations, and began to spread among all the sons of men. And it was among the sons of men. And among the daughters of men these things were not spoken, because that Lamech had spoken the secret unto his wives, and they rebelled against him, and declared these things abroad, and had not compassion" (Moses 5:52–53).

The depths of depravity to which participants in secret combinations invariably sink is foreign to the nature of most women, who have no taste for such evil and rightly rebel against it. But like her wicked sisters in the Bible, the daughter of Jared had no such natural revulsion toward evil. She stands out among women not only as evil but also as unnatural.

245

The story of the daughter of Jared is the classic story of a woman who used every resource at her disposal to obtain power. Rather than inspiring those around her to goodness, compassion, and charity, she prodded them to murder and evil. Righteous daughters of God do not use their beauty or their intelligence to promote evil or stimulate the men around them to seek power in unrighteous ways. Exerting this type of influence and responding to the temptation to seek power always ends in disaster and destruction for individuals and for nations.

There is much to be learned from her portrait. But perhaps there is even more to be learned from the portraits of Adah and Zillah, whose rebellion against the evil of Lamech established a standard of behavior that is not as well known as it ought to be. Their choice was undoubtedly difficult, but evil cannot be countenanced, ignored, or tolerated, even when it is perpetuated by those closest to us. In a world where so much sin is hidden, covered up, or rationalized, the portraits of Adah and Zillah in the Lord's gallery may teach us important truths.

CHAPTER 29

WOMEN OF FAITH
AND SACRIFICE

We move now to stand before the portraits of several faithful
Lamanite and Nephite women. In them we see great
beauty and dignity. They are some of the most faithful women in
the scriptures.

In the Doctrine and Covenants the Lord states: "To some it is
given by the Holy Ghost to know that Jesus Christ is the Son of
God, and that he was crucified for the sins of the world. To others
it is given to believe on their words, that they also might have
eternal life" (D&C 46:13–14). The missionary accounts of the
four sons of Mosiah introduce us to women who believe on their
words. Their beautiful portrayal of trusting faith and their willingness to act upon it make them examples for all believers.

LAMONI'S QUEEN:
I HAVE NO WITNESS SAVE THY WORD

When Ammon was taken into Lamoni's custody, his dignity
and willingness to serve quickly gained the king's confidence. His
defense of the king's flocks opened the way for him to teach the
king the gospel. The king believed him, prayed, and fell to the
earth (see Alma 18:41–43).

After two days, the queen, who had not heard Ammon's teaching, "having heard of the fame of Ammon, therefore she sent and desired that he should come in unto her" (Alma 19:2). When Ammon arrived, "she said unto him: The servants of my husband have made it known unto me that thou art a prophet of a holy God, and that thou hast power to do many mighty works in his name; therefore, if this is the case, I would that ye should go in and see my husband, for he has been laid upon his bed for the space of two days and two nights; and some say that he is not dead, but others say that he is dead and that he stinketh, and that he ought to be placed in the sepulchre; but as for myself, to me he doth not stink" (Alma 19:4–5).

Based on the testimony of her husband's servants, Lamoni's queen believed Ammon could bring her husband out of his deep sleep. Ammon visited the king, understood what was happening to him, and explained: "He is not dead, but he sleepeth in God, and on the morrow he shall rise again; therefore bury him not" (Alma 19:8). Ammon then asked her, "Believest thou this?" Perhaps, like Naaman, the queen might have liked him to use his power immediately. Unlike Naaman, she replied, "I have had no witness save thy word, and the word of our servants; nevertheless I believe that it shall be according as thou hast said" (Alma 19:9).

It is difficult to believe when we have had no witness except the words of others, yet that is often what the Lord requires. It might seem to us that the Lord does things backwards. We say to him, "Show me, and I will believe." He replies, "Believe, and I will show you." The scriptures testify that we will "receive no witness until after the trial of [our] faith" (Ether 12:6).

The trusting faith of this Lamanite queen so impressed Ammon that he proclaimed, "Blessed art thou because of thy exceeding faith; I say unto thee, woman, there has not been such great faith among all the people of the Nephites" (Alma 19:10). The queen was so sure of Ammon's words that "she watched over the bed of her husband, from that time even until that time on the morrow which Ammon had appointed that he should rise" (Alma 19:11).

In accordance with her faith and in fulfillment of Ammon's promise, Lamoni arose and "stretched forth his hand unto [his wife] and said: Blessed be the name of God, and blessed art thou." Overcome with joy Lamoni sank again, "and the queen also . . . , being overpowered by the Spirit" (Alma 19:12–13). She who had believed the words of Ammon was now to receive her own witness and add her testimony to her husband's. Their testimonies would begin the wonderful work of conversion among the Lamanites. Her words closely parallel those of her husband when she arose from the ground and saw her people who had gathered in amazement: "O blessed Jesus, who has saved me from an awful hell! O blessed God, have mercy on this people! And when she had said this, she clasped her hands, being filled with joy, speaking many words which were not understood; and when she had done this, she took the king, Lamoni, by the hand, and behold he arose and stood upon his feet" (Alma 19:29–30).

What a wonderful scene these words describe. Lamoni and his wife stand side by side, testifying to the people. Hers was the first testimony to the Lamanite people by one of their own. Together, husband and wife testified and taught. The servants added their witness and soon many "did believe in their words . . . and they became a righteous people" (Alma 19:35).

Like Lamoni's queen, the women my companions and I taught during my mission were ready to believe. Patiently they waited, desiring baptism, while we taught their husbands. As soon as these women received the witness, they desired the blessings of the gospel for themselves and others. I was often impressed with their simple faith.

I recall one evening on my mission teaching a young woman from Italy about the Word of Wisdom. She asked, "My Heavenly Father does not want me to drink?" When we assured her that was true, she went to her cupboard and took to the sink all the bottles of wine and other alcoholic drinks that were there. Without a word, she opened them one after another and poured them down the drain.

The husband of another woman informed us that she would

not be interested in hearing the gospel but that we could teach him. As we did so, his wife quietly washed the dishes behind a curtain that separated their living room from the kitchen. It always seemed to take her a long time to complete her dishes. We learned later that each night she had stood silently behind the curtain, listening intently and believing every word. Her faith later brought her husband into the Church.

We taught many such wonderful women. They were our greatest allies, and their faith led in many cases to the conversion of whole families.

Our skeptical world demands various types of signs before truth is considered verified. Generally we expect to know before we act. Yet the Lord sometimes asks us simply to believe the testimony of others and to act on that belief until he sends the promised confirmation. It is refreshing to gaze upon the portrait of Lamoni's queen, who believed and testified, and to remember a trust and faith greater than that "among all the people of the Nephites" (Alma 19:10).

ABISH: MAINTAINING FAITH IN ISOLATION

Next to the portrait of Lamoni's queen is that of Abish, "one of the Lamanitish women." She also believed because of the words of another. She had been "converted unto the Lord for many years, on account of a remarkable vision of her father" (Alma 19:16). That vision sustained her faith for many years. She sets a unique example for us all, especially for those who are isolated from the supports of the outward Church. Perhaps without a full understanding of the gospel, the ordinance of baptism, or the gift of the Holy Ghost, this Lamanite woman kept her faith. Surrounded by unbelievers, she clung to the faith she had learned from her father. Her faith centered on the Savior, and in her father's testimony. What was true of her was true of all the Anti-Nephi-Lehies, for we read, "as many of the Lamanites as believed . . . and were converted unto the Lord, never did fall away" (Alma 23:6).

We have heard many "Abish stories" from Eastern Europe.

Wonderful Saints there kept their faith. They endured isolation much as she did, with little support except the Spirit and their prayers during World War II and Communist domination. We continue to hear of Saints who accept the gospel in countries where the Church is not officially recognized and where no missionaries are yet allowed. In other areas the Church is just beginning to be established. Members worship in tiny branches. I think of these Saints, and I am awed by the strength of their convictions and their faith.

Abish is an inspiration to every member, whether far from the full programs of the Church or fully involved in them. The Lord needs more people like Abish, who can serve and strengthen the people of their own lands, women and men who maintain their testimony, relying on the Lord for confirmation and support. So few women are mentioned by name in the Book of Mormon. How blessed we are to have the inspiring portrait of Abish preserved to uplift the many Saints who hold tight to their faith in the most demanding circumstances.

With the burning desire to share what she knew, Abish must have rejoiced when she heard her king testify that he had seen the Redeemer and saw the queen "overpowered by the Spirit" (Alma 19:13). In the great mercy and wisdom of the Lord, Abish witnessed all this.

"She knew that it was the power of God; and supposing that this opportunity, by making known unto the people what had happened among them, that by beholding this scene it would cause them to believe in the power of God, therefore she ran forth from house to house, making it known unto the people" (Alma 19:17). It is easy to visualize Abish, filled with happiness and faith, running from door to door. The testimony she had longed to declare needed no longer to be locked inside. She felt sure that the people needed only to see the miraculous manifestation of power to believe. The people could see for themselves and share her joy and faith.

The childlike faith of Abish strikes us deeply. But many did not share her gift. Gathering to witness the scene she had felt was wonderful, they argued. One even tried to kill Ammon. Contention resulted, and when "the woman servant who had caused the multitude to be gathered together came, and when she saw the contention which was among the multitude she was exceedingly sorrowful, even unto tears" (Alma 19:28). Her sorrow could not be contained. She wept openly. Going to the queen, she raised her up, and with the queen's awakening the soul of the Lamanite people began to awaken.

One of the few women named in the Book of Mormon, Abish continues to inspire many who must maintain the integrity of their beliefs virtually alone. Her portrait is reflected in the thousands of Saints who prepare the way in their families, communities, or countries for the spread of the gospel, as they wait faithfully for the full blessings of the Church.

MOTHERS OF THE STRIPLING WARRIORS: THEIR GREATEST GIFT

The next portraits in this area of the gallery are of the mothers of the stripling warriors. Few stories are more inspiring than the account of the Lamanite stripling warriors. We are touched each time we hear the Primary children sing, "We are as the army of Helaman. / We have been taught in our youth" (*Children's Songbook*, 173).

The story of these women begins earlier, in the book of Alma. As the sons of Mosiah enjoyed the freedom to preach, many thousands of Lamanites were converted. The mothers of the stripling warriors were among this group, which came to be called the Anti-Nephi-Lehies because they desired to be "distinguished" from those who did not believe (Alma 23:16). They were distinguished not only in name but also in behavior. They became one of the most powerful examples in the scriptures of being in the world but not of the world. When they arrived in the land of Jershon, "they were among the people of Nephi, and also numbered among the people who were of the church of God. And they were also distinguished for their zeal towards God, and also towards men; for they were perfectly honest and upright in all things; and they were firm in the faith of Christ, even unto the end" (Alma 27:27). They were distinguished among the Lamanites, as well as among the Nephites.

These Lamanite mothers teach us to be distinguished from the world through our honesty, uprightness, and firmness in the faith. It takes far less effort to adopt the outward marks of the world than to develop the inner qualities fostered by the Spirit. What a powerful example the stripling warriors received from the manner in which their parents chose to distinguish themselves. It is not surprising that these sons also distinguished themselves in firmness of faith.

THEY DID BURY THEM DEEP IN THE EARTH

The Anti-Nephi-Lehies are remembered for burying their weapons of war: "This they did, it being in their view a testimony to God, and also to men, . . . that rather than shed the blood of their brethren they would give up their own lives. . . . And thus we see that, when these Lamanites were brought to believe and to know the truth, they were firm, and would suffer even unto death rather than commit sin" (Alma 24:18–19).

The decision to bury the weapons was shared in by the wives, sisters, and daughters. They were severely tried by that commitment. In the first battle 1,005 men were killed before the hearts of the attacking Lamanites were changed. We read: "Now when the Lamanites saw that their brethren would not flee from the sword . . . but that they would lie down and perish, . . . they did forbear from slaying them; and there were many whose hearts had swollen in them for those of their brethren who had fallen. . . . And there was not a wicked man slain among them" (Alma 24:23–24, 27).

What profound effect would the death of 1,005 husbands, brothers, and sons have had on the women? The joy in the additional converts could not compensate for the sorrow of lost loved ones. Yet those who died "praised God even in the very act of perishing under the sword" (Alma 24:23). In time the Anti-Nephi-Lehies were attacked again. Once again they "refused to take their arms, and they suffered themselves to be slain according to the desires of their enemies" (Alma 27:3). How many of the stripling warriors were reared by their mothers alone because their fathers had died to honor their covenant? In spite of all these trials, "as many as . . . were converted unto the Lord, never did fall away" (Alma 23:6).

What an amazing testimony they leave us. They never doubted the justice or the love of God. "He loveth our souls as well as he loveth our children" they testified (Alma 24:14). None turned away in disillusionment, wondering why a loving God could allow such slaughters to take place among them. In time they were delivered by the Nephites who gave them lands and protected them, but before that time came, their faith underwent one of the severest trials named in scripture.

I believe the faith of the striplings' mothers was forged in the crucible of persecution before they were finally rescued by the kindness of the Nephites. They became acquainted with God in their extremities. It is sometimes difficult to maintain faith in the face of overwhelming suffering or persecution, yet these beautiful converts "would suffer death in the most aggravating and distressing manner which could be inflicted by their brethren" (Alma 27:29) and still believed in a God of love and deliverance. That is the faith they passed on to their sons.

WE DO NOT DOUBT OUR MOTHERS KNEW IT

Helaman wrote that the young men of the Anti-Nephi-Lehis "were exceedingly valiant for courage . . . but behold, this was not all—they were men who were true at all times in whatsoever thing they were entrusted. Yea, they were men of truth and soberness, for they had been taught to keep the commandments of God and to walk uprightly before him" (Alma 53:20–21). From whom did they learn to be true in whatsoever thing they were entrusted, if not from their parents who paid the price of faith in the land of Nephi? When facing their first battle, they assured Helaman that all would be well. "They did not fear death . . . yea, they had been taught by their mothers, that if they did not doubt, God would deliver them. And they rehearsed unto me the words of their mothers, saying: We do not doubt our mothers knew it" (Alma 56:47–48).

These women had great faith in the Lord's power to deliver. They taught this faith to their sons, who were full of conviction when the trial of faith commenced. When Helaman saw that his "two thousand and sixty [sons] were firm and undaunted," he remembered "the words which they said unto me that their mothers had taught them" (Alma 57:20–21). We have some of these teachings in the letter Helaman wrote to Captain Moroni. "And now, their preservation was astonishing to our whole army, yea, that they should be spared while there was a thousand of our brethren who were slain. And we do justly ascribe it to the miraculous power of God, because of their exceeding faith in that which they had been taught to believe—that there was a just God, and whosoever did not doubt, that they should be preserved by his marvelous power. Now this was the faith of these of whom I have spoken; they are young, and their minds are firm, and they do put their trust in God continually" (Alma 57:26–27).

This just God had once saved their mothers from spiritual death. These same mothers had cried out, as did Lamoni's queen, "O blessed Jesus, who has saved me from an awful hell!" (Alma 19:29). Even though they had seen husbands and brothers die defenseless under the Lamanites, God was still just. This same Jesus would save their sons if they did not doubt.

What the stripling warriors said about their mothers is impressive. They said not "our mothers taught us" but "our mothers knew it." The mothers gave their sons something more important than teachings—they gave them testimony. One of the greatest gifts a mother gives her children is the gift of her own faith and testimony. Children need the gift of knowing that their mothers know the truthfulness of the gospel.

STIR UP THEIR FAITH TO FEEL AFTER GOD

Joseph Smith taught that the great patriarchs had "stirred up the faith of multitudes to feel after [God]—to search after a knowledge of his character, perfections and attributes, until they became extensively acquainted with him." The Prophet continued, "We have seen that it was human testimony, and human testimony only, that excited this inquiry, in the first instance, in their minds. It was the credence they gave to the testimony of their fathers, this testimony having aroused their minds to inquire after the knowledge of God; the inquiry frequently terminated, indeed always terminated when rightly pursued, in the most glorious discoveries and eternal certainty" (*Lectures on Faith* 2:34, 56).

My mother stirred my faith, as did the mothers of the stripling warriors. I never doubted that my mother knew God watched over his children. I knew how she felt about the Book of Mormon and the Savior. I knew of her faith in the counsels of the prophets. I knew she knew Joseph Smith was a prophet and that the priesthood had power to bless and heal. I knew she believed in prayer and tithing and fasting. Since I was old enough to reason, I knew what my mother knew, and that knowledge inspired me to know for myself. It excited my own faith to feel after God as she had done.

The portrait of these Lamanite mothers illustrates the influence and power of a mother's testimony. Mothers who share their testimony freely and often with their children, both through their words and actions, will see their own striplings feel after God and receive "glorious discoveries and eternal certainty."

As we take a last look at the faces of these Lamanite wives and mothers, we are grateful for the way they have enriched our lives. Like them we will believe the sincere testimony of others. We will cling to our faith, even when we stand alone. Like theirs, our faith in a just and loving God does not falter. We desire to be distinguished through inward righteousness and faith rather than by the outward marks of the world. Above all, we seek to stir up the faith of our children to feel after God through the power of our own testimonies. May our own children echo the words of the stripling warriors, "We do not doubt our mothers knew it" (Alma 56:48).

THE WOMEN OF AMMONIHAH:
NO GREATER SACRIFICE

A group portrait hangs near those of Lamoni's queen, Abish, and the mothers of the stripling warriors. Those Lamanite women saw their husbands, sons, and brothers face death because of their beliefs. This portrait shows the faces of women who themselves faced martyrdom.

Alma found success in almost every city where he went during his mission to reform the Church, but in the city of Ammonihah he confronted a people hardened in apostasy. His first convert was a man "of no small reputation" named Amulek (Alma 10:4). Amulek took Alma into his house and accepted his teachings. He told the people that Alma "blessed mine house, he hath blessed me, and my women, and my children, and my father and my kinsfolk; yea, even all my kindred hath he blessed" (Alma 10:11).

The people of Ammonihah refused to repent. They chased the believing men out of the city, and "sent men to cast stones at them" (Alma 14:7). Then, to mock Alma and Amulek's warning that refusal to repent would result in their being "cast into a lake of fire and brimstone" (Alma 14:14), they "brought their wives and children together, and whosoever believed or had been taught to believe in the word of God they caused that they should be cast into the fire" (Alma 14:8). Amulek's own wife and children may have been burned while he was forced to watch.

"When Amulek saw the pains of the women and children who were consuming in the fire, he also was pained; and he said unto Alma: How can we witness this awful scene? Therefore let us stretch forth our hands, and exercise the power of God which is in us, and save them from the flames" (Alma 14:10).

Alma, however, was constrained by the Spirit not to intercede on their behalf and comforted Amulek with the assurance that "the Lord receiveth them up unto himself, in glory" (Alma 14:11).

Faith sometimes requires the ultimate sacrifice. These

Nephite women were willing to pay that price. If the Lamanite women were not required to lay down their own lives they were willing to do so, and they lost husbands, brothers, and sons—which they might have regarded as being even more terrible than losing their own lives. In Ammonihah, the men escaped, but the women and children paid the supreme price, and "the Lord receiv[ed] them up unto himself, in glory." They have a place with the Father throughout the eternities. What Alma promised Amulek concerning the women and children of Ammonihah extends to all who have sacrificed for their beliefs. Though we may be asked to sacrifice all we have and love, even our own lives, the Father will receive us to himself in glory.

CHAPTER 30

MANY HEARTS DIED, PIERCED WITH DEEP WOUNDS

In the next room of the scriptural gallery are grouped the portraits of women spoken of in the Book of Mormon who found themselves the victims of abuse in one form or another. Among these women were the wives and daughters of the Nephites during the time of Jacob, the twenty-four young Lamanite women who were kidnapped by the wicked priests of King Noah, Morianton's maid during the wars at the time of Captain Moroni, and the women and children who endured tremendous suffering during the last battles between the Nephites and Lamanites. It is wicked that the abuse of women and children should continue to this day and that even Latter-day Saint women should find themselves in abusive situations. Yet the portraits in this room of the gallery offer great hope and insight.

NEPHITE WIVES AND DAUGHTERS

The writings of Jacob in the Book of Mormon express without equivocation the evils of abuse, particularly when that abuse is committed by a husband or father. Jacob was instructed by his brother Nephi to record in the small plates only those things that were "most precious . . . sacred . . . or great" (Jacob 1:2, 4). He chose to preserve his instructions concerning the pain the husbands and fathers had caused their wives and children by their unrighteous desires.

The prophet Jacob was conscious of the "tender and chaste and delicate" feelings of the women and wished to give them the "pleasing word of God, yea, the word which healeth the wounded soul" (Jacob 2:7–8). He chastised the husbands and fathers for their "grosser crimes" and quoted the Lord's words: "I, the Lord God, delight in the chastity of women. . . . I, the Lord, have seen the sorrow, and heard the mourning of the daughters of my people . . . , because of the wickedness and abominations of their husbands. . . . they shall not lead away captive the daughters of my people because of their tenderness, save I shall visit them with a sore curse, even unto destruction" (Jacob 2:23, 28–33). Jacob added his own admonition, concluding with the often tragic results of rejection and abuse: "Ye have done greater iniquities than the Lamanites. . . . Ye have broken the hearts of your tender wives, and lost the confidence of your children, . . . and the sobbings of their hearts ascend up to God against you. And because of the strictness of the word of God, which cometh down against you, many hearts died, pierced with deep wounds" (Jacob 2:35).

In contrast to the deep wounds inflicted by Nephite husbands and fathers, Jacob spoke of the family unity and love that existed among the Lamanites: "[They] are more righteous than you. . . . Behold, their husbands love their wives, and their wives love their husbands; and their husbands and their wives love their children" (Jacob 3:5, 7).

Modern prophets, too, have spoken plainly about the evils of abuse, offering comfort and recognition to women of today who suffer as their sisters suffered in the days of Jacob. President Gordon B. Hinckley stated: "My heart reaches out to . . . [those] who by the circumstances in which they find themselves feel oppressed and smothered—all but destroyed. I regret that there are some men who are egotistical and evil, who are insensitive and even brutal. They are to be both condemned and pitied. I believe that any man who offends a daughter of God will some day be held accountable, and the time will come when he will stand before the bar of judgment with sorrow and remorse" ("Rise to the Stature of the Divine within You," 95). President Hinckley also spoke of "the terrible, inexcusable, and evil phenomenon of physical and sexual abuse. It is unnecessary. It is unjustified. It is indefensible" (Conference Report, October 1994, 73).

Perhaps the great value of Jacob's decision to include in the Book of Mormon his words regarding these "grosser crimes" lies not so much in his condemnation of the husbands and fathers or in his description of the painful consequences of abuse as in the counsel he gives to the victims of abuse, whom he called, significantly, the "pure in heart" (Jacob 3:1). Even though they did not enjoy the love and tenderness which they deserved from their husbands and fathers, they were counseled to do at least five things:

First, "look unto God with firmness of mind" (Jacob 3:1). "Firmness of mind" suggests a consistent, unwavering focus on the Lord with the firm expectation that his love and mercy will in time heal wounds and mend shattered lives. Jacob reiterated this "firmness" as he concluded his counsel. Elder Richard G. Scott gave similar counsel to abuse victims: "Recognize that you are a beloved child of your Heavenly Father. He loves you perfectly and can help you as no earthly parent, spouse, or devoted friend can" (Conference Report, April 1992, 44).

Second, "pray unto [God] with exceeding faith" (Jacob 3:1). Elder Scott gave similar counsel to that of Jacob: "Healing best begins with your sincere prayer asking your Father in Heaven for help" (Conference Report, April 1992, 44). Jacob indicated that praying with faith will bring three results: God "will console you in your afflictions," "plead your cause," and "send down justice upon those who seek your destruction" (Jacob 3:1).

Third, "lift up your heads" (Jacob 3:2). There are many reasons for those who have received the wounds of abuse to hang down their heads in sorrow and pain. Sadly, victims often hang down their heads in guilt or shame. Elder Scott declared: "I solemnly testify that when another's acts of violence, perversion, or incest hurt you terribly, against your will, you are not responsible and you must not feel guilty" (Conference Report, April 1992, 44). The Church publication *For the Strength of Youth* assures victims of abuse that they "are not guilty of sin. If you have been a victim of any of these terrible crimes, be assured that God still loves you!" (15).

Fourth, "receive the pleasing word of God" (Jacob 3:2). We may receive the word of God through the Holy Spirit, who is also called the Comforter; the teachings and counsel of our leaders, particularly the prophets and apostles; and the scriptures. Assurances and counsel specific for each situation may be found by turning to these sources in times of confusion, fear, or sorrow.

Finally, "feast upon [God's] love; for ye may, if your minds are firm, forever" (Jacob 3:2). Whether abused, abandoned, constantly criticized, or rejected, we may often be left thirsting for love and acceptance. Jacob assures us all that not only does our Father in Heaven love us but we may feast on his love, the never-failing source of spiritual nourishment.

TWENTY-FOUR LAMANITE DAUGHTERS

The portraits of the young Lamanite women show the fear and suffering inflicted on them by the wicked priests of King Noah. Led by Amulon, the wicked Nephite priests caused suffering for both their own wives and children and also for the Lamanite women they kidnapped. Fearful for their own safety and slowed in their flight by their families, the wicked priests left their wives and children to the mercy of the Lamanite army and saved themselves. Fortunately the pleadings and the beauty of the Nephite women pacified the Lamanites, and they were spared. "The priests of king Noah, being ashamed to return to the city of Nephi . . . therefore they durst not return to their wives and their children. And having tarried in the wilderness, and having discovered the daughters of the Lamanites, they laid and watched them; and when there were but few of them gathered together to dance, they came forth out of their secret places and took them and carried them into the wilderness" (Mosiah 20:3–5).

It is not difficult to imagine the terror of these Lamanite daughters, though we do not hear of them again until a Lamanite army discovered the hiding place of the wicked priests while they were pursuing Limhi's people. "Amulon . . . sent forth their wives, who were the daughters of the Lamanites, to plead with their brethren, that they should not destroy their husbands. And the Lamanites had compassion on Amulon and his brethren, and did not destroy them, because of their wives" (Mosiah 23:33–34).

I have often wondered how the fear and violence of their capture by Amulon and the other priests turned into pleading for husbands. It may suggest that, given a terrifying situation from which they had no means of escape, these twenty-four young women somehow adjusted, forgave, and made the best life they could for themselves and their children. That solution may not be ideal, but their struggles and reconciliation may provide insight and counsel for some individuals today.

MORIANTON'S MAID

Next we see the portrait of the courageous maidservant of Morianton. During the great Nephite and Lamanite wars, Morianton and those who followed him tried to flee to the land northward, which "would have been a cause to have been lamented" (Alma 50:30). The plan would have been successful had it not been for one of Morianton's maidservants. "Morianton being a man of much passion, therefore he was angry with one of his maid servants, and he fell upon her and beat her much" (Alma 50:30).

The decision of the maidservant may be instructive to others who find themselves in situations of physical abuse. "And it came to pass that she fled, and came over to the camp of Moroni, and told Moroni all things concerning the matter" (Alma 50:31). When abuse reaches the level inflicted by Morianton, the correct response is to do what this woman did: Flee the situation, and seek help from those who can assist. Very important, also, is the maidservant's telling "all things concerning the matter." Abuse need not be tolerated by any woman or child.

In this case, the actions of the maidservant not only removed her from the abusive situation but saved the whole Nephite nation from a lamentable situation. Moroni was able to stop Morianton's flight and restore the security of the people.

Joseph Smith was a gentle, meek, and forgiving man. Rarely did he react strongly or with anger, yet one of the few times in his life that he fought another man was on account of that man's treatment of his wife. Joseph wrote: "I'll tell you a story: A man who whips his wife is a coward. When I was a boy, I once fought with a man who had whipped his wife. It was a hard contest; but I still remembered that he had whipped his wife; and this encouraged me, and I whipped him till he said he had enough" (*History of the Church*, 5:285). Even as a boy, Joseph knew that this kind of behavior was inexcusable and must be stopped.

WOMEN IN TIMES WITHOUT CIVILIZATION

The last group of portraits in this section of the gallery depicts the faces of the Nephite and Lamanite women and children who were victims of the savage warfare between their peoples. Mormon wrote his son Moroni a letter that Moroni included in the last chapters of the Book of Mormon. In this letter Mormon described the atrocities both sides were committing. The letter emphasizes the suffering of the women and children:

"The Lamanites have many prisoners . . . men, women, and children. And the husbands and fathers of those *women* and *children* they have slain; and they feed the women upon the flesh of their husbands, and the children upon the flesh of their fathers. . . . And notwithstanding this great abomination of the Lamanites, it doth not exceed that of our people in Moriantum. For behold many of the *daughters* of the Lamanites have they taken prisoners; and after depriving them of that which was most dear and precious above all things, which was chastity and virtue—And after they had done this thing, they did murder them in a most cruel manner, torturing their bodies even unto death. . . . There are many *widows* and their *daughters* who remain in Sherrizah; and that part of the provisions which the Lamanites did not carry away, behold, the army of Zenephi has carried away, and left them to wander whithersoever they can for food, and many *old women* do faint by the way and die. . . . And as many as have fled to the army of Aaron have fallen victims to their awful brutality. O the depravity of my people! They are without order and without mercy . . . and the suffering of our *women* and our *children* upon all the face of this land doth exceed everything; yea, tongue cannot tell, neither can it be written. . . . Behold, my son, I cannot recommend them unto God lest he should smite me" (Moroni 9:7–21; emphasis added).

This shocking portrayal is of a people who had been "a civil and a delightsome people" only a few years previous (Moroni 9:12). Mormon summarized this treatment of women and children: "O my beloved son, how can a people like this, that are *without civilization*— . . . how can we expect that God will stay his hand in judgment against us?" (Moroni 9:11, 14; emphasis added).

One critical measure of a civilized people is its treatment of women and children. Regardless of the advancements a society may make in any other field, be it artistic, technological, scientific, or political, if it fails to treat women and children in a respectful, gentle, and dignified manner, that society is "without civilization." What is true of a whole people is also true of individuals. If one person abuses another, he is considered by the Lord to be "without civilization."

If we may render aid or alleviate the suffering caused by abuse, we must do so. And, of course, we must be sure that we do not commit such evils ourselves. In time, with the Lord's help, we pray that abuse of every kind will cease. Until then, however, we may revisit the portraits in this room of the gallery to find insight, encouragement, and renewed resolve to fight against such evils.

CHAPTER 31

VIENNA JAQUES, A WOMAN OF CONSECRATION

The portrait of Vienna Jaques is one both of remarkable faith and of enduring faithfully to the end. In Doctrine and Covenants 90, the Lord revealed his will to Joseph Smith concerning "my handmaid Vienna Jaques." At the time of this revelation there were two centers of Church population—Kirtland, Ohio, and Jackson County, Missouri. The Lord told the Prophet that Vienna "should receive money to bear her expenses, and go up unto the land of Zion; and the residue of the money may be consecrated unto me, and she be rewarded in mine own due time." Once she arrived in Missouri, the Lord instructed that she should "receive an inheritance from the hand of the bishop; that she may settle down in peace inasmuch as she is faithful, and not be idle in her days from thenceforth" (D&C 90:28–31).

These instructions are remarkable in light of the facts of Vienna's life and the situation in Missouri at the time. The money she was to receive to bear her expenses was her own money. Vienna had joined the Church in the East after considerable reflection and study. Then she traveled to Kirtland to see the man she firmly believed was a prophet of God. After a visit of several weeks, she returned to Boston to convert her mother, sister, and nieces. She settled her affairs in Boston and returned to Kirtland with about fourteen hundred dollars. In Kirtland she followed the Lord's instructions to consecrate her resources to the Church.

The Prophet wrote to Vienna, expressing his gratitude for her consecration and telling her the whisperings of the Spirit he had received concerning her: "Joseph, thou art indebted to thy God for the offering of thy Sister Vienna, which proved a savor of life as pertaining to thy pecuniary concerns. Therefore she should not be forgotten of thee, for the Lord hath done this, and thou shouldst remember her in all thy prayers and also by letter, for she oftentimes calleth on the Lord saying, O Lord, inspire thy servant Joseph to communicate by letter some word to thine unworthy handmaiden, and say all my sins are forgiven, and art thou content with the chastisement wherewith thou hast chastised thy handmaiden?" Joseph further wrote, "Let your heart be comforted; live in strict obedience to the commandments of God, and walk humbly before Him, and He will exalt thee in His own due time. I will assure you that the Lord has respect unto the offering you made" (Smith, *History of the Church*, 1:408).

The Lord, cognizant of Vienna's desires to know of her standing before him, answered her prayers as she requested. The Prophet responded, that she might know the Lord was pleased with her sacrifice. But even though she was "faithful," as the revelation directed her to be, Vienna never "settle[d] down in peace" in Missouri. Within a few months of the date of this revelation, 8 March 1833, the persecutions in Missouri began, leading eventually to the expulsion of the Saints from the state. During this time of trial and throughout the next few years, many Saints left the Church. That was not true of Vienna, however. Her faith in the Prophet and the cause of Zion remained steadfast. In this way, her portrait is like that of many other women in the scriptures who, though apparently denied the blessings they were promised, continued in faith, never faltering nor turning away in bitterness or cynicism.

The peace Vienna Jaques was promised did not come until the Church was established in Salt Lake. At age sixty, she drove her own wagon across the plains, arriving in Utah in October 1847. True to the instruction given her, Vienna refused to be idle, remaining active in worthy pursuits for the rest of her life. She lived to the age of ninety-two, and when she died, Wilford Woodruff, who was then president of the Church, spoke at her funeral.

The beauty and power of Vienna's portrait is reflected in the faces of thousands of other women whose lives have followed the pattern hers did. She and other sisters of the Restoration may not be well known to many today, but the Lord knows them well. He has heard their prayers and accepted their consecrations, and he will reward them fully for their quiet, faithful contributions to the building up of his kingdom on the earth.

CHAPTER 32

LUCY MACK SMITH, THE MOTHER OF THE PROPHET

Every book of scripture opens with the portrait of noble women. In the Old Testament and Pearl of Great Price we are introduced to Eve. The life of Christ in the New Testament begins with Mary, and the Book of Mormon begins with Sariah faithfully blessing her family. Likewise there are many noble women of the Restoration; one of the noblest was Lucy Mack Smith, mother of the Prophet Joseph Smith. Hers is the portrait we see before us now.

Lucy Mack Smith is spoken of in Doctrine and Covenants 137 and in the Pearl of Great Price in Joseph Smith–History. As the mother of the first latter-day prophet, she was called to prepare Joseph for his role in the Restoration, and she was among the very first to believe his message of restored truth.

After the First Vision, Joseph responded to his mother's concern for him with the words, "I am well enough off. . . . I have learned for myself that Presbyterianism is not true" (Joseph Smith–History 1:20). Lucy had been "proselyted to the Presbyterian faith, and . . . joined that church" (Joseph Smith–History 1:7), but from the very beginning of the Restoration, she believed and supported her son. Through the long years of persecution and betrayal, she strengthened, comforted, and counseled him. She saw her husband and four of her sons buried as a result of the persecutions they suffered.

The Prophet recorded the names of "the faithful few" in a book he entitled "The Book of the Law of the Lord." These were souls "such as have stood by me in every hour of peril." Of his mother he wrote:

"Words and language are inadequate to express the gratitude that I owe to God for having given me so honorable a parentage.

"My mother also is one of the noblest and the best of all women. May God grant to prolong her days and mine, that we may live to enjoy each other's society long" (Smith, *History of the Church*, 5:124, 126).

On his deathbed Joseph Smith Sr. turned to Lucy and said, "Mother, do you not know, that you are one of the most singular women in the world? . . . you have brought up my children for me by the fireside, and when I was gone from home, you comforted them. You have brought up all my children, and could always comfort them when I could not. We have often wished that we might both die at the same time, but you must not desire to die when I do, for you must stay to comfort the children when I am gone" (Smith, *History of Joseph Smith by His Mother*, 313).

Lucy's strength and remarkable character were known to the Lord. In January 1836, Joseph was shown a vision of the celestial kingdom. Within the gates of that kingdom, he "saw Father Adam and Abraham; and my father and my mother . . ." (D&C 137:5). Years before her death, Lucy Mack Smith knew she would inherit a place in the highest degree of glory. What comfort this revelation must have given her in the years of suffering and trial that followed.

What must the Lord know about an individual before he confirms their exaltation in the celestial kingdom? "After a person has faith in Christ," Joseph Smith wrote, "repents of his sins, and is baptized for the remission of his sins and receives the Holy Ghost . . . , then let him continue to humble himself before God, hungering and thirsting after righteousness, and living by every word of God, and the Lord will soon say unto him, Son, thou shalt be exalted. When the Lord has thoroughly proved him, and finds that the man is determined to serve Him at all hazards, then the man will find his calling and his election made sure" (*Teachings of the Prophet Joseph Smith,* 150).

Lucy lived up to those conditions, and therefore, it was her privilege to know, twenty years before her death, that her exaltation was assured. The following incident, recorded in her history of the Prophet, shows us the strength of her character:

Joseph and Hyrum were suffering the horrible effects of cholera, which attacked them while they were in Zion's Camp, and they joined in prayer to beseech the Lord to spare their lives. "'We still besought the Lord, with all our strength, to have mercy upon us, but all in vain. It seemed as though the heavens were sealed against us, and that every power that could render us any assistance was shut within its gates. We then kneeled down the third time, concluding never to rise to our feet again until one or the other should get a testimony that we should be healed; and that the one who should get the first intimation of the same from the Spirit, should make it known to the other.'

"... the cramp began to release its hold; and, in a short time, Hyrum sprang to his feet and exclaimed, 'Joseph, we shall return to our families. I have had an open vision, in which I saw mother kneeling under an apple tree; and she is even now asking God, in tears, to spare our lives, that she may again behold us in the flesh. The Spirit testifies, that her prayers, united with ours, will be answered.'

"'Oh my mother!' said Joseph, 'how often have your prayers been the means of assisting us when the shadows of death encompassed us'"(Smith, *History of Joseph Smith by His Mother,* 228–29).

In a discourse he gave on the resurrection, the Prophet spoke of his desire to greet those most dear to his heart when the graves were opened. He had seen a vision of the resurrection and knew the joy of embracing loved ones. "When we lie down we contemplate how we may rise in the morning; and it is pleasing for friends to lie down together, locked in the arms of love, to sleep and wake in each other's embrace and renew their conversation. . . . So plain was the vision, that I actually saw men, before they had ascended from the tomb, as though they were getting up slowly. They took each other by the hand and said to each other, 'My father, my son, my mother, my daughter, my brother, my sister.' And when the voice calls for the dead to arise, suppose I am laid by the side of my father, what would be the first joy of my heart? To meet my father, my mother, my brother, my sister; and when they are by my side, I embrace them and they me" (Smith, *History of the Church*, 5:361–2).

In light of these sentiments it is not difficult to understand why Lucy Mack Smith told the Saints of Nauvoo: "I feel that the Lord will let Brother Brigham take the people away. Here, in this city, lay my dead; my husband and children; and if so be the rest of my children go with you, (and would to God they may all go), they will not go without me; and if I go, I want my bones brought back in case I die away, and deposited with my husband and children" (Smith, *History of the Church*, 7:471).

The commitment to her family and the unity her commitment helped to create are clearly visible in this portrait of Lucy Mack Smith, mother of the Prophet of the Restoration. May her commitment and strength of purpose continue to inspire us whenever we think of her.

CHAPTER 33

EMMA HALE SMITH,
AN ELECT LADY

We turn now to the portrait of Emma Hale Smith, wife of the great Prophet of the Restoration. Her portrait is different from many of the previous ones we have seen, for it is composed of instructions given to Emma and not specific events from her life.

Early in the Restoration, the Lord gave a revelation to Emma Smith that depicts the characteristics he desires in his daughters as they participate in his latter-day kingdom and seek to attain celestial glory. This revelation, recorded in what is now Doctrine and Covenants 25, was given to Emma, "an elect lady, whom I have called" (v. 3). The last verse of the revelation explains, "And verily, verily, I say unto you, that this is my voice unto all" (v. 16). It presents a pattern of exaltation for all women who would be "elect ladies," for one who is elected by the Lord is one chosen to serve.

The revelation begins with a greeting: "Hearken unto the voice of the Lord your God, while I speak unto you, Emma Smith, my daughter; for verily I say unto you, all those who receive my gospel are sons and daughters in my kingdom" (D&C 25:1).

Anyone who reads this greeting could substitute her own name for Emma's. There is little in this revelation that cannot be applied to every woman. For instance, the Lord told Emma he would give her a revelation concerning his will and promised she would "receive an inheritance in Zion" (D&C 25:2). That is the reward for all who can learn from and apply the principles taught in Doctrine and Covenants 25.

WALK IN THE PATHS OF VIRTUE

Emma is encouraged to be "faithful and walk in the paths of virtue before me." Notice that it is the *paths,* not *path,* of virtue. The word *virtue* has many meanings, all of which can clarify what the paths of virtue are. Today the primary meaning of *virtue* may be "chastity," and without doubt, one of the paths of virtue is obeying the law of chastity. Those who walk this path believe virtue is "most dear and precious above all things" (Moroni 9:9).

But there are other meanings of *virtue* as well. One of them is described in the thirteenth Article of Faith: "If there is anything virtuous, lovely, or of good report or praiseworthy, we seek after these things." When the Lord counseled Emma to walk in the paths of virtue, he was encouraging her to actively seek the finest literature, entertainment, music, art, friendships, and environments. Similarly, in the Book of Mormon, the prophet Mormon admonished his people to "judge," "search diligently," "lay hold on," and "cleave unto every good thing" that "persuadeth," "inviteth and enticeth to do good, and to love God, and to serve him" (Moroni 7:13–28). Mormon called this type of virtue-directed life a "peaceable walk."

As we saw in the portrait gallery of the Old Testament, Ruth lived her life in the paths of virtue. Boaz described her as "a virtuous woman" (Ruth 3:11), whose portrait is a study of compassion, selflessness, service, loyalty, and industry. She walked the paths of virtue.

When the Nephite men wished to compromise the virtue of the Nephite daughters, Jacob chastened in words that add to our understanding of the paths of virtue. Jacob testified that the feelings of the wives were "exceedingly tender and chaste and delicate before God, which thing is pleasing unto God" (Jacob 2:7). He expressed his fear that his word would "wound their delicate minds" (v. 9) and spoke of the Lord's concern that his sons not take advantage of his daughters' tenderness (see v. 33). *Tender, chaste,* and *delicate* are marvelous words to describe the paths of virtue. The Lord is pleased when his daughters exhibit these traits.

Tenderness suggests a compassionate, sensitive, gentle character. Joseph Smith told the first Relief Society that "this is a charitable Society, and *according to your natures;* it is natural for females to have feelings of charity and benevolence. You are now placed in a situation in which you can act according to *those sympathies which God has planted in your bosoms.* If you live up to these principles, how great and glorious will be your reward in the celestial kingdom!" (*Teachings of the Prophet Joseph Smith,* 226).

Jacob also used the word *delicate,* which suggests a certain reverence towards life and the avoidance of light-minded, vulgar, or suggestive things. The path of virtue is a path of refinement. This characteristic is reflected in a person's feelings, dress, language, demeanor, and so forth. Refinement is a dying virtue, but Latter-day Saint women continue to cultivate it and teach it to their sons and daughters. They know that light-mindedness, vulgarity, and irreverence almost always go hand in hand to destroy our sensitivity to tender, chaste, and delicate feelings. For example, the Lord's counsel in the Doctrine and Covenants 88:121 to avoid loud or excessive laughter means to avoid vulgar, irreverent humor, not to avoid seemly and appropriate joyousness. The path of refinement avoids light-minded speeches and laughter.

Emma is promised that the Lord "will preserve thy life, and thou shalt receive an inheritance in Zion" (D&C 25:2). That is the natural and desirable destination of the paths of virtue.

MURMUR NOT BECAUSE OF THINGS WHICH ARE WITHHELD

After calling Emma "an elect lady," the Lord counseled her not to murmur "because of the things which thou hast not seen"

(D&C 25:4). We are not told what Emma had not seen, but we can imagine. Emma played a great supportive role while Joseph translated the Book of Mormon. She spoke of the plates being wrapped in cloth and of her moving them in order to clean. What tremendous self-restraint she must have had to not look under the cloth. Having assisted in the work of translation, Emma surely would have desired to see the plates. Though she was denied this privilege and in spite of later difficulties, Emma never denied her testimony of the Book of Mormon or of Joseph's prophetic call.

All of us are tempted to murmur when we feel worthy to receive desired blessings and cannot understand why the Lord withholds them. It is most difficult during these times to avoid murmuring and to trust the wisdom of the Lord. Some day we will see the wisdom of the Lord, but until then, we must try not to murmur. Doctrine and Covenants 25 reminds us to trust the Lord's wisdom until we receive understanding.

A COMFORT UNTO MY SERVANT, JOSEPH

Emma was called to be a "comfort unto my servant, Joseph Smith, Jun., thy husband, in his afflictions, with consoling words, in the spirit of meekness" (D&C 25:5). Considering all the persecutions, trials, and anxieties that Joseph Smith—and with him, his family—experienced, this calling of Emma's was especially important. Joseph spent his life and energy caring for, blessing, and comforting the Church. He was a tender and considerate husband and father. We know he was deeply grateful that Emma fulfilled her calling of comforting and consoling him in such an admirable manner.

Joseph Smith gave counsel to the first Relief Society that is directly related to the calling of giving comfort. "Let this Society teach women how to behave towards their husbands," he instructed, "to treat them with mildness and affection. When a man is borne down with trouble, when he is perplexed with care and difficulty, if he can meet a smile instead of an argument or a murmur—if he can meet with mildness, it will calm down his soul and soothe his feelings; when the mind is going to despair, it needs a solace of affection and kindness" (*Teachings of the Prophet Joseph Smith*, 228).

LIBERTY JAIL

The Prophet's advice makes me think of his experiences in Liberty Jail and the beautiful revelations he received there, recorded now in Doctrine and Covenants 121, 122, and 123. Joseph Smith had reached a low point, and his "mind [was] going to despair" (*Teachings of the Prophet Joseph Smith*, 228). He pleaded with the Lord and cried: "O God, where art thou? And where is the pavilion that covereth thy hiding place? How long shall thy hand be stayed, and thine eye . . . behold from the eternal heavens the wrongs of thy people and of thy servants, and thine ear be penetrated with their cries? Yea, O Lord, how long shall they suffer these wrongs and unlawful oppressions, before thine heart shall be softened toward them, and thy bowels be moved with compassion toward them?" (D&C 121:1–3).

Just before recounting the Lord's answer of peace Joseph recorded, "We received some letters last evening—one from Emma, one from Don C. Smith, and one from Bishop Partridge—all breathing a kind and consoling spirit. We were much gratified with their contents. . . . and when we read those letters they were to our souls as the gentle air is refreshing. . . . those who have not been enclosed in the walls of prison without cause or provocation, can have but little idea how sweet the voice of a friend is; it moves the mind backward and forward, from one thing to another, until finally all enmity, malice and hatred, and past differences, misunderstandings and mismanagements are slain victorious at the feet of hope; and when the heart is sufficiently contrite, then the voice of inspiration steals along and whispers, ['My son peace be unto thy soul' . . .]" (*History of the Church*, 3:293).

The comforting words in Emma's letter produced in her husband a spirit that invited the Lord to reveal to him some of the most loved and beautiful words in latter-day revelation. They were the catalyst for the comfort that only the Lord's Spirit can bring. How often did Emma's influence give Joseph the calm he needed to receive inspiration? Surely the calling of Emma to serve as a comfort with consoling words was a most necessary and important calling associated with the Restoration.

IN THE SEVENTH TROUBLE

At another trying period of Joseph's life he was in hiding on an island in the Mississippi. Joseph sent word that he wished to see Emma, his brother Hyrum, and a few others. Joseph wrote of the events that followed: "I was much rejoiced to meet my dear wife once more. . . . Spent the forenoon chiefly in conversation with Emma on various subjects, and in reading my history with her—both felt in good spirits and very cheerful" (*History of the Church*, 5:92).

Joseph recalled the night they visited on the island. "How glorious were my feelings when I met that faithful and friendly band, on the night of the eleventh, on Thursday, on the island . . . with what unspeakable delight, and what transports of joy swelled my bosom, when I took by the hand, on that night, my beloved Emma—she that was my wife, even the wife of my youth, and the choice of my heart. Many were the reverberations of my mind when I contemplated for a moment the many scenes we had been called to pass through, the fatigues and the toils, the sorrows and sufferings, and the joys and consolations, from time to time, which had strewed our paths and crowned our board. Oh what a commingling of thought filled my mind for the moment, again she is here, even in the seventh trouble—undaunted, firm, and unwavering—unchangeable, affectionate Emma!" (*History of the Church*, 5:107).

What a tender and eloquent tribute! Many a husband and child have known the feelings the Prophet so beautifully expressed. To be a comforter is a call of tremendous significance. I believe Mary and Martha and others had such an effect on the Savior. Indeed, elect ladies of any era in time have had this same effect on their families and on their friends.

THOU SHALT GO WITH HIM AT
THE TIME OF HIS GOING

Emma was counseled to "go with [Joseph] at the time of his going" (D&C 25:6). An elect lady sustains her husband in his various responsibilities, just as Eve labored with Adam. Obedience to this commandment often requires considerable sacrifice. Lucy Mack Smith wrote of Emma, "I have never seen a woman in my life, who would endure every species of fatigue and hardship, from month to month, and from year to year, with that unflinching courage, zeal, and patience, which she has ever done; for I know that which she has had to endure . . . she has breasted the storms of persecution, and buffeted the rage of men and devils, which would have borne down almost any other woman" (*History of Joseph Smith by His Mother*, 190–91).

EXPOUND THE SCRIPTURES AND
EXHORT THE CHURCH

The Lord told Emma, "And thou shalt be ordained under his hand to expound scriptures, and to exhort the church, according as it shall be given thee by my Spirit. For he shall lay his hands upon thee, and thou shalt receive the Holy Ghost, and thy time shall be given to writing, and to learning much" (D&C 25:7–8). Emma was to improve her mind, specifically by studying the scriptures and the revelations. Moreover, the Lord told Emma to "expound scriptures," not just learn them, and to "exhort the church." *Expound* and *exhort* are two words used in Doctrine and Covenants 20 to describe responsibilities of the priesthood. Men and women thus have a similar commission in this area.

Joseph Smith gave us an important key to understanding what it means to expound the truths of the scriptures. After being baptized and receiving the Holy Ghost, Joseph wrote: "We were filled with the Holy Ghost, and rejoiced in the God of our salvation. Our minds being now enlightened, we began to have the scriptures laid open to our understandings, and the true meaning and intention of their more mysterious passages revealed unto us in a manner which we never could attain to previously, nor ever before had thought of" (Joseph Smith—History 1:73–74).

It does not require great scholarship or many commentaries to understand the scriptures. It requires the Holy Ghost and what President Gordon B. Hinckley called "a love affair with the word of the Lord and that of his prophets" (*Church News,* 17 March 1985, 3). President Spencer W. Kimball spoke of the great need for the sisters of the Church to be able to expound scriptures: "We want our homes to be blessed with sister scriptorians . . . After all, who has any greater need to 'treasure up' the truths of the gospel (on which they may call in their moments of need) than do women and mothers who do so much nurturing and teaching" (*Teachings of Spencer W. Kimball,* 321).

It requires the Holy Ghost to expound scripture and exhort the Church properly, and Emma was promised Joseph would "lay his hands upon thee, and thou shalt receive the Holy Ghost" (D&C 25:8). Teaching and exhorting by the Spirit occurs every day in the Church. I first learned the gospel from the scriptural understanding of my mother, and I have been edified and instructed by sister scriptorians throughout my life. They have brought a sensitivity and refinement of insight to their under-standing of the scriptures.

THY TIME SHALL BE GIVEN TO LEARNING MUCH

As if to place a capstone on the principle of growth in knowl-edge (particularly, but not exclusively, revealed knowledge), the Lord told Emma to devote her time to "learning much" (D&C 25:8). Although this learning begins with the scriptures and the words of the prophets, it may be broadened to include all truth. The Lord has instructed us to "teach one another the doctrine of the kingdom," including "things both in heaven and in the earth, and under the earth; things which have been, things which are, things which must shortly come to pass; things which are at home, things which are abroad; the wars and the perplexities of the nations, and the judgments which are on the land; and a knowledge also of countries and of kingdoms" (D&C 88:77, 79).

Because "the glory of God is intelligence" (D&C 93:36), the prophets have encouraged us to "learn much" in order to serve God with all of our mind as well as with all of our heart and strength. Once we accept this truth, we will see that our opportunities for learning are limitless.

Learning much includes using and developing talents. Emma was encouraged to use her talents in selecting hymns for the Church (see D&C 25:11). Music is one example of learning that the Lord can use to further his work. I remember the clear voice of a Primary chorister singing:

> The golden plates lay hidden
> Deep in the mountainside,
> Until God found one faithful,
> In whom he could confide.
> (*Children's Songbook*, 86)

Her voice took me to Cumorah, and I knew, because her voice told me in the strength of her music, that Joseph Smith really saw those plates. This was the foundation of my testimony of Joseph Smith and the Book of Mormon. My life was significantly blessed by her talent.

The desire to learn much among the women of the Church has given the Lord a vast array of tools to further his work of edifying and exalting his sons and daughters. Our lives continue to be blessed by Spirit-nurtured learning.

THY HUSBAND SHALL SUPPORT THEE

The Lord instructed Emma that she need "not fear, for thy husband shall support thee in the church" (D&C 25:9). Because of the many demands upon his time made by the Church and because "in temporal labors [Joseph did] not have strength" (D&C 24:9), Emma worried about the day-to-day support of the family.

This is often a difficult subject, even though the counsel of the Brethren has been consistent. In the Doctrine and Covenants the Lord taught that "women have claim on their husbands for their maintenance, until their husbands are taken. . . . All children have claim upon their parents for their maintenance until they are of age" (D&C 83:2, 4).

I recall many comments I heard after President Ezra Taft Benson addressed the mothers of the Church. In that address he quoted President Spencer W. Kimball's words: "'Women are to take care of the family—the Lord has so stated—to be an assistant to the husband, to work with him, but not to earn the living, except in unusual circumstances. Men ought to be men indeed and earn the living under normal circumstances.' (*The Teachings of Spencer W. Kimball*, ed. Edward L. Kimball [Salt Lake City: Bookcraft, 1982], 318.)

"President Kimball continues: 'Too many mothers work away from home to furnish sweaters and music lessons and trips and fun for their children. Too many women spend their time in socializing, in politicking, in public services when they should be home to teach and train and receive and love their children into security.' (*Teachings of Spencer W. Kimball*, 319.) . . .

"Finally, President Kimball counsels: 'I beg of you, you who could and should be bearing and rearing a family: wives, come home from the typewriter, the laundry, the nursing, come home from the factory, the cafe. No career approaches in importance that of wife, homemaker, mother—cooking meals, washing dishes, making beds for one's precious husband and children. Come home, wives, to your husbands. Make home a heaven for them. Come home, wives, to your children, born and unborn. Wrap the motherly cloak about you and, unembarrassed, help in a major role to create the bodies for the immortal souls who anxiously await.

"'When you have fully complemented your husband in home life and borne the children, growing up full of faith, integrity, responsibility, and goodness, then you have achieved your accomplishment supreme, without peer, and you will be the envy [of all] through time and eternity.' (Fireside address, San Antonio, Texas.)" (*Come, Listen to a Prophet's Voice*, 30–31).

A HOLY PLACE

The home is a holy place where the Latter-day Saints will stand against the forces of the adversary. When they are filled with love and the Spirit, our homes become like temples.

The temple is a sanctuary, a shadow from the heat, a place of refuge from the storm (see Isaiah 4:6). The temple is "a house of prayer, a house of fasting, a house of faith, a house of learning, a house of glory, a house of order, a house of God" (D&C 88:119). These are wonderful images for the home also. Our own homes must become like the Lord's house.

A woman who is the guiding spirit of her own house of prayer, fasting, faith, learning, glory, order, and godliness has found a proper place.

SEEK THE THINGS OF A BETTER WORLD

After assuring Emma that Joseph would support her, the Lord repeated a principle that guided the life of Sarah. "And verily I say unto thee that thou shalt lay aside the things of this world, and seek for the things of a better" (D&C 25:10). This principle demands sacrifice. It applies to modern-day prophets' counsel for mothers to remain in the home as well as to other choices in which families lay aside the things of this world in their search for celestial priorities. Laying aside "the things of the world" often requires changing the desires of the mind and heart. The Lord desires a singleness of heart. Emma was counseled to seek for the things of a better world.

Moroni spoke of that better world and the results of actively seeking it: "Wherefore, whoso believeth in God might with surety hope for a better world, yea, even a place at the right hand of God, which hope cometh of faith, maketh an anchor to the souls of men, which would make them sure and steadfast, always abounding in good works, being led to glorify God" (Ether 12:4). The desire for a better world and the hope that it is attainable inspires us to be involved in good works. It adds stability to life and leads us to glorify the Lord.

Sometimes we overestimate the things of this world because we underestimate the things of a better. We fail to realize that "since the beginning of the world men have not heard, nor perceived by the ear, neither hath the eye seen, O God, beside thee, what he hath prepared for him that waiteth for him" (Isaiah 64:4). Nor do we sufficiently consider the transitory nature of the things of this world. Joseph Smith observed that "*Destruction*, to the eye of the spiritual beholder, seems to be written by the finger of an invisible hand, in large capitals, upon almost everything we behold" (*Teachings of the Prophet Joseph Smith*, 16). Therefore, to lay aside the things of this world for those of a better is to give up the transitory in favor of the eternal.

BEHOLD THE THINGS OF THIS WORLD

Some years ago a member of our ward related a dream. She found it helped her lay aside the things of this world, because it taught her the ultimate source of joy in the Lord's better world. In her dream she was walking down the street of a large city. The huge buildings towered above her, and she felt small and insignificant. At the head of the street was the huge stone head of an idol. It towered as high as the buildings and brooded over the whole city. All at once the wind began to blow and caused the buildings to sway. Suddenly they exploded into millions of tiny pieces, like a barn hit by a tornado. The debris of the city flew by her and was gone. Within moments there was nothing left of the city but the huge stone head. It, too, was no match for the wind, which picked the head up as if it were made of paper and shattered it into dust that blew past at great speed.

All this happened in seconds. As the remains of the city and the idol were scattered in the wind, a voice from the heavens spoke, calling her by name: "Behold the things of this world!" Then there was a great calm. All that was left was the green earth and a little hill off to the side. "Where is my family?" she thought frantically. She looked for her husband and children and saw them standing together at the top of the hill waiting for her. The joys of the Lord's better world center on the family.

The Lord's preface to the Doctrine and Covenants states, "They seek not the Lord to establish his righteousness, but every man walketh in his own way, and after the image of his own god, whose image is in the likeness of the world, and whose substance is that of an idol, which waxeth old and shall perish in Babylon, even Babylon the great, which shall fall" (D&C 1:16).

The elect daughters of God throughout the Church do not walk after an "image . . . in the likeness of the world," but rather follow the images of the noble women of the scriptures and the image of the Savior (see Alma 5:14).

LIFT UP THY HEART AND REJOICE

After instructing Emma to make a selection of hymns, the Lord told her to "lift up thy heart and rejoice" (D&C 25:13). The scriptures are filled with references to cheerfulness, joy, and happiness. In no fewer than forty sections of the Doctrine and Covenants is this encouraging counsel given. The Lord desires us to be happy.

Many references to rejoicing are linked in the scriptures to the atonement of the Savior. We are imperfect beings and like Nephi often feel like exclaiming, "When I desire to rejoice, my heart groaneth because of my sins; nevertheless, I know in whom I have trusted" (2 Nephi 4:19). We may rejoice and be of good cheer because we trust in the forgiving mercy of the Savior. Despite the temptations that so easily beset us, forgiveness is offered. Jesus is good, patient, long-suffering, merciful, compassionate, wise, and forgiving. We trust in him because of these characteristics. Paraphrasing the fourth Article of Faith we might say, "We believe the first principle of the gospel is faith in the goodness, mercy, patience, and willingness to forgive of the Lord Jesus Christ. Because he has these attributes, we have great reason to rejoice."

The spirit of rejoicing will help spread the gospel throughout the world. President Spencer W. Kimball stated that "much of the major growth that is coming to the Church in the last days will come because many of the good women of the world . . . will be drawn to the Church in large numbers. This will happen to the degree that the women of the Church reflect righteousness and articulateness in their lives and to the degree that the women of the Church are seen as distinct and different—in happy ways— from the women of the world" (*Teachings of Spencer W. Kimball,* 322–23).

CLEAVE UNTO THE COVENANTS

The same sentence in Doctrine and Covenants 25 that contains the Lord's invitation to rejoice instructs Emma to "cleave unto the covenants which thou hast made" (D&C 25:13). True happiness comes not only through the mercy of the Savior but also from the knowledge that our lives are in accordance with the will of God. Lehi taught his sons, "If there be no righteousness there be no happiness" (2 Nephi 2:13). Righteousness naturally produces rejoicing. One definition of righteousness is obedience to the covenants of the gospel. Jesus, although "acquainted with grief" (Isaiah 53:3), was the most joyful man ever to walk the earth, for he always did that which pleased his Father (see John 8:29). To truly lift up one's heart and rejoice, we must cleave unto the covenants we have made.

There are two ways in which we cleave unto our covenants: by constantly trying to live in accordance with the promises we have made and by renewing them frequently through partaking of the sacrament and returning as often as possible to the temple. In other words, we cleave to our covenants through obedience and renewal. This process helps create the joy the Lord linked with this counsel to Emma.

LET THY SOUL DELIGHT IN THY HUSBAND

Emma is encouraged to "continue in the spirit of meekness, and beware of pride. Let thy soul delight in thy husband, and the glory which shall come upon him" (D&C 25:14). *Meekness* is the antithesis of pride. Because the Lord used the word *continue,* it seems evident that Emma had achieved a measure of the spirit of meekness.

The Lord's counsel that Emma delight in Joseph is wonderful

counsel for the elect woman of today. All the honor that comes upon one partner comes upon the other, for they are one. There should be no competition between men and women in marriage or in the Church.

I have watched my mother-in-law delight in my father-in-law for the past twenty-five years. Much of the strength of their exemplary, eternal marriage comes in their mutual "delight" in each other.

MY MOST PRECIOUS THING

Recently I witnessed an example of a woman's delighting in her husband and the effect that delight had on him. While teaching a class, I asked what was each class member's most precious thing. A young wife replied without hesitation and with deep sincerity, "My most precious thing is my husband." It was a tender moment, because he was sitting next to her. He was embarrassed by her answer, but no one in the room could doubt the effect of her words. A few moments later I noticed that he had taken her hand and held it throughout the remainder of the lesson.

When the virtuous woman delights in her husband and in others, she creates in them a confidence that helps them become all that the Lord desires. This delight brings out the best in those who receive it. It creates in them a desire to delight in others also, including the woman who first delighted in them. A mother's delight in her children can be life-changing, for children as well as husbands thrive on sincere praise and love.

THE STRONGEST ANCHOR

President Joseph F. Smith related how the need to retain his mother's love and delight became a barrier against temptation:

"When I was fifteen years of age, and called to go to a foreign country to preach the gospel . . . the strongest anchor that was fixed in my life, and that helped to hold my ambition and my desire steady, to bring me upon a level and keep me straight, was that love which I knew she had for me who bore me into the world.

" . . . This feeling toward my mother became a defense, a barrier between me and temptation, so that I could turn aside from temptation and sin by the help of the Lord and the love begotten in my soul, toward her whom I knew loved me more than anybody else in all the world, and more than any other living being could love me" (*Gospel Doctrine*, 314–15).

Keeping the delight of a loved one is a source of constant encouragement to dignity and righteousness. It brings out all that is noble in us. Much of the good and the glory that is achieved in the world is inseparably linked to the delight of an elect lady.

A CROWN OF RIGHTEOUSNESS

The Lord's concluding counsel to Emma is an exhortation: "Keep my commandments continually, and a crown of righteousness thou shalt receive" (D&C 25:15). The call to keep God's commandments needs no commentary. It is the determining factor for a daughter of God. The word *continually* suggests a constancy of life that is built by habit and reinforced by the will. Emma was promised that if she obeyed continually, a crown awaited her. In other words, she would become a queen in heaven.

Just as a man is promised in Doctrine and Covenants 121:46 an "unchanging scepter" and an "everlasting dominion," if he continues in righteousness, so too is the elect lady promised her crown. Standing side by side as kings and queens, men and women will receive eternal life. In this eternal relationship they honor the Father. Together they reign as an everlasting unit, receiving the blessings of eternal lives, creating worlds for the continuing glory of their Father in Heaven.

THE ELECT LADY

In Doctrine and Covenants 25 the Lord has described not only an elect lady but a celestial one. This portrait of an elect and celestial lady depicts some of the highest ideals for the sisters of the Church. In this way section 25 is akin to section 121 of the Doctrine and Covenants, in which the ideals of righteous priesthood are portrayed. This detailed portrait from section 25 combines elements from the women of earlier dispensations whose likenesses have been preserved for us in the Lord's portrait gallery of the scriptures. Through this final portrait in the halls of latter-day scripture, the Lord counsels his daughters to focus on the things he knows will result in their temporal and eternal happiness.

Great blessings will flow to the Church and fulfillment will come into their own lives as the elect ladies of today faithfully walk in the paths of virtue, seeking the lovely and the praiseworthy. Great blessings will come because they do not murmur, choosing rather to comfort and console. Blessings will come as they go with their husbands and children to support and help them, expounding the scriptures, and exhorting others to higher lives of devotion. Blessings will come as they learn much in many different areas of life while fulfilling the critical role of guardian of the home. Joy will spread into every area of their lives as they sacrifice the things of this world to seek the things of a better. Rejoicing will grow through cleaving to covenants and keeping commandments and through realizing that their loving delight inspires others to righteousness, honor, and glory.

Though few would ever feel their own faces could fill the frame of this celestial portrait, their desires and efforts will help to create that celestial crown. They will see its outline in their own portraits as their election is made sure and they are invited to rule and reign beside their companions throughout eternity.

THE CORRIDORS OF TIME

We have come to the end of our journey through the scriptural portrait gallery. We have examined many of the faces framed by the pages of the scriptures and discussed some of the truths and insights these women impart to us. But we have only begun to discover all that there is to be learned from the women of the scriptures.

Our situation with respect to these women reminds me of the miracle of Jesus feeding the multitude of thousands of men, women, and children with only "five barley loaves, and two small fishes." Then, "when [Jesus] had given thanks, he distributed to the disciples, and the disciples to them that were set down; and likewise of the fishes as much as they would. When they were filled, he said unto his disciples, Gather up the fragments that remain, that nothing be lost. Therefore they gathered them together, and filled twelve baskets with the fragments of the five barley loaves, which remained over and above unto them that had eaten" (John 6:9–13).

Like the great multitude that followed Jesus, hungering for his word, the women of the Church seek the Savior's love and teachings. Filled with compassion toward them, he understands the many pressures and challenges they face each day. The Savior's words to his disciples are as true today as they were at the Sea of Galilee, "They need not depart; give ye them to eat" (Matthew 14:16).

But how can the experiences of the women in the scriptures satisfy the hunger of today's diverse women? With the help of the Spirit, the five small loaves and fishes of the women in the scriptures begin to grow. All may eat until their needs are filled, for despite the brevity of some of the stories, the Lord desires that nothing be lost. Even after we feast on the lives and lessons of these wonderful women, there is always more left for our future edification. That is the miracle of the Lord's best books. Although I have shared insights and edification I have received from these women, many more baskets of truth and power remain to nourish us later.

The mirrors in the celestial room of the temple are another manifestation of this principle of abundance. Before beginning my responsibilities in the Jordan River Temple, I often have time to sit quietly in the celestial room. I am usually alone, and the stillness invites thoughts of eternal things. I love to stand before the mirrors in the center of the room and watch the lights of the chandelier multiply down the corridors of time. Almost always, the words of Joseph Smith come to mind. He spoke of "a welding link of some kind or other between the fathers and the children. . . . For we without them cannot be made perfect. . . . for it is necessary in the ushering in of the dispensation of the fulness of times . . . that a whole and complete and perfect union, and welding together of dispensations, . . . should take place, and be revealed from the days of Adam even to the present time" (D&C 128:18).

I cannot help but think, as I look into the mirrors, that I am looking at the chain of which the Prophet spoke. Each new reflection is another generation, another link, in that eternal chain that creates a "whole and complete and perfect union, and welding together of dispensations." Sometimes I long to step into the mirrors and walk back through the generations that bind me to my first parents, greeting each mother and father who gave me life.

We are of the house of Israel. The scriptures are our family records. The lives of the women in those records strike deep chords within our hearts, for we are welded to every dispensation. How wonderful it would be to wander the halls of time until we met our ancient mothers and sisters. We know only their inspiring portraits now. What heights of joy will be born in our hearts when we see their faces in eternity and enjoy that moment so beautifully described by the Lord to Enoch? "Then shalt thou and all thy city meet them there, and we will receive them into our bosom, and they shall see us; and we will fall upon their necks, and they shall fall upon our necks, and we will kiss each other" (Moses 7:63).

We are the family of our Father in Heaven, bound to each other and to every generation by our mutual devotion to truth, our love of our Father and his Son, and our commitment to the great plan of salvation. It should not surprise us that we love to read of the struggles and joys of our ancient mothers and sisters. All are important to us, even those whose lives are not much more than a shadow. If I have missed some reality in the dimness of those shadows, I hope other eyes will see better and edify us with the clarity of their vision. Nevertheless, I feel a deep respect and profound reverence for all the daughters of God.

All of us, women and men, owe a debt of gratitude to the Lord's daughters, and so I conclude by saying to them, Thank you. Thank you for the life you gave us through sacrifice and sorrow. Thank you for your examples of compassion, gentleness, and mercy. Thank you for your hunger for truth and righteousness, your constant striving for perfection. Thank you for the service, the devotion, that gives so selflessly. Thank you for your quiet faith in God and your rejoicing in his gospel. Thank you for the sensitivity that opens our eyes and hearts to spiritual things. Thank you for showing us the beautiful and the refined.

We are created in the image of God, male and female. I have seen God's majesty and strength in the great men I have known and studied. I have seen his purity in the guileless innocence of little children. But it has been in women that I have seen his heart.

SOURCES

Benson, Ezra Taft. *Come, Listen to a Prophet's Voice*. Salt Lake City: Deseret Book, 1990.

Children's Songbook of The Church of Jesus Christ of Latter-day Saints. Salt Lake City: The Church of Jesus Christ of Latter-day Saints, 1989.

Cowley, Matthew. Conference Report, October 1953.

Dummelow, J. R., ed. *The One Volume Bible Commentary*. New York: Macmillan, 1936.

Ehat, Andrew F., and Lyndon W. Cook, eds. *The Words of Joseph Smith*. Provo, Utah: Religious Studies Center, Brigham Young University, 1980.

First Presidency and Quorum of the Twelve Apostles of The Church of Jesus Christ of Latter-day Saints. "The Family: A Proclamation to the World." *Ensign*, November 1995, 102.

Farrar, Frederic W. *The Life of Christ*. 1874. Reprint: Salt Lake City: Bookcraft, 1994.

For the Strength of Youth [pamphlet]. Salt Lake City: The Church of Jesus Christ of Latter-day Saints, 1990.

Frost, Robert. "Into My Own," in *The Poetry of Robert Frost*. New York: Holt, Rinehart and Winston, 1966.

Hinckley, Bryant S. *Sermons and Missionary Services of Melvin Joseph Ballard.* Salt Lake City: Deseret Book, 1949.

Hinckley, Gordon B. *Teachings of Gordon B. Hinckley.* Salt Lake City: Deseret Book, 1997.

———. Conference Report, October 1978.

———. Conference Report, October 1994.

———. Conference Report, October 1996.

———. "Rise to the Stature of the Divine within You." *Ensign,* November 1989.

———. "True to the Faith." *Ensign,* June 1996.

———. *Church News,* 17 March 1985, 3.

Holland, Jeffrey R. Conference Report, April 1996.

Holland, Jeffrey R., and Patricia T. Holland. *On Earth As It Is in Heaven.* Salt Lake City: Deseret Book, 1989.

Hunter, Howard W. Conference Report, October 1982.

Josephus, Flavius. *Antiquities of the Jews.* In *Josephus: Complete Works.* Translated by William Whiston. Grand Rapids, Mich.: Kregel Publications, 1974.

Journal of Discourses. 26 vols. London: Latter-day Saints' Book Depot, 1854–86.

Kimball, Spencer W. *The Teachings of Spencer W. Kimball.* Edited by Edward L. Kimball. Salt Lake City: Bookcraft, 1982.

———. "The Blessings and Responsibilities of Womanhood." *Ensign,* March 1976.

———. "The False Gods We Worship." *Ensign,* June 1976.

———. "The Uttermost Parts of the Earth." *Ensign,* July 1979.

Lee, Harold B. *Decisions for Successful Living.* Salt Lake City: Deseret Book, 1973.

———. *Ye Are the Light of the World.* Salt Lake City: Deseret Book, 1974.

Maxwell, Neal. Conference Report, April 1978.

McConkie, Bruce R. *Doctrinal New Testament Commentary.* 3 vols. Salt Lake City: Bookcraft, 1965–73.

McKay, David O. "True Beauty." *Young Woman's Journal* 17 (August 1906).

Monson, Thomas S. Conference Report, October 1989.

Oaks, Dallin H. Conference Report, October 1993.

Old Testament [student manual for Religion 301]. Salt Lake City: The Church of Jesus Christ of Latter-day Saints, 1980.

Packer, Boyd K. Conference Report, October 1980.

————. *The Holy Temple*. Salt Lake City: Bookcraft, 1980.

————. Regional Representatives' Seminar, 2 April 1982. Unpublished.

Scott, Richard G. Conference Report, April 1992.

Smith, Lucy Mack. *History of Joseph Smith by His Mother*. Edited by Preston Nibley. Salt Lake City: Bookcraft, n.d.

Smith, Joseph. *History of The Church of Jesus Christ of Latter-day Saints*. Edited by B. H. Roberts. 2d ed., rev. 7 vols. Salt Lake City: The Church of Jesus Christ of Latter-day Saints, 1932–51.

————. *Lectures on Faith*. Compiled by N. B. Lundwall. Salt Lake City: N. B. Lundwall, n.d.

————. *Teachings of the Prophet Joseph Smith*. Selected by Joseph Fielding Smith. Salt Lake City: Deseret Book, 1938.

Smith, Joseph F. *Gospel Doctrine: Selections from the Sermons and Writings of Joseph F. Smith*. Salt Lake City: Deseret Book, 1939.

Smith, Joseph Fielding. *Doctrines of Salvation*. 3 vols. Salt Lake City: Bookcraft, 1954–56.

Strong, James, ed. *The New Strong's Exhaustive Concordance of the Bible*. Nashville, Tenn.:Thomas Nelson Publishers, 1984.

Talmage, James E. *Articles of Faith*. Salt Lake City: The Church of Jesus Christ of Latter-day Saints, 1949.

————. "The Eternity of Sex." *Young Woman's Journal* 25 (October 1914).

Young, Brigham. *Discourses of Brigham Young*. Selected by John A. Widtsoe. Salt Lake City: Deseret Book, 1941.

INDEX

Aaron, 65
Abigail, 68, 99–101
Abigails, modern-day, 100
Abish, 250–52
Abishes, modern, 250–51
Abraham: posterity of, 25; name of,
    changed, 26
Absalom, 111
Abuse: victims of, 259, 263–64;
    consequences of, 261; alleviating,
    265
Adah, 245
Adam and Eve, 7–8, 67–68;
    commitment of, 9; and sacrifice,
    19; unity of, 20–21
Adoption, 63–64, 123–24
Adultery, 111, 113; woman taken in,
    219–20
Agency, 46
Ahab, 133–34
Ahasuerus, 140
Ahijah, 133
Akish, 244–45
Alma, 257–58
Ammon, 247–49, 252
Ammonihah, women of, 257–58
Amnon, 111, 113
Amram, 62

Amulek, 257–58
Amulon, 262
Ananias, 231–32
Anger, 100, 103
Anna, 183–87
Annas, modern-day, 184–87
Answers, 31
Anti-Nephi-Lehies, 250–56
Antipas, Herod, 221–23
Apathy, 36
Apostasy, 161, 231
Apostles, living, 70
Apphia, 235
Aquila, 228–31
Ark of God, 104
Armoni, 108
Athaliah, 135–37
Atonement, 10, 94, 221, 285
Attractiveness, physical, 157–58
Austin, Harriet, 73–74

Baal, worship of, 134
Babylon: spiritual, 33–34; queen of,
    138–40
Balance, principle of, 93
Ballard, Melvin J., on childlessness,
    14–15
Barak, 68, 77–78

Bathsheba, 68, 110–11
Battles, spiritual, 79
Beauty, 170–71
Belial, sons of, 103
Belief, 155, 248
Belshazzar, 138
Benson, Ezra Taft, 282
Bethel, 56
Bilhah, 58
Birthright, 27
Bitterness, 103, 156
Blessedness, 170
Blessings: promised, 25; temple, 48;
    and consecration, 94–95; from
    faith and service, 118; suitable,
    124; patriarchal, 206; to the
    Church, 289
Boaz, 74, 89–90, 274
Book of Life, names recorded in,
    224–25
Book of Mormon, 276

Caligula, 222
Canaan, woman of, 211–13
Cancer, 156, 181
Celestial kingdom, 270–71
Character, 158; decisions of, 27
Charity, 86–90, 128, 149; of soul, 160
Chastity, 22–23, 37–38; and virtue,
    170–71
Childbearing: 12–15, 19, 53–54, 180;
    wonder at, 13
Childlessness, 14–15, 24, 91, 180–81
Children: rearing, 8, 19, 82–83;
    rebellious, 20, 83, 136, 165; and
    agency, 46; exceptional, 63;
    adopted, 63–64; desire for, 91;
    instilling qualities of godhood in,
    103; grief over, 109, 154; abuse of,
    159; influence of mothers on, 173;
    Christ and, 203–5; importance of,
    204–5
Church of Jesus Christ of Latter-day
    Saints, The, 73–74; truth of, 131;
    description of, 161; teaching of,
    177; exhorting the, 279–80
Circumcision, 66–67
Civilization, without, 264–65

Claudia, 235
Combinations, secret, 243–45
Comforter, calling as, 278
Commands, willingness to obey, 42
Commitment, 9
Companionship, eternal, 8
Compassion, 109, 115, 149, 191; lack
    of, 219
Competition of wife, 53
Condemnation, 220
Confession, 216, 220
Conscience, laws of, 60–61
Consecration, 94–95, 231–33, 266
Conversion, 49–50, 73–74
Converts, 71–74
Counsel, seeking, 44
Couples, missionary, 187
Courage, 239; of Deborah, 75–76
Covenant: marriage in the, 46–47,
    50; weight of, 79–81; symbol of
    Lord's, 104; baptismal, 202
Covenants, 128, 286
Cowley, Matthew, 96
Crucifixion, 172
Cruelty, 98
Cursing God, 155–56

Daniel, 138–39
David, 68, 99–101; and Michal,
    105–7
Death, 154, 191–92
Deborah, 68, 75–78
Deborahs, modern-day, 76 -77
Decency, 141
Deception, 52, 85
Delilah, 83–85
Desire, 17
Destruction, spiritual, 144
Devotion, 91
Dinah, 114
Discernment, spirit of, 76
Disciples, 192
Disobedience, 61
Divorce, 241
Dominion, unrighteous, 17–18, 84
Down's Syndrome, 63
Duty, 144

Earth, 165
Education, 149
Eli, wicked sons of, 103
Elijah, 117–19, 134
Elisabeth, 171, 180–83, 186
Elisabeths, modern-day, 181
Elisha, 68, 120–23, 126, 189
Elkanah, 91–98
Empathy, 109, 202
End, enduring to the, 73, 156, 230–31
Endor, witch of, 107–8
Enoch, 28, 165, 292
Equality, 70
Esther, 138, 141–45
Esthers, modern-day, 142, 144
Eternal life, 153
Eternity: as covering, 27–28; courting for, 52
Eunice, 233–34
Eve: as help meet, 7; metaphor of, 9; portrait of, 10; as transgressor, 11–12; sorrow of, 12–13; as life-giver, 15
Evil: justifying, 61; victims of, 102; of Ahab, 133–34; influence of, 136; women and, 245
Exaltation, 153, 270–71
Exodus, 64

Faith, 44; of Sarah, 24, 28, 93; of Amram and Jochebed, 62; and works, 71–72; of Deborah, 75–76; of Hannah, 92; and blessings, 118; reconfirming, 119; and miracles, 120–21; in healing, 125–26, 207; of Mary the mother of Jesus, 172; fruits of, 186; of Mary and Martha, 191–93; and miracles, 225; of Eunice and Lois, 233–34; and sacrifice, 257 58
Faithful, remaining, 73, 154, 156
Faithfulness, 120–21, 125, 225
Fall, the, 10; necessity of, 11
Fallibility, 66
Family: proclamation on, 143–44; unity of Lamanite, 270; commitment to, 272; support of,

281–82; as center, 284; of God, 292
Farrar, Frederic W., 192
Fears, 31
Food storage, 149
Forgiveness, 216, 263
Frost, Robert, 119

Gadianton, 243
Gallery, scriptural, 2–3
Garden of Eden, 18
Gifts, 195; spiritual, 76
Glory, celestial, 8
God: refusal to worship any but, 23; sons of, 48; fearing, 61, 152; Ruth's commitment to, 87; faithful to, 154–55; cursing, 155–56; vision of, 173; power of, 225; justice of, 255; glory of, 281
Godhood, qualities of, 103
Gospel, truths of the, 131; spreading the, 199–200; affirming the, 226
Grieving, 109

Habakkuk, 174
Hagar, 25–26, 29–31
Hagars, 31
Haman, 142
Hannah, 68, 91–98
Hannahs, modern-day, 95
Happiness, 132
Healing: gift of, 76, 125–26; of Savior, 206–9
Heart, treasure in, 174–75
Heavenly Father, faith centered in, 93
Help meet: Eve as, 7; wives of Solomon as, 132–33
Herodias, 221–23
Hinckley, Gordon B.: on children, 83; on morality, 113–14; on widow's mite, 209–10; on abuse, 260–61; on the scriptures, 280
Hoglah, 69–71
Holland, Jeffrey R., 117
Holland, Patricia, on mothering, 15–16
Holy Ghost. *See* Holy Spirit

Holy Spirit, the: as guide, 2; as balance, 36; and spiritual gifts, 76; influence of the, 92; wisdom and peace of the, 100; and Mary, the mother of Jesus, 173; and Elisabeth, 182; companionship of the, 280

Home: protection provided by, 7; as holy place, 283

Honor, 149–50

Hope, 218

Hophni, 103–4

Hosea, 162

Huldah, 126–28

Huldahs, modern-day, 127–28

Humility, 170

Hunter, Howard W.: on Rebekah, 43; on commitment, 55–56

Husband, bloody, 67

Husbands and wives, 8, 10

Hymns, 281, 285

Ichabod, 104

Idleness, 150–51

Images of women, 2

Immorality, tragedy of, 111

Infanticide, 60

Infants, sacrifice of, 132

Inheritance, laws of, 69–70

Intelligence, 281

Isaac, 26, 68

Isaacs, 31

Ishmael, 25; daughters of, 240

Ishmaels, 31

Israel: Exodus of, 64–65; mother in, 77–78; famine in, 117–19; wives of Solomon and, 133

Jacob, 52, 58–59, 68, 260

Jael, 78

Jaques, Vienna, 266–68

Jared, daughter of, 243–46

Jehoram, 135–36

Jehoshabeath, 136

Jehovah, worship of, 134

Jehu, 136

Jephthah's daughter, 79–81

Jeremiah, 126

Jericho, 73

Jeroboam, 133

Jesus Christ: as covering, 28; faith centered in, 93; lineage of, 111; bride of, 160–63; birth of, 171; crucifixion of, 172; anointing of, 193–94; as beginning and end, 198–99; blesses children, 203–5; and healing, 206–9; declares himself, 217–18; compassion of, 290–91. *See also* Savior

Jethro, 66

Jews, return of, 138

Jezebel, 133–36

Jezebels, modern-day, 136

Joash, 136

Job, 154

Job's wife, 154

Jochebed, 62, 68

John the Baptist, 221

Jordan River Temple, 291

Joseph, 114–15, 175

Josiah, 126

Joy, 173–74

Judging, 38, 76, 219–20

Judgment, loss of, 136

Justice, 70, 255

Kimball, Spencer W., 9; on temple marriage, 10; on presiding, 17; on conversion, 50; on Rhoda, 226; on the scriptures, 280; on role of women, 282; on growth of the Church, 285–86

Kindness, 123, 150

Knowledge, growth in, 280

Laban, 79

Lady, elect, 273, 288–89

Lamanites, 250–52, 260, 262–64

Lamech, 245

Lamoni, queen to, 247–50

Latter-day Saints, 145, 158, 177–78; abuse of, 259

Law of Moses, 94, 177

Lazarus, 191–92

Leaders, Lord's choice of, 65–66; following, 178–79

Leah, 52
LDS Social Services, 123–24
Lee, Harold B., 9
Legality and morality, 108
Levi, 53
Liberty Jail, 277
Life, book of, 234
Lives, eternal, 48
Lois, 233–34
Lord: lending a child to the, 97–98;
    trust in the, 118; woman that
    feareth, 152–53
Lot: wife of, 32–34; daughters of,
    35–36
Love: unfeigned, 85; unselfish,
    89–90; and passion, 114;
    wickedness and, 114; and
    miracles, 225
Loyalty, 143
Lust, 113, 114–15, 244–45
Lydia, 227–28
Lydias, modern-day, 228
Lying, 232

Magdalene, Mary, 188, 196–200
Mahlah, 69–71
Maidservants, giving of, in marriage,
    58–59; Morianton's, 263–64
Man, stereotypes of, 7
Marriage: first, 9; temple, 10, 48; and
    unrighteous dominion, 17–18;
    laughter in, 45; outside covenant,
    47–48; plural, 98; of David and
    Michal, 106–7; to Christ, 160–63;
    trials in, 241; delighting in,
    286–87
Mary (in book of life), 235
Mary (mother of Jesus), 169–79
Mary and Martha (of Bethany),
    188–96
Marys, modern-day, 178
Maxwell, Neal A., 296–97
McConkie, Bruce R., 192
McKay, David O., 170–71
Mephibosheth, 108
Michal, 68, 105–7
Midwives, 61
Milcah, 69

Miracle, 119, 120–22, 225
Miriam, 64–66, 68; challenges Moses,
    65
Mission, Moses', 63
Missionaries, 73, 97; couples as, 187;
    sister, 200, 228; and trials, 240–41
Mite, widow's, 209–10
Modesty, 141; virtue and, 115, 144
Monson, Thomas S., 224
Morality and legality, 108
Mordecai, 142
Mortality, lessons of, 18
Moses, 60; mission of, 63
Mosiah, sons of, 252
Mother, title of, 15
Mothers: influence of, 7, 77, 136; role
    of, 8; of stripling warriors, 252–56;
    responsibility of, 282–83
Mourning, 20, 98, 201–3
Murder, 264–65
Museums, 2–3

Naaman's wife's maid, 125–26
Nabal, 99–101
Name, perpetuating, 35–36, 37–38
Naomi, Ruth and, 86–90
Nazarite, 81–82, 94
Nephi, 79, 239
Nicodemus, 217
Noah, granddaughters of, 47–48
Noah (daughter of Zelophehad),
    69–71
Noah (king), 262–63

Oaks, Dallin H., on the Fall, 11–12
Oaths, 80
Obadiah, widow of, 120
Obedience, 118, 216
Offense, 100, 212–13
Offerings, 210
Omer, 243
Onitah, daughters of, 22–23
Ordinances, importance of, 66–67,
    177
Orpah, 87

Packer, Boyd K.: on scriptures, 1; on
    worldliness, 57

Pain, 53, 98, 102
Parenting, 19
Partridge, Edward, 277
Passions, 101; bridling, 114
Peace, 127, 277
Peninnah, 98
Persis, 235
Personality, 158
Pharaoh, daughter of, 62–63, 68
Pharaoh's daughters, modern-day,
   63–64
Phebe, 234–35
Phinehas, wife of, 103–4
Pilate's wife, 68
Portraits: metaphorical, 160–67;
   latter-day, 239; celestial, 289
Posterity: of Abraham, 25; of Judah,
   37–38; of Jacob, 54; of midwives,
   61; of Jephthah, 80
Potiphar's wife, 114–15
Power, abuse of, 134–36
Prayer, 19, 44, 210; answers to, 31,
   92–93, 181; in heart of mother,
   151–52; and priesthood, 176–77
Preparation, spiritual, 149, 182
Pride, 98, 158
Priesthood, 17; responsibility of
   holders of, 148, 177; honoring
   the, 176–77
Priscilla, 228–31
Procreation, misuse of gift of, 112
Prophetess, 65, 75
Prophet, description of, 139
Prophets, living, 70, 226
Propriety, 141
Proving, 131
Puah, 60–61, 68
Punishment, fear of, 107–8
Purim, 143

Rachel, 52–55
Rage, 100
Rahab, 68, 71–74, 133
Rahabs, modern-day, 73
Rape, 113
Rebekah, 39–44, 68; obedience of,
   43; grief of, 46
Rebekahs, modern-day, 41–42

Rebellion, 36
Recommend, temple, 232
Reconciliation, 263
Refinement, 275
Regret, 101
Rejoicing, 173, 285
Relationships, 8; covenant, 67
Relief Society, 149
Repentance, 10, 72, 111–12; Elijah
   calls famine to bring Israel to,
   117–19, 134; and affliction,
   118–19; of woman of sin, 216; call
   by John the Baptist to, 221
Respect, 144
Responsibility, 118; weight of, 190
Rest, 190
Restoration, sisters of the, 268
Resurrection, 54–55, 271–72
Reuben, 53
Reverence, 152
Reward, 89
Rhoda, 226
Rigdon, Sidney, 67
Righteousness, 17, 51–52, 286; of
   women, 66, 68, 85, 116, 136, 139;
   and peace, 127; clothed in, 163;
   crown of, 288
Rizpah, 108–9
Rizpahs, modern-day, 109
Rubies, value above, 147–53, 164
Rule, 17
Ruth, Naomi and, 86–90, 133, 274
Ruths, modern-day, 88

Sacrifice, 19, 144, 283; of women,
   14, 91; human, 22; of Jephthah's
   daughter, 80–81; and obedience,
   118; of infants, 132; of Christ,
   172; willingness to, 230; and
   faith, 257–58
Salome, 201–3
Salvation: plan of, 11, 165, 185;
   spiritual, 14
Samaria, woman of, 217–19
Samson, 81–85; mother of, 81–83
Samuel, 91, 95–98
Sapphira, 231–33
Sarah: childlessness of, 24; faith of,

24–25; name change of, 26; test of faith of, 28
Sarahs, 31
Sariah, 239–42
Satan, 10, 154
Saul, 99, 105
Savior: lineage of the, 89–90; Mary, mother of the, 169–70; delight in, 174; expressing gratitude for, 185; offerings to the, 194–95; blessings of, 201; trust in, 208; mercy of, 220. *See also* Jesus Christ
Scott, Richard G., on abuse, 261–62
Scriptures: as guide, 1, 291; reflections of women in the, 2; gallery of portraits from, 3; verifying the, 127–28; expounding the, 279–80
Self-importance, 157
Selfishness, 113
Self-righteousness, 219
Service, 79, 118, 184, 203; joy of, 124; fruits of, 186; to the Lord, 189–90
Shadrach, Meshach and Abednego, 23
Sheba, queen of, 129–32
Shechem, 114
Shiphrah, 60–61, 68
Shunammite woman, 68, 122–25, 189
Sin, 161; results of, 110–11; tragedy of, 111; yoke of, 214–15; awareness of, 220
Sisera, 78–79
Smith, Don C., 277
Smith, Emma Hale, 130, 273–89
Smith, George Albert, 9
Smith, Hyrum, 271
Smith, Joseph: on Eve, 11, 15; on character, 27; and Lot's daughters, 35–36; chastening of, 67; on faith, 93; sufferings of, 156; on Three Witnesses, 182–83; on Mary, 197; on First Vision, 227; and stirring up faith, 255–56; on abuse, 264; and Vienna Jaques, 267; mother

of, 269; on exaltation, 270–71; wife of, 273; on nature of women, 275; counsels Relief Society, 276–77; and Emma, 281, 284
Smith, Joseph, Sr., 270
Smith, Joseph F., 14, 151, 227, 287–88
Smith, Joseph Fielding, 11
Smith, Lucy Mack, 269–72, 279
Snow, Erastus, 45–46
Sodom, 32–33
Solitude, 190
Solomon, 68, 111, 129–30; wives of, 132–33
Sorrow: preventing, 100; portraits reflecting, 102
Sorrows, 13, 20, 46, 53; of Hannah, 91–92, 96; of Mary and Martha, 193
Soul, beauty of the, 152
Speech, character in, 150
Spirit: sorrowful, 91–92; multiplying things of the, 122; recognizing the, 123; receiving, 190
Spirituality, 158
Standard, double, 38
Strength, 143, 149–50
Students, trails of, 241
Suffering, 102–3, 156
Suicide, 109, 241
Support, 281–82
Sympathy, 128

Tabitha, 224–26
Talmage, James E., 10, 193; on woman of Canaan, 211
Tamar, 37–38, 111–14
Teachers, 186
Teaching, 82–83, 184, 280
Tears, 197–98
Temple: marriage, 10, 48; worship, 57; as sanctuary, 283
Testifying, 131–32
Testimony, 126, 254, 256
Testing, 122
Thanks, 96
Three Witnesses, 182–83
Tirzah, 69–71

Tongues, gift of, 76
Transgressions, sexual, 115
Trials, 91, 156, 181; magnifying our, 240–41
Trust, 118, 154–56, 176, 208
Truth: wisdom and, 130; symbolic, 160; gospel, 164

Unity, 20–21, 82
Uriah, 110–11

Vashti, 140–41
Victims, 261–62, 264–65
Virtue: value of, 22–23, 51–52; and modesty, 115; women of, 133; chastity and, 37–38, 170, 264–65; meaning of, 274
Vows, 80–81; of Nazarite, 94; power in, 95

Warfare, victims of, 264–65
Warriors, stripling, 252–56
Water, living, 217–19
Well, woman at the, 217
Wickedness, 33–34, 114, 116, 165; of Jezebel, 133–35
Widow: trust of the, 116–20; service of the, 184; offering of the, 209–10
Widows, 265
Widow's row, 186
Wife, role of, 67
Wilcox, Laura, 41–42, 88, 97, 148, 151–52
Wilcox, Norma, 33–34, 151–52, 256
Williams, Frederick G., chastening of, 67
Wisdom, 130–32, 150, 164
Witchcraft, 107
Witnesses, God's, 187
Wives: influence of, 7, 77; of covenant, 46–47; role of, 67
Woman: seductive, 147; contentious,

147, virtuous, 147–53; with issue of blood, 206–9; laden with sin, 215; at well, 217–19; taken in adultery, 219–20
Women: as single parents, 1, 121–22; childlessness of, 1, 14; role of, 2; as examples, 3, 185; God hears prayers of, 31; sorrow of, 46, 53; righteous, 66, 68, 85, 116, 136, 139; as help meet, 7, 67, 132–33; and equality, 70; service to Lord of, 79; unrighteous dominion of, 84; understanding, 99; virtuous, 133; strength and loyalty of, 143; Latter-day Saint, 145, 177–78, 232–33; worldly, 157–58; value of, 164; respect for, 176; wicked, 331–23; becoming virtuous, 223; believing, 227–28, 250; nature of, 245; abuse of, 259; feelings of, 260; suffering of, 264–65; working, 283
Woodruff, Wilford, 51–52, 268
Word of Wisdom, 36–37, 249
Work, 19
Works, faith and, 71–72, 225
World, lone and dreary, 18

Young, Brigham, 272; on Eve, 11; on mothers, 15; on marriage, 39–40, 49–50; on love, 48; on first resurrection, 54–55; on converts, 74; on beauty, 158

Zacharias, 172, 180
Zarephath, 116–20
Zeal, fanatical, 36
Zelophehad, daughters of, 69–71
Zeresh, 145–46
Zillah, 245
Zilpah, 58
Zion, daughters of, 157
Zipporah, 66–68